Re-Envisioning Transformation

Re-Envisioning Transformation

Toward a Theology of the Christian Life

DAVID C. SCOTT

WIPF & STOCK · Eugene, Oregon

RE-ENVISIONING TRANSFORMATION
Toward a Theology of the Christian Life

Copyright © 2018 David C. Scott. All rights reserved. Except for brief quotations in critical publications or reviews, no part of this book may be reproduced in any manner without prior written permission from the publisher. Write: Permissions, Wipf and Stock Publishers, 199 W. 8th Ave., Suite 3, Eugene, OR 97401.

Wipf & Stock
An Imprint of Wipf and Stock Publishers
199 W. 8th Ave., Suite 3
Eugene, OR 97401

www.wipfandstock.com

PAPERBACK ISBN: 978-1-5326-3240-2
HARDCOVER ISBN: 978-1-5326-3242-6
EBOOK ISBN: 978-1-5326-3241-9

Manufactured in the U.S.A.   08/31/18

Contents

Preface | ix
Acknowledgments | xi

Chapter 1: Introduction | 1
1.1 The Contemporary Landscape | 1
    1.1.1 The Transformation Problem | 1
    1.1.2 The Evangelical Problem | 4
1.2 The Purpose of this Book | 7
1.3 Transformation and the Christian Life | 9
1.4 The Meaning of "Evangelical" | 13
    1.4.1 Deconstructing Evangelicalism | 13
    1.4.2 A Biblical-Theological Approach | 16
1.5 Representative Literature | 19
1.6 The Way Forward | 31

Chapter 2: The "Systematic Spirituality" of J. I. Packer | 34
2.1 Introduction | 34
2.2 Prolegomena | 37
2.3 The Nature of God | 42
2.4 Creation and Redemption | 44
    2.4.1 God in Creation | 44
    2.4.2 God in Christ | 48
2.5 Union with Christ | 51
2.6 Living in Christ | 55
    2.6.1 Divine Initiation | 55
    2.6.2 Human Response: Co-operation with God | 57

2.6.3 Human Response: Rational Primacy | 60

2.6.4 Growth in Community | 64

2.6.5 Transformation in the World | 69

2.7 Conclusion | 72

Chapter 3: The "Synthetic Vision" of Maximus Confessor | 74

3.1 Introduction | 74

3.2 Christology and Integration | 76

    3.2.1 Introduction | 76

    3.2.2 Christ and the Trinity | 78

    3.2.3 The Two Natures of Christ | 79

    3.2.4 Christ the Mediator | 80

3.3 Anthropology and Deification | 82

    3.3.1 Introduction | 82

    3.3.2 The Three Modes of Personhood | 83

    3.3.3 Humanity and the Cosmos | 86

3.4 Bibliology, Cosmology, and Ecclesiology | 87

3.5 Integrating Knowledge and Praxis | 90

    3.5.1 Introduction | 90

    3.5.2 Forms of Divine Knowledge | 91

    3.5.3 Theoria and Praxis | 92

3.6 Conclusion | 93

Chapter 4: Dialogue and Analysis | 96

4.1 Introduction | 96

4.2 Framing Transformation | 97

    4.2.1 Propositional Doctrine | 97

    4.2.2 Lived Experience | 99

4.3 Foundational Categories | 99

    4.3.1 The Triune God | 99

    4.3.2 The Person of Christ | 101

    4.3.3 Death and Resurrection | 103

    4.3.4 Holy Scripture | 104

    4.3.5 Summation | 107

4.4 Anthropology and Transformation | 107

    4.4.1 Transitional Modes | 107

4.4.2 Relational Mode I: Divine-Human | 110
4.4.3 Relational Mode II: Intra-Self | 112
4.4.4 Relational Mode III: Intra-Human | 113
4.4.5 Ecclesial Mode I: The Gathered Church | 115
4.4.6 Ecclesial Mode II: The Scattered Church | 117
4.5 Knowledge and Transformation | 119
    4.5.1 Introduction | 119
    4.5.2 Rational Knowledge | 119
    4.5.3 Knowledge-in-Union | 121
    4.5.4 Applied Knowledge | 124
4.6 Conclusion | 125

Chapter 5: Transformational Theology I —Theoretical Framework | 127

5.1 Introduction | 127
5.2 The Ground of Transformation | 128
    5.2.1 Trinitarian Dynamics | 128
    5.2.2 Anthropological Implications | 129
    5.2.3 Christology and Transformation | 133
5.3 The Context for Transformation | 135
    5.3.1 Definitive Union with Christ | 135
    5.3.2 The Nature and Position of Scripture | 136
    5.3.3 Experiential Union with Christ: Living in the Trinity | 138
    5.3.4 Experiential Union with Christ: Personhood and Community | 139
5.4 Conclusion | 141

Chapter 6: Transformational Theology II —Lived Experience | 143

6.1 Introduction | 143
6.2 Integral Knowledge | 144
    6.2.1 Revelation and Transformation | 144
    6.2.2 The Means of Divine Knowledge | 145
6.3 Formational Worship I: Orientation Toward God | 145
    6.3.1 An Integrated Response to God | 145
    6.3.2 The Essence of Divine Engagement | 146

6.4 Formational Worship II: Scripture and Physicality | 148
    6.4.1 Introduction | 148
    6.4.2 Engaging with Scripture | 148
    6.4.3 Transformation and Physicality | 150
6.5 Formational Worship III: Ecclesial Modes | 151
    6.5.1 The Gathered-Scattered Dialectic | 151
    6.5.2 The Rational-Linguistic Center | 152
    6.5.3 Integrating Presence and Act | 153
    6.5.4 Transformation as Witness | 155
6.6 Conclusion | 156

Chapter 7: Conclusion | 158
7.1 Introduction | 158
7.2 The Need for Christian Distinctiveness | 159
7.3 The Importance of a Rational-Linguistic Center | 160

Glossary | 163
Bibliography | 169

Preface

THE ABSENCE OF MARKED change in the lives of self-identified "evangelicals" has led them to explore different approaches to transformation. Some have sought to adopt ancient and/or new spiritual practices in the hope that this leads to spiritual growth. Others have perceived value in the insights derived from different academic disciplines in order to embrace a more "holistic" expression of human development. Some people, disillusioned by the divine call for ecclesial sanctification, have defined the transformational task around a need for cultural relevance and "changing the world." Across all these approaches the diversity of views imply that there is no common or cohesive vision of transformation from a Christian perspective, and that it is not possible to progress toward one.

In recent years, the academic interest in Christian formation has led to many studies exploring a broad approach—some from a multidisciplinary perspective. Despite the expanding number of academic works on Christian formation, there has been no attempt to outline a truly comprehensive and unified theological framework on the subject. This book attempts to fill that gap. The purpose of this volume is to look at the possibility of moving toward a vision of transformational theology that is cohesive, integrated, broad, effectual, and distinctly Christian. It is hoped that the vision of the Christian life presented will serve God's people as they continually strive together—by his grace—to be transformed to reflect the image of Christ to the world.

Acknowledgments

I AM GRATEFUL TO Martyn Percy and Philip Sheldrake for their support in guiding the research project that led to this book. Their depth of knowledge, insight, and feedback during the writing process has been invaluable and significantly improved the quality of this work.

I would also like to express my gratitude to Michael Lloyd for taking the time to review the manuscript and for offering helpful feedback. I am also grateful to Alister E. McGrath and Augustine Casiday for kindly providing comments on chapters 2 and 3 respectively.

Finally, I would like to thank the staff at Wipf and Stock Publishers, and Jennie Pollock for all her editorial support.

Soli Deo Gloria

Chapter 1

Introduction

1.1 THE CONTEMPORARY LANDSCAPE

1.1.1 The Transformation Problem

THERE IS AN ETERNAL call on God's people to be transformed and come to reflect the glory of Christ throughout creation.[1] At the same time, there is a draw toward alternative visions of transformation that are—at best—not "distinctly Christian." Although there is much talk amongst Christians about what transformation is (and how it occurs), the different perspectives offered are often contradictory and piecemeal. Instead of there being a common transformational vision that the church is seeking to move toward, the focus can shift to being more human-centered—suggesting an ecclesial landscape characterized by fragmentation and relativism.

Rather than providing a solution to this "transformation problem," the "evangelical world" would appear to affirm it. The ostensible absence of authentic transformation in the lives of many self-identified evangelicals has certainly contributed to the proliferation of approaches to Christian formation that have been put forward in recent years. In the early 1970s, church historian Richard Lovelace commented on the failure of so-called "evangelical" Christians to grow in spiritual maturity, a phenomenon he coined the "sanctification gap."[2] More recently John Coe has called this gap

---

1. See Rom 8:29; Eph 5:27; 2 Cor 3:18; 1 Jn 3:2; Rev 21:10–11.
2. Lovelace, "Sanctification Gap." See also Porter, "Sanctification in a New Key."

"the awareness of an immense distance between where we should, could, or ought to be spiritually and where we in fact are."[3]

In an attempt to rectify this, some commentators have called for renewal based upon the understanding that so-called "evangelical spirituality" is narrow, rather than broad and holistic.[4] It has been assumed that self-identified evangelicals in pursuit of real change, depth, and authenticity need to look outside of their "tradition."[5] In recent years the necessity for renewal has led to a greater ecumenical "ressourcement," where self-identified evangelicals have become exposed to an ever-increasing array of "spiritual practices," and multifarious understandings of what constitutes a "deeper" Christian life.[6] This trend towards experimentation can be seen most evidently within the "spiritual formation movement" which surfaced in the late 1970s. Those involved were concerned to see authentic transformation within the church—partly in reaction to a perceived overemphasis on conversion experience and correct doctrine.[7]

Despite the merits of this movement in highlighting the need for authenticity and spiritual maturity it has not had continued success. The plurality of approaches to spiritual growth this movement has spurred has done little toward facilitating a comprehensive or cohesive understanding of the Christian life.[8] At best, the openness to diverse theories and practices has provided a view that is "piecemeal." Rather than facilitating a common and integrated perspective, it has led to an emphasis on specific areas at the expense of others. Furthermore, instead of grounding spiritual growth in a solid Protestant soteriology, the movement has expressed overdependence on a series of imperatives and practices, or "spiritual disciplines,"

---

3. Coe, "Spiritual Theology," 4.

4. See Chan, "Spiritual Practices," 247. Some of the studies advocating the broadening of an "evangelical" view are Parker, "Evangelical Spirituality"; Seddon, *Gospel and Sacrament*; Cocksworth, *Holding Together*; Chan, "New Directions"; Smith, *Evangelical, Sacramental & Pentecostal*.

5. This understanding is expressed in Foster, *Streams of Living Water*; Demarest, *Satisfy Your Soul*.

6. Parker, "Evangelical Spirituality," 123; Chan, "New Directions," 219; "Spiritual Practices," 249. The need for ecumenical "ressourcement" is reflected in Maas and O'Donnell, *Spiritual Traditions*; Foster, *Streams of Living Water*; Boa, *Conformed to His Image*; Beasley-Topliffe, *Dictionary of Christian Spiritual Formation*; Buschart and Eilers, *Theology as Retrieval*.

7. Some influential figures at the start of this movement were James Houston, Eugene Peterson, Dallas Willard and Richard Foster. The movement has been noted for both positive and negative contributions, see Armstrong, "Rise, Frustration, and Revival"; Langer, "Spiritual Formation"; Porter, "Spiritual Formation Movement."

8. Porter, "Doctrine of Sanctification," 421.

demonstrating a misunderstanding of the critical connection between belief and practice.

Within the "evangelical world," the conflicting approaches to Christian formation that are offered suggest a landscape characterized by confusion, pluralism, fragmentation, relativism, individualism, pragmatism, and subjectivism. To some degree this serves to reflect the cultural zeitgeist. Steve Porter has argued that many self-identified evangelicals "become disillusioned and frustrated with the Christian life, as they are confronted with a welter of divergent perspectives."[9] Much of the contemporary search for authenticity in the Christian life appears to have added an unnecessary level of complexity—and perhaps elitism—beyond that which is presently accessible to the ordinary Christian who simply desires to be a "faithful follower of Jesus."

In reference to the wide variety of incompatible and conflicting approaches put forward as possible ways of understanding the nature and process of spiritual growth,[10] Porter states: "Confusion reigns when there is no meta-theory which deals appropriately with divergent theoretical voices."[11] Such confusion stems from individualism, where the focus remains on personal preference rather than obedience to the divine will.[12] Douglas Groothuis warns against such self-styled spirituality, which, at its root, has no concern for absolute truth. He believes that what is needed is a "spirituality as set within a framework of objective truth. Otherwise, Christian spirituality will be seen as simply another pragmatic, relative, subjective option."[13]

Amongst some evangelical groups, there has been growing concern to reform spirituality in accord with biblical teaching.[14] At best, evangelicalism has been seen to be about persons seeking to be biblically faithful—standing under Scripture so that it may be allowed to continually form them. Those aligning with this approach would argue that any alternative method

9. Ibid., 426.

10. This plurality is seen in various studies. For example, see Gundry, *Five Views*; Alexander, *Christian Spirituality*; Demarest, *Satisfy Your Soul*; Boa, *Conformed to His Image*; Howard, "Advancing the Discussion." See also Chan, "New Directions"; Armstrong, "Rise, Frustration, and Revival."

11. Porter, "Doctrine of Sanctification," 420.

12. It has been suggested that there is a specific path that individuals are required to take depends on their own "personality type" or "spirituality type." See Sager, *Gospel-Centered Spirituality*; Ware, *Discover Your Spiritual Type*; McGuinness, *Growing Spiritually*; Thomas, *Sacred Pathways*.

13. Groothuis, *Truth Decay*, 165–66.

14. An attempt at expressing a biblical understanding of sanctification can be seen in Peterson, *Possessed by God*. For an outline of a broad biblical perspective on the Christian life, see Davis, *Infinite Journey*.

of reforming the Christian life only takes away from—rather than adds to—the possibility of spiritual depth, transformation, and authenticity. This suggests that reliance upon anything outside of the biblical text (as a central means through which to explore Christian formation) weakens a commitment to the authority and sufficiency of Scripture, and leads to a distorted perspective.

Those advocating a more biblical focus would concur that a "rational-linguistic" form of communication has a central and irreplaceable function within the Christian life.[15] The term "rational-linguistic" would denote a logocentric method of communication that reveals cognitive knowledge. It is "rational" in terms of involving mind-to-mind communication (to be understood), and "verbal"—involving the spoken word. In the Christian faith, what is to be communicated in such manner is the fullness of biblical teaching—of which the gospel of Christ is the center—in correspondence with the objective revelation of God already spoken forth in history.

Certainly, many recognize that the dual need is to reform based upon a commitment to the biblical gospel, and Scripture as *the* central source and authority, while acknowledging the proper place for tradition, experience, and reason.[16] The assumption here is that a core understanding of Christian formation (and the central practices and principles that lead to it) are revealed clearly in Scripture. In light of this, the only reform and renewal thought to be required is that which is in accord with scriptural teaching and involves the right use of Scripture as *the* foundational "spiritual practice."[17]

1.1.2 The Evangelical Problem

The divergence of contemporary approaches to Christian formation can be seen to reflect the present conflict around evangelical identity. The term "evangelical" is becoming progressively more ambiguous. It has been used to express anything and everything; consequently, in one sense it has come to mean nothing. Today, the supposed cross-denominational evangelical

---

15. The reason for any move away from rational-linguistic communication may be because it is seen as a limited medium that relies too much on the inadequacies of human language and the rational faculties. It could also be construed that a rational-linguistic focus leads toward a narrow and restricted expression of Christian formation, rather than a holistic one.

16. See Carson, "When Is Spirituality Spiritual?"; Whitney, "Defining the Boundaries"; Plummer, "Spiritual Disciplines"; McClendon, "Bible in Spirituality"; *Paul's Spirituality in Galatians*.

17. For example, see Adam, *Hearing God's Words*; Ferguson, *From the Mouth of God*; *Devoted to God*.

movement is often thought to be so broad, fragmented, and diverse that it is increasingly difficult to define the commonalities.[18]

The well-known quadrilateral put forward by historian David Bebbington (i.e., "biblicism," "crucicentrism," "conversionism," and "activism") is often referred to as a means of understanding the central characteristics of evangelicalism.[19] However, this framework was not put forward as a means of determining orthodoxy and orthopraxy. Indeed, Bebbington's phenomenological study of self-identified evangelicals does not provide any objective criteria for discernment. Because of its flexibility and ambiguity, Bebbington's framework allows space for some form of relativist plurality to be permitted over and above true unity around theological convictions.[20] Today, the evidence of this plurality is demonstrated in the diverse beliefs seen across the so-called "evangelical landscape."[21]

As well as there being diversity in beliefs, the lived practices and expressions of faith demonstrated in the lives of self-identified evangelicals also seem to be increasingly diverse. From a phenomenological perspective, it is difficult to describe a distinctly "evangelical spirituality" because there is so much fragmentation, complexity, and variety. It is certainly questionable whether this exists as a distinct and fresh expression, given that it has grown out of a wide range of traditions that preceded it, from both within and outside of Protestantism. Bruce Hindmarsh affirms that "evangelicalism emerges as a devotional movement in continuity with older traditions of Christian spirituality."[22] Given its broad heritage, so-called "evangelicalism" does not appear to express anything new, and so never forms an isolated spirituality.

---

18. Various perspectives have been expressed in Naselli and Hansen, *Four Views*. Within a British context this is demonstrated in Warner, *Reinventing English Evangelicalism*; Clifford, *21st Century Evangelicals*; Holmes, "Evangelical Theology."

19. Bebbington, *Evangelicalism in Modern Britain*, 2.

20. Steve Porter makes an important point about the presence of pluralism within "evangelicalism": "The problem with pluralism of any kind is that if we do not actually have knowledge of the reality in question independently of the plurality of perspectives, then we cannot develop any criteria to determine which perspectives or which parts of various perspectives correspond to the reality in question. And if we do not have the means to discriminate between the various perspectives or their parts, then all perspectives and each part becomes either equally valid or equally invalid. Relativism or skepticism prevails—take your pick" ("Doctrine of Sanctification," 421).

21. For the range of views, see Boyd and Eddy, *Across the Spectrum*. In *The Bible Made Impossible*, Christian Smith suggests that a plurality of perspectives stems from the lack of biblical clarity. Kevin Vanhoozer believes that Smith "fails to distinguish the naive biblicism characteristic of *solo scriptura* from the critical biblicism that characterizes *sola scriptura*" ("May We Go Beyond," 764).

22. Hindmarsh, "Seeking True Religion," 119.

Though many commentators have made attempts to properly define the parameters and distinctive characteristics of an "evangelical spirituality" their descriptions have far less in common than one would like.[23] Ian Randall has provided one of the more comprehensive phenomenological studies.[24] The conclusions of his research suggest tensions and irreconcilable differences—reinforcing the kaleidoscopic and eclectic nature of "evangelical spirituality"—to the point where one wonders if it represents anything cohesive at all. In the end, any notion of a coherent spirituality within the movement appears to be a construct of the historian and sociologist. In reference to Randall's research, David Parker states:

> The vast number of examples of different types and varied instances of spirituality that appear in this work sometimes giving the appearance of a mere catalogue or smorgasbord rather than a coherent movement with substantive content presents a challenge of categorisation. Although the structure (from Keswick onwards, in opposites and variations) provides a useful analytical scheme, which the author exploits fully, there are many instances where exceptions, anomalies, tensions, and paradoxes are noted, suggesting that the data is perhaps more complex than the author's theoretical framework allows. Furthermore, Bebbington's quadrilateral, a key factor in the analysis, may not be a sharp enough instrument to handle what is certainly revealed to be a 'kaleidoscopic' phenomenon.[25]

Of course, the problem here is not the mere presence of plurality and diversity. There is a need for broadness within the Christian life that is God-given in nature.[26] However, there is a problem with an uncritical embrace of everything as a possible source and expression of the divine good. Although

---

23. For example, see Hingley, "Evangelicals and Spirituality"; Gordon, *Evangelical Spirituality*; Parker, "Evangelical Spirituality"; Gillett, *Trust and Obey*; Randall, *Evangelical Experiences*; *What a Friend*; "Recovering Evangelical Spirituality"; Chan, "New Directions"; Olsen, "Perspectives on Spirituality"; Howard, *Christian Spiritual Formation*; "Evangelical Spirituality"; Ridgely, "Connected Christians"; Schwanda, *Emergence of Evangelical Spirituality*; "Evangelical Spiritual Disciplines."

24. See Randall, *Evangelical Experiences*. Diversity is also apparent in sociological research on the spiritual lives of self-identified evangelicals, see Clifford, *Time for Discipleship?*

25. Parker, "Review of Evangelical Experiences," 375.

26. A broad evangelical approach is suggested in Tiller, *Puritan, Pietist, and Pentecostalist*. For attempts at balanced and holistic approaches to the Christian life, see Hollinger, *Head, Hands & Heart*; Beeke, *Developing Healthy Spiritual Growth*. The need for a "broad" approach that draws from across the Christian tradition has been advocated in Foster, *Streams of Living Water*.

so-called "evangelicalism" may be understood to contain diverse God-given expressions that are healthy, necessary, and complementary, it can also be seen to express a plurality that is both contradictory and conflicting. While forms of diversity are proper and needed in any given context, the presence of a relativistic plurality is inherently problematic because it denotes irreconcilable differences that stem from the corrupt human will; as opposed to a paradoxical unity-in-diversity that reflects the Triune God. True God-given diversity can only occur as a result of persons having a unified and singular identity.

Although some understand evangelicalism to be a wide and diverse movement, many would see it as being more restorationist in terms of seeking to draw the church back toward a prototypal faith—being united around specific doctrinal and ethical tenants. Theologians such as J. I. Packer have tried to defend the unity within the movement.[27] The reason for doing so is clear—without the recognition and demonstration of a unified expression of belief and praxis, there remains openness to embrace conflict that emanates from fallen human nature, rather than reflecting a unity-in-diversity that stems from divine intention. If there is objective truth that God is willing and able to make known, then by definition it is illogical for persons to celebrate, affirm, and accept contradictory and incompatible perspectives. A true evangelical path stands or falls on the possibility of persons being able to grow in the knowledge and expression of a common and universal narrative.

1.2 THE PURPOSE OF THIS BOOK

In light of the aforementioned "transformation problem" evident across the ecclesial landscape, the central aim of this book will be to outline an original theological synthesis that points the church toward the need to express and live out a full, integrated, effectual, and distinctly Christian vision of transformation. It will be argued that the only way to move toward a cohesive vision of transformational theology is through an approach grounded in rational-linguistic truth.[28]

---

27. This is demonstrated in Packer and Oden, *One Faith*. Various other attempts have been made to outline the common beliefs among self-identified evangelicals. For example, see Stott, *Evangelical Truth*; Wright, *Cape Town Commitment*.

28. The notion of "transformational theology" is understood in this book as a systematic theological framework that is orientated toward the central goal of the Christian life—namely, transformation into the image of Christ.

The intention will be to develop a model that demonstrates a broad, balanced, and internally consistent approach to Christian formation—in terms of both understanding and practice. An effectual transformational theology needs to fully express integration, through eliminating dualism and dichotomy. This book will show that it is possible to construct a holistic model that holds together the important elements of Christian formation rather than isolating them and/or placing undue emphasis on one area at the expense of others. The premise is that formation does not occur by means of an isolated "part," for no element can be understood except in relation to everything else. Therefore, the need is to express an organized outline of transformational theology that allows for a focus on the nature of the connections between all the parts, embracing a cohesive whole rather than being piecemeal.

A premise of this book is that the problem outlined can only be solved by exploring a proper relation between the concerns of both theology and spirituality (i.e., suitably integrating doctrine, experience, and praxis). It is suggested that an integrated approach to Christian formation requires the construction of a well-developed framework for a "theology of the Christian life," where an appropriate understanding of the Christian life can be located within the proper theological schema. Therefore, the need is to provide a way of formulating a model that fully embraces orthodox beliefs and practices—a theology of formation that does not allow a dualistic separation between doctrine and life.

A suitable framework of transformational theology must be seen to demonstrate a broad and diverse understanding, while also expressing common characteristics. It is argued that there is a need for this framework to be grounded in a distinctly "proto-evangelical" center—which is characteristically rational-linguistic in nature—under the premise that the framework can only show both breadth and integration through a clearly defined center. The term "proto-evangelical" here—which will be looked at later on in this chapter—is being used to refer to an understanding that is grounded in the original core message of the Christian faith. Namely, the "first gospel" which God the Father spoke forth—in his Son—which was proclaimed as "good news" by the early church, in accord with the Scriptures. Consequently, it also denotes a core commitment to the witness and authority of the Scriptures, which God has already spoken in history.

There is a need for a comprehensive model to be constructed that holds together the primary concerns of transformational theology without the proto-evangelical center being compromised. In developing an integrated framework, there will be exploration into central characteristics of Christian growth and the principal means of nurturing formation. In doing so, the purpose will be to demonstrate the necessity of embracing unity-in-diversity. This will mean showing the need for common points of agreement about the nature and practice of Christian formation, while at the same time integrating broad concerns—without conflict.

1.3 TRANSFORMATION AND THE CHRISTIAN LIFE

In this next section, there will be a brief introduction to the central subject matter of this book—the Christian life—with a focus on the nature and process of transformation. The subsequent section will set the trajectory for a "proto-evangelical" perspective.

The starting point for understanding the Christian life is recognizing that it is rooted in the redemptive narrative. The biblical story describes human existence as being "disordered" as a result of persons being alienated from God. Scripture also portrays God's relation to his people as being redemptive in nature. In Christ, God has revealed himself in human flesh—demonstrating both divine and human life in its fullness. Through his salvific work, Christ brings forth the possibility of reconciliation with God, so that God's people may be able to more fully reflect his life to the world. Christ has confronted the world with a call to repentance and counter-cultural living. His teachings call for radical obedience—for persons to continually turn away from a self-glorifying and disorderly existence—toward a life lived in relation to the Triune God.

An imitation of Christ's earthly life must stem from personal faith in the risen Christ; otherwise, it leads toward autonomous personal morality. Through faith, lived experience is to be grounded in Christ's death and resurrection, with the continual movement of persons losing their life to find new life. As individuals continually seek to follow Christ, they can increasingly come to reflect his image more. The Christian life is also to be characterized by the work of the promised Holy Spirit, who has been poured out upon the church as a result of Christ's salvific work. It is only through the presence and power of the indwelling Spirit that persons can live in a distinct way. Rather than being an individualistic experience, formation occurs as a result of persons seeking to follow Christ together, in the power of the Spirit, the end goal of transformation being corporate, rather than private.

This book focuses specifically on exploring the nature of the Christian life through use of the transformation motif. Different terms and phrases are used when referring to the central need in the Christian life, for example: spiritual growth, spiritual [trans-]formation, Christian [trans-]formation, spiritual development, spiritual maturity, holiness, sanctification, discipleship, piety, and godliness. Without overlooking the clear nuances and distinct meanings of each of these—the common trajectory they indicate is a movement toward Christian distinctiveness—a process that may best be encapsulated by the term "[trans-]formation."[29] Although this motif only represents one angle from which to examine the Christian life, its value lies in the fact that it denotes the central telos—the goal being that persons are to be changed into the image of Christ.

Transformation is of primary concern given that it is a mark of authenticity, and a sign of God being actively at work in a person's life. Given the depths of human depravity, there may be disillusionment over the possibility of experiencing authentic transformation, and the question may be asked as to whether substantial change can occur before the eschaton.[30] Though it is true that the absolute fulfillment of the telos will occur at the eschaton, the Scriptures positively affirm that distinctiveness in the lives of God's people is both possible and necessary in this present age.[31] The question only concerns the degree to which the inseparable relation between eternity and history will allow the in-breaking of Christ's risen life in the current witness of his church.

As already noted, self-identified evangelicals have continued to explore the possibility of authentic transformation in a variety of different ways. Some of the approaches taken have been characterized by a notable shift of focus away from a need for personal and ecclesial transformation, toward a "wider" vision that is supposedly more "holistic" and "inclusive."[32] This drive toward so-called "whole-life" transformation may in part be due to

---

29. The importance of the word is demonstrated in Waaijman, "Transformation." Though the terms *formation* and *transformation* could be used interchangeably, it is suggested that "formation" denotes marginal change, while "transformation" points to a more marked and dramatic change. *Christian formation* is perhaps the most suitable phrase to describe a distinctly Christian approach to development.

30. The struggle for transformation has been expressed in Porter, "Gradual Nature of Sanctification." There has been some research carried out to determine how Christian formation occurs, see Macchia, *Becoming a Healthy Disciple*; Waggoner, *Shape of Faith to Come*; Barna, *Growing True Disciples*; Geiger et al., *Transformational Discipleship*; Bergler, *From Here to Maturity*. There are also various published studies that explore how change occurs, see Cloud and Townsend, *How People Grow*; Chester, *You Can Change*; Lane and Tripp, *How People Change*; Crabb, *Inside Out*; Powlison, *How Does Sanctification Work?*

31. An attempt to understand transformation as a central motif in Pauline theology can be found in DeSilva, *Transformation*.

32. There are many examples of "holistic" approaches that have sought to integrate the concerns of human development with Christian formation. See Feldmeier, *Developing Christian*; Brown, Dahl, and Reuschling, *Becoming Whole and Holy*; Chandler, *Christian Spiritual Formation*; *Holy Spirit and Christian Formation*.

disillusionment over the lack of evidential sanctification within the church. It also reflects a desire to integrate all areas of human life—and to understand the connections—rather than to compartmentalize or dichotomize. This has led many to shift their focus toward areas of human development outside of a redemptive schema, with some seeking to "integrate" by expressing an understanding of Christian formation that incorporates insights on development from other disciplines.[33]

There have also been approaches put forward that are "holistic" in terms of focusing on the need for the church to place a central emphasis on bringing about various forms of empirical change across society.[34] Within these approaches, God's present redemptive mission is primarily portrayed as being about fulfilling all "human needs." As a result, ecclesial mission is broadened to include all that individual Christians do in their societal roles to meet the needs that are common to all.[35]

The main problem is, that in seeking to be "broad," the missional focus can easily shift from being distinctly Christian (i.e., away from the fundamental need for the glory of Christ to be revealed through his church). Here, ecclesial mission is portrayed as incorporating the *same* vocational activities that are—to a great extent—already present across society. This is evidence that these activities are not necessarily synergetic with persons becoming conformed to reflect the glory of the risen Christ.

Though the "inclusivism" of such approaches may be thought to lead to "holistic" (or "whole-life") transformation, it can lead the church toward having the exact same focus and concerns as secular culture, rather than its primary focus—and distinct mission—being to make the glory of Christ known to the ends of the earth.

---

33. See Perrin, *Studying Christian Spirituality*, 219–57. Adrian Van Kaam made an ambitious attempt at a "holistic" transformational theology. A helpful summary of Van Kaam's contribution is seen in Wilhoit, "Only God's Love Counts."

34. Disillusionment with personal or ecclesial transformation can result in persons shifting to focus on human-centered goals (i.e., looking for a more concrete and universalistic understanding of "transformation"), which involves society becoming subject to the socio-political action of the church, in an attempt to "redeem culture." For commentary on how the central purpose of the church can become distorted see Nugent, *Endangered Gospel*. See also Little, "What Makes Mission Christian?"

35. This approach has arisen out of the "transformational development movement." Here the term *transformation* has been used to describe "holistic" forms of change that occur as a result of all that Christians do for the common good. This confuses the distinct mission of the church with the wide range of God-given callings within society that individual Christians and non-Christians have. This movement has been well documented in Tizon, *Transformation after Lausanne*. Academic articles on "transformational development" have appeared in *Transformation: An International Journal of Holistic Mission Studies*. In particular, see Sugden, "Transformational Development."

The emphasis within this book is the distinct transformation that can only be seen to occur in the life of the Christian community. It is only as a result of identification with the salvific work of Christ and through a dynamic relationship with the living God that Christian formation can take place. The process through which formation occurs cannot be controlled or fully understood—it transcends a reductionist, prescriptive, or formula-driven approach. However, individuals create opportunities for it to occur through continually nurturing their faith. Rather than beginning with a precise and/or narrow definition of transformation from a Christian perspective, what follows is a simple yet broad definition that will later be developed upon in a holistic way:

> A. *Transformation begins with the work of the divine agency.* Christian formation is grounded in the redemptive work of the Triune God. God initiates formation in human life based on his will and purposes—and provides the means for it to occur.
>
> B. *Transformation requires intentional human co-operation with "A"—the divine agency.* Christian formation occurs where persons demonstrate the purposeful willingness and appropriate response to what God is seeking to do in their lives. This requires both a desire to change and a continual commitment to live in consecration and obedience to God.
>
> C. *The purpose of "A"+"B" is for persons to be progressively conformed to the image of Christ.* Christ expresses the fullness of the divine life in human flesh. The goal of Christian formation is for the whole church to reveal the image of Christ, to the glory of God.

When grounded in a soteriological narrative, together, these three elements articulate how Christian formation can be differentiated from human development in both its central goal and its principal means. The three-point definition allows for a proper understanding of Christian growth and formation that transcends fragmented expressions. The central dynamic here is a "personal relationship" with God, where God initiates, and persons respond—God revealing himself and individuals choosing to co-operate with him so that they may come to reflect his character more. The definition above provides the ground upon which to develop a broad, holistic, and distinctly Christian vision of transformational theology.

1.4 THE MEANING OF "EVANGELICAL"

1.4.1 Deconstructing Evangelicalism

This book sets out to explore a "proto-evangelical" view of transformation. In this section, there will be an attempt to deconstruct "evangelicalism" as a phenomenon constructed upon historical and social science methodologies, before reconstructing a biblical-theological (and protological) understanding that holds to a rational-linguistic center. It is proposed that this proto-evangelical method provides the only meaningful understanding of the term "evangelical."[36]

The term "evangelical" has become notoriously hard to define.[37] D. A. Carson notes: "Giving definition to evangelicalism is not only difficult, but is growing even more difficult as a wider and wider group of people apply the label to themselves. It may be, as some have suggested, that the term will eventually so lack definition as to be theologically useless—much like the term *Christian* today."[38] Given that the term "evangelical" is often designated to an eclectic variety of groups, there is an increasing need to ask what type of evangelical we are talking about.[39] As Colin Hansen states: "Simply labeling ourselves evangelical no longer suffices. We are conservative, progressive, post-conservative, and pre-progressive evangelicals. We are traditional, creedal, biblical, pietistic, anti-creedal, ecumenical, and fundamentalist. We are 'followers of Christ' and 'Red Letter Christians.' We are everything, so we are nothing."[40] Because of the variety of meanings that have come to

---

36. D. A. Carson has expressed the need for a biblical-theological method to be applied. He affirms: "I have long argued that 'evangelicalism' must be defined first and foremost theologically, or else it will not be long before the term will become fundamentally unusable to its core adherents" ("Domesticating the Gospel," 43–44). Works that focus on a more biblical-theological understanding are Lloyd-Jones, *What Is an Evangelical?*; Armstrong, *Coming Evangelical Crisis*; Sproul, *Getting the Gospel Right*; Mohler, "Confessional Evangelicalism."

37. For an introductory discussion on the various perspectives, see Naselli and Hansen, *Four Views*. Different attempts to define evangelicalism can be found in Larsen, "Defining and Locating Evangelicalism"; Noll, "What Is 'Evangelical'?"; "Defining Evangelicalism"; Bebbington, "Definition of Evangelicalism"; Hutchinson and Wolffe, *Global Evangelicalism*; Stiller et al., *Evangelicals around the World*.

38. Carson, *Gagging of God*, 444.

39. Brian Harris has warned: "Evangelicalism is in danger of becoming a hyphenated movement. Increasingly its adherents find it necessary to qualify what kind of evangelical they are" ("Beyond Bebbington," 201).

40. Naselli and Hansen, 9.

be associated with the term "evangelical," the word has become virtually meaningless.[41]

Although evangelicalism may be defined in a variety of different ways, there are essentially only two ways to go about the task of looking for a definition—through either a *historical-sociological* method or a *biblical-theological* method. Bruce Hindmarsh explains:

> The most common way to define evangelicalism is by trying to determine the distinctive, universally shared characteristics of the movement. This can be done from the inside, as it were, by an evangelical theologian such as J. I. Packer, who writes from a conviction about what evangelicalism *ought* to be, or from the outside, by a historian such as David Bebbington . . . who describes from a more neutral point of view what it seems the movement *is* (or what it *was*). Whereas Packer identifies a syllabus of ten doctrinal convictions that *ought* to characterize evangelicals, such as the authority of Scripture, the supremacy of Christ as Savior and Lord, the necessity of faith and holiness, and so on, Bebbington argues that only four characteristics have really distinctively characterized evangelicals throughout their history, namely, their emphasis on personal conversion, the Bible, the cross of Christ, and active Christian service.[42]

There are commonalities, but also vast differences between the approaches of Packer and Bebbington. Packer's biblical-theological approach involves seeing evangelicalism as a renewal movement that is based on doctrinal norms, while Bebbington defines evangelicalism historically—based upon what he sees as phenomenological commonalities across a broad movement. In defining evangelicalism within a historical-sociological framework, Bebbington has sought to find some similarities across the evolving beliefs and experiences of Protestant groups.[43]

---

41. D. G. Hart affirms: "Evangelicalism needs to be relinquished as a religious identity because it does not exist. In fact, it is the 'wax nose' of twentieth century American Protestantism" (*Deconstructing Evangelicalism*, 16).

42. Hindmarsh, "Contours of Evangelical Spirituality," 150.

43. For a discussion of some weaknesses in Bebbington's theory, see Stewart, "David Bebbington's Thesis." See also Haykin and Stewart, *Emergence of Evangelicalism*; Stewart, *In Search of Ancient Roots*. The underlying problem with Bebbington's approach is his understanding of the origins of the movement. Brian Harris summarizes the controversy over Bebbington's thesis thus: "Bebbington argues that the origins of the evangelical movement should be linked to the renewal movements of the eighteenth century and that evangelicalism should be dated to the pivotal events of the 1730s that marked the start of an extended period of spiritual awakenings. As this challenges the notion of gospel successionism popularized by leading evangelicals such as Packer and Stott, who

Although Bebbington's quadrilateral may in some way describe the broad commonalities amongst self-identified evangelicals, it is unable to provide means of expressing or holding to aspirational norms. Consequently, it leaves room for pluralism, divisiveness, and contradiction within the so-called "evangelical world." For Bebbington, evangelicalism is more about the present and evolving state of the beliefs and behaviors of a wide variety of social and ecclesial groupings than it is about firm theological convictions or aspirational virtues. Furthermore, Bebbington's framework does not provide any characteristics that are exclusive to evangelicalism—and so suggests a false view of unity and cohesiveness in one subset of the church. Many, if not all, of the four characteristics he describes would apply in some way to other Christians who do not identify as "evangelical."[44]

From a phenomenological perspective, so-called "evangelicalism" has become so broad that the possibility of a common "evangelical" identity appears to be futile. Robert Warner has pointed out the increasing diversity within what he understands as "evangelicalism," demonstrating that it is an increasingly fragmented movement.[45] Ironically, his accurate observations of self-identified evangelicals ultimately only serve to reinforce the futility of the observation itself. "Evangelicalism," sociologically understood, is indeed evolving and moving, because those self-identified as "evangelical" have themselves defined what it is—both in terms of beliefs and practices—it has become a "wax nose." Clearly, a historical-sociological method is unable to find a solid and workable framework because it is rooted in a subjective observation of subjective experience—and consequently subject to the relativism that arises from this. It will invariably include observing the plurality of beliefs, behaviors, and experiences of fallen and fallible human beings.[46] In

---

argue that evangelicalism is essentially New Testament Christianity, as recovered by the Reformation, reinforced by the Puritans and popularized by the awakenings from the 1730s onwards, it is not surprising that some have been critical of Bebbington's work" ("Beyond Bebbington," 202).

44. Regarding the quadrilateral, Albert Mohler affirms that "these criteria are so vague as to be fairly useless in determining the limits of evangelical definition. Construed in such general terms, it is hard to see how many Roman Catholics and liberal Protestants would not consider themselves included. They, too, believe that lives need to be changed, hold 'a particular regard for the Bible,' place a stress on the sacrifice of Christ on the cross, and seek an activist demonstration of their faith. So, even as Bebbington's descriptive argument is helpful, it hardly solves the problem of evangelical identity and definition" ("Confessional Evangelicalism," 73).

45. See Warner, *Reinventing English Evangelicalism*.

46. The problem is that a sociological method will always allow forms of individualism and relativism. Whether something is right or true (or "evangelical") becomes subjectively determined by specific individuals and/or groups who are self-identified as evangelical, rather than by an objectively revealed Word. A sociological method

summary, any attempts to properly observe and describe a true movement of God—from a phenomenological perspective—prove to be futile. In the truest sense, this kind of "evangelicalism" is a mirage—it does not exist.[47]

1.4.2 A Biblical-Theological Approach

As an alternative to a historical-sociological understanding, it is suggested that the term "evangelical" can—in its truest sense—only be defined by its protological foundation, i.e., divine revelation in redemptive history. It is only a biblical-theological understanding that provides the means for an objective and meaningful definition of the term "evangelical."[48] And only this can orientate a proto-evangelical understanding of Christian formation.

In seeking to follow a biblical-theological method, Packer has tried to describe evangelicalism through the lens of theological orthodoxy. His approach has involved laying out doctrinal markers that he sees as being necessary and common to self-identified evangelicals.[49] While these markers may be congruent with orthodoxy, to define the essence of what it means to be evangelical, the imperative should not be to start with a focus on the specific boundaries of a movement, but instead to define its core convictions. An understanding of what it means to be evangelical has to arise out of a clearly defined center (and how to relate to that center), so that persons may be able to increasingly come to express the norms and aspirations of both orthodoxy and orthopraxy.

---

cannot lead to any true consensus because there is the observance of beliefs and practices that—to a greater or lesser extent—will always be distorted by the sinful nature of humanity.

47. When Christian identity is not framed by biblical language it can become subject to language that is sociological and/or political, which leads to tribal labels (e.g., "conservative," "moderate," "liberal," "charismatic," "open/progressive," and so forth). Such designations are a simplistic attempt to pigeonhole groups and individuals. Moreover, these labels inevitably lead to the positive acceptance and affirmation of contradictory and discordant perspectives, under the guise of "inclusivity," "broadness," and "diversity."

48. D. A. Carson affirms: "I hold that 'evangelical' and 'evangelicalism' are most useful when they are held to their etymology in the evangel, 'the gospel [God] promised beforehand through his prophets in the Holy Scriptures regarding his Son' (Rom 1:2–3), on the assumption that such an 'evangel' is held with firmness and sincerity of heart. In this light, evangelicalism as a movement must be seen to be determined by its center, not by its outermost boundary—and even that center must, in the light of its own confession, constantly be held up to the examination of Scripture" (*Gagging of God*, 448).

49. See Packer and Oden, *One Faith*; Packer, "Reflection and Response," 179–81.

Notably, Packer's understanding of evangelicalism is not only rooted in "confessional" orthodoxy, but also in evidence of a transformed existence. Regarding this, he states: "Should persons who endorse this ideal notionally fail to pursue it practically, the right thing to say of them is that they are not real evangelicals."[50] The point Packer is making is that being truly evangelical involves seeking to conform to *both* the doctrinal ideal (the "conceptual norm") and the behavioral ideal (the "aspirational norm"). While this is necessary for evidence of authenticity, the achievement of these ideals is always something individuals are called to work toward. Indeed, a person's commitment to remain faithful to a clearly defined center should lead to a change in their beliefs and actions, which causes them to be increasingly conformed to the image of Christ.

As already noted, a biblical-theological understanding is grounded in the protological concerns of God's redemptive action in history. Only when the definition of evangelical is determined in relation to these "first things" can it have any real value—for being rooted in the proper historical ground leads to suitable convictions and aspirations. Don Payne points out that Packer understands evangelicalism as being "rooted in Reformational theology, Puritan-type pietism, and eighteenth and nineteenth century ideals of evangelistic outreach."[51] However, while Packer does not see himself apart from the post-reformation "evangelical tradition," he does recognize the need for "norming norms" which stem from historical continuity with the "Great Tradition."[52] Packer refers to the

> mutation of the former self-image of evangelicals as the marginalized faithful remnant within liberal-led Protestantism into a sense of being truly the core of God's church on earth. Evangelicalism is more and more viewing itself as the mainstream in relation to which non-evangelicals, whether so by adding to the biblical faith or subtracting from it, are deviating eddies.[53]

While Packer believes that evangelicalism is both historical and theological in nature, his understanding of it remains within the context of "gospel successionism." Consequently, he does not see it as simply being a narrow post-reformation movement affirming "confessional" truths but, first and foremost, as representing those seeking to bring the church back within the "Great Tradition"—characterized by a genuine commitment to the apostolic gospel. According to Packer, evangelicalism is

50. Ibid., 182–183.
51. Payne, *Theology of the Christian Life*, 18.
52. Packer, "Reflection and Response," 179–85.
53. Packer, "Stunted Ecclesiology?" 120.

> the Christianity, both convictional and behavioral, which we inherit from the New Testament via the Reformers, the Puritans, and the revival and missionary leaders of the eighteenth and nineteenth centuries. . . . The reason why I call myself an evangelical and mean to go on doing so is my belief that as this historic evangelicalism has never sought to be anything other than New Testament Christianity, so in essentials, it has succeeded in its aim.[54]

It is proposed that using a biblical-theological method to understand the term "evangelical" will enable a proto-evangelical approach—because it appeals to protological concerns around the redemptive climax of the drama of God in human history. Here, God has already fully and objectively revealed himself by his Word (i.e., in his Son and the Scriptures)—through his Spirit. This is the "first gospel" which God the Father spoke forth in his Word—the Son—who lived the perfect life, died on the cross, was resurrected—and is presently exalted—reigning as Lord and Savior. Such was witnessed by the early church and verbally proclaimed as "good news," in accord with the Scriptures. Consequently, the term proto-evangelical would also denote a core commitment to the witness and authority of the Scriptures.

The church has always been called to faithfully pass down the "spoken Word," in congruence with the historic gospel. Such is to be communicated as rational-linguistic truth, so that it may be understood and lived in relation to. The possibility of persons being able to faithfully receive and respond to this starts with the presupposition that there is a personal, sovereign, and transcendent God—an omniscient being, possessing absolute truth—who chooses to share this with humanity. If God is able to communicate himself so that persons can come to true knowledge and understanding of him—and respond appropriately—then formation can occur. Revelation is not first and foremost rooted in a subjective experience. It begins as the objective drama of God in history, being *a priori* and independent of any human knowledge or acknowledgment of it.[55] If God has already spoken his Word in history, then it does not need a human witness to be deemed true—he has already declared it to be so.

---

54. Packer, "Uniqueness of Jesus Christ," 102.

55. Albert Mohler states: "If Scripture is not objectively true, independent of our acknowledgment, and if God is not objectively real, independent of our knowledge of him, then we are without hope. If Jesus Christ did not die on the cross as our substitute and if he was not resurrected on the third day, if we have not been justified by faith and if his righteousness has not been imputed to us, then we are dead in our sins. Christianity is predicated upon a claim to absolute truth, though we never claim that, in our fallenness, our knowledge is ever absolute. To surrender this ground is to surrender the faith itself" ("Evangelical," 39).

In summary: at its best evangelicalism is a renewal movement committed to the "Great Tradition," and to bringing the church back to what it understands to be "true Christianity," by continually subjecting its beliefs and practices to the Scriptures, within which the "good news" of the gospel of Christ is the center.[56] To be truly evangelical would be to speak of "guarding" and "preserving" that which has already been objectively spoken forth. Such is the aspirational task of those who seek to be faithful stewards of the gospel and the Scriptures—as they have been given—to defend and proclaim the truth as God has willed, and try to faithfully live in light of it.[57]

Based on this understanding, where the "church" ceases to do this—it ceases to be truly evangelical—in both intention and practice. Moreover, any problems within so-called "evangelicalism" occur on the basis of persons not wholly embracing the fullness of the evangel, in which orthodox tradition rests. In order to develop a broad and holistic understanding of transformational theology, the need is not merely to explore a variety of Christian traditions but, more precisely, to be open to the evangel wherever it is found. In doing so, there is the possibility of persons critiquing where their own tradition has strayed from the biblical gospel and the authority of Scripture itself. In this book, it is argued that the only means through which a proto-evangelical model of transformational theology can be constructed, is by being grounded in the rational-linguistic communication of the Scriptures—in which the gospel of Christ is the center.[58]

1.5 REPRESENTATIVE LITERATURE

This next section will introduce some contemporary approaches to Christian formation within the "evangelical world." It will look at the contribution of representative figures who have sought to express different ways of

---

56. John Stott affirms: "if evangelical theology is biblical theology, it follows that it is not a newfangled 'ism,' a modern brand of Christianity, but an ancient form, indeed the original" (*Christ the Controversialist*, 33).

57. Alister McGrath states: "Evangelicalism is determined to 'let God be God,' and to receive, honor, and conceive him as he chooses to be known, rather than as we would have him be. At its heart, evangelicalism represents a relentless and serious attempt to bring all our conceptions of God and ourselves to criticism in the light of how and what God wishes to be known" (*Passion for Truth*, 37–38).

58. This communication is firstly understood by its content (the "material principle"), which is the substance of the gospel of Christ based upon scriptural teaching—the objective historicity of Christ's coming as God's self-revelation in human flesh, culminating in his death, resurrection, and exaltation. Secondly, it is understood by its authority (the "formal principle"), appealing to Scripture to shape and define in light of the gospel—Scripture being understood as authoritative, sufficient, and perspicuous.

renewing perspectives on [trans-]formation within the church. There will be a brief discussion on the material of four different "evangelical" thinkers, introducing how each of them has sought to "re-envision transformation."[59] All of them provide works that offer a critique of so-called evangelical approaches, and/or set out to propose a new way forward for understanding Christian formation.

Richard Lovelace

In the 1970s an important commentator on spiritual renewal was church historian Richard Lovelace. Lovelace desired to see "spiritual theology" at the center of renewal, and for self-identified evangelicals to study Christian spirituality.[60] His seminal work is *Dynamics of Spiritual Life*, which he calls "a manual of spiritual theology, a discipline combining the history and the theology of Christian experience."[61] In this book, he speaks of the absence of spiritual maturity present among self-identified evangelicals (i.e., the "sanctification gap") and sets out a vision for "holistic" spiritual renewal.[62]

In exploring the true nature of renewal, Lovelace believes that personal formation should not be separate from other areas of regeneration in church and society. He sets out a broad vision that offers a base for ecumenical renewal. Lovelace supposes that self-identified evangelicals have something to offer the wider church theologically, while—at the same time—understanding the need to listen to the evangel of Christ being preached and enacted in other Christian traditions. He firmly believes that evangelicalism must hold to biblical authority and bring theological reformation and integration, including needing to increase theological depth through biblical education. Lovelace also proposes a need to "live orthodoxy," which he understands to

---

59. Alongside these four voices (and J. I. Packer—whose work will be examined in the next chapter), other notable "evangelical" writers on Christian spirituality in the last forty years would include Robert Webber, James Houston, Richard Foster, Eugene Peterson, David Benner, Alister McGrath, Donald Bloesch, Ian Randall, Evan Howard, John Coe, Robert Mulholland, Bruce Demarest, Steve Porter, Gordon Smith, Jerry Bridges, Don Whitney, Michael Allen, Joel Beeke, James Wilhoit, Glen Scorgie, Gary Thomas, Sinclair Ferguson, Peter Adam, James K. A. Smith, Tom Schwanda, Kyle Strobel, Kelly Kapic, Diane Chandler, and Larry Crabb.

60. Lovelace understands the term *spiritual theology* to denote the integration between spirituality and theology, rather than seeing it as being synonymous with spirituality alone.

61. Lovelace, *Dynamics of Spiritual Life*, 11. A short revision of this book appeared later as *Renewal as a Way of Life*.

62. This was first recorded in his article "The Sanctification Gap."

involve holding to propositional truth and doctrine, while understanding that a genuine commitment to orthodoxy is only found in living it.[63]

However, Lovelace does not set out to root his approach within a comprehensive framework of theological orthodoxy. Instead, he attempts to develop integrative models for renewal based upon both post-reformation history and Scripture. He presents what he calls a "unified field theory" of spirituality that seeks to reconcile different areas of Christian experience—and sets out the broad parameters for "holistic" renewal.[64] Rather than solely focusing on personal formation, Lovelace seeks to embrace various dimensions of renewal—individual, corporate, and societal—with the understanding that they are all interconnected—holding together the need for a relationship with God, personal growth, community life, theology, mission, and so forth.[65] Lovelace does not set out to provide an exegetical basis for formation or renewal; the "biblical models" for renewal that he puts forward can only be described as being characterized by select biblical principles.

Lovelace's influential work has set out important parameters for understanding an integral approach to renewal in the church. However, he has not sought to provide a systematically constructed model. What Lovelace offers is a comprehensive manual of insightful principles, not an organized attempt to deliver a cohesive theological model for "holistic" transformation. It is questionable whether he provides the most effective integral agenda for renewal, given that his approach is not rooted in a systematic theological framework. While others have looked outside of the "evangelical tradition" toward a wider variety of sources, Lovelace looks to it for "ressourcement."[66] However, he also speaks about the need for self-identified evangelicals to listen to voices outside their tradition, where others have preserved biblical values that they lack. He believes that looking to history helps to "force us back toward biblical balance and authentic spirituality."[67] In response, it could be argued that being *truly* evangelical is not about holding to so-

63. Lovelace, *Dynamics of Spiritual Life*, 271–87.

64. Ibid., 17.

65. There have been more comprehensive attempts at providing a "holistic" approach; many of these suggest a shift in emphasis toward "societal transformation." Notable works that have affirmed this approach are: Samuel and Sugden, *Mission as Transformation*; Myers, *Walking with the Poor*.

66. Some works have encouraged people to explore wider than the so-called "evangelical tradition." For example, see Foster, *Streams of Living Water*; Webber, *Common Roots*; *Evangelicals on the Canterbury Trail*.

67. Lovelace, "Evangelical Spirituality," 35. The contribution of historical theology for Christian formation studies is explored in Peters, "Historical Theology"; Hall, "Spiritual Formation."

called "evangelical tradition," but rather about seeking to be rooted in protological concerns within redemptive history. Such would lead toward an understanding that is more acceptable outside of the so-called "evangelical world."

Dallas Willard

Since the late 1970s, there has been a resurgence of Protestant literature on ascetical theology.[68] Much of this material has emphasized the need to practice what have been coined "spiritual disciplines." Dallas Willard has been an important voice at the forefront of the resurgence. Steve Porter describes five key books that make up the "Willardian Corpus" as being "a unified and comprehensive account of spiritual growth in Christ."[69] Together, the principal concepts within Willard's major works suggest a well-ordered understanding of the nature and process of Christian formation.

At the core of Willard's thought is a concern for Christians to move beyond the experience of "transactional salvation" toward being committed and mature disciples of Christ.[70] His writings show he has a solid grasp of the fundamental characteristics of a transformational relationship with Christ. Willard articulates some basic parameters of formative theology and discipleship, laying an emphasis on the need for persons to follow Christ's leading, and on human co-operation that leads to transformation into Christlikeness.

His framework for a transforming relationship is laid out in his first book, *Hearing God*.[71] Here, Willard provides a context for the ascetical theology that arises in his second book, *The Spirit of the Disciplines*, where he explores the nature of human co-operation and praxis. Willard focuses on the idea that engagement in disciplines and "spiritual practices" enables persons to co-operate with divine resources, which changes human behavior and leads to character modification.

Willard's central theoretical model for formation is developed in a later work, *Renovation of the Heart*, where he provides a "holistic" understanding of Christian formation based on his own integrated theological

68. The beginning of this literary resurgence is often attributed to Foster, *Celebration of Discipline*.

69. Porter, "Willardian Corpus," 240.

70. His understanding of discipleship is outlined in Willard, "Discipleship."

71. Willard bases his whole system of formation upon the possibility of persons coming to a true knowledge of God. He fully outlines his epistemology in a later work *Knowing Christ Today*.

anthropology. Willard seeks to describe the nature of transformation toward Christlikeness that occurs in different dimensions of a person—mind, heart/will/spirit, body, social, and soul—as a result of them interacting with the constant movements of God's grace. He understands this transformation to be a divinely led process that allows the whole of a person's being—from the inside out—to come into harmony with the will of God.

Willard shows due concern for the lack of transformation he perceives amongst self-identified evangelicals, recognizing that "transactional salvation" is often pursued apart from a life of discipleship with Jesus. His desire is for persons to experience authentic change, rather than to rely on "cheap grace" and their initial conversion. Willard's remedy for the lack of transformation is to emphasize the need for the church to recapture the essence of the message Christ taught—the message he believes to be the proto-evangelical gospel.[72] He supposes that the principal requirement is for us to discover what Jesus really meant in his teachings, so that the transforming life of God may be experienced now in all its fullness, across all of life.[73]

Willard does not see the need to ground transformation in doctrinal propositions. Instead, he identifies the problem as being when persons seek to believe the correct doctrine without a demonstration of real change in their lives. Consequently, there is little function for dogma in his schema. Rather than believers simply assenting to a set of propositions, Willard affirms that the principal requirement is for them to enter into a personal relationship with Jesus as disciples, to learn his way—hearing, observing, and imitating in order to take on his characteristics. Willard has acknowledged that there is a need to responsibly reconcile the practice of spiritual disciplines within a soteriological framework.[74] However, his overwhelming focus has been on the moral teachings of Christ, rather than on what Jesus said about himself and his salvific mission.

Although Willard's corpus reveals that he is deeply concerned with authentic transformation, it does not demonstrate that he has allowed the center of change to be the biblical gospel. Nor does it show that he has held together the categories of "law" and "gospel" appropriately. Willard appears to lay great emphasis on the need for obedience to the spoken imperatives of Christ as the main driving force behind transformation. As a result, faith in the exalted Christ and identification with his death and resurrection are

---

72. Black, *Theology of Dallas Willard*, xv. Willard's understanding of Christ's message is expressed in two of his books, see Willard, *Divine Conspiracy*; *Great Omission*.

73. See Willard and Black, *Divine Conspiracy Continued*. In this later work, there is an expression of a "broader," more "inclusive" vision of the Kingdom of God, demonstrating a shift toward societal transformation.

74. See Willard, "Spiritual Formation."

not always given the central function as a catalyst for change in the life of the believer.

Ultimately, Willard's vision of the Christian life is not transformational enough. He defers from emphasizing eternal salvation in order to focus more on the need for transformation in this present age and so applies a false dichotomy between the two. Willard's concern for the process of transformation in this life leads him to assimilate justification and sanctification, rather than allowing sanctification to be wholly driven by justification. Given that reflecting the image of the risen Christ is the goal of the Christian life, transformation in this present age must principally be seen to occur as a result of union with Christ in his present exalted state.

Despite Willard's desire to emphasize the teachings of Christ, his methodology is not always grounded in a solid exegesis of Scripture. Therefore, a robust biblical theology of the soteriological drama is not made a necessary backdrop for present transformation. Willard writes as a philosopher rather than a theologian, and this is evident in the framework for his understanding of anthropology and formation, which are based on a mixture of historical and biblical sources, alongside social sciences.[75] Because of the diversity of Willard's sources stemming from his cross-disciplinary method, he does not focus on developing a systematic framework that integrates all the necessary biblical-theological concerns. Consequently, he is unable to provide a suitable basis for an integrative understanding of Christian formation. Although a focus on definitive union with Christ and propositional doctrine are (as will be pointed out in this book) integral to transformation, Willard appears to see an emphasis on these areas as creating the problem, rather than being the solution.

Given that Willard has been critical of a systematic theological method, it is unsurprising that he does not attempt to provide a cohesive transformational theology rooted in biblical-theological categories. In leaving a large divide between doctrine and life, he does not provide a way of sufficiently exploring the proper interaction between the concerns of theology and spirituality (i.e., praxis does not become fully integrated within orthodox theological categories). His methodology does not lead him

---

75. Various works on Christian formation have drawn from the social sciences. Bruce Demarest has noted how many contemporary approaches have sought to include insights from developmental psychology (see "Reflections on Developmental Spirituality"; *Seasons of the Soul*). Other studies incorporating the social sciences have been Conn, *Spirituality and Personal Maturity*; Balswick et al., *Reciprocating Self*; Estep and Kim, *Christian Formation*; Tisdale, "Psychology and Spiritual Formation"; Collicutt, *Christian Character Formation*. David Benner has made a significant contribution, taking a "psychospiritual" approach to formation that integrates spiritual and psychological growth (Howard, "Psychospiritual Model").

toward constructing a suitably proto-evangelical model of transformational theology because his protological center is the teachings of Christ, rather than the core gospel itself. Ultimately, the gospel of God cannot chiefly be identified with the words of Christ, for it is only Christ himself who is *the* Word—spoken by the Father, through the Spirit.

Simon Chan

Another notable contributor to the contemporary conversation has been Simon Chan. Chan has understood there to be a deficiency with the "evangelical spiritual tradition," and offered a vision of how it can be rejuvenated. Like others, he points out supposed problems and omissions, and proposes a new way forward.[76] Chan has called for a renewal of "evangelical spirituality" based upon "historical continuity," which would involve the need to become more "catholic" by focusing on what it shares in common with the wider church.[77] He has highlighted the need for "ressourcement" from other traditions—ultimately pointing toward a more convergent approach that places a stronger focus on liturgy and "spiritual practices"—while attempting to integrate them with "evangelical doctrine."

Chan recognizes that there has been a resurgence of material that emphasizes the practice of spiritual disciplines.[78] He identifies what he understands to be traditional "evangelical" practices and advocates an enlarging of the list.[79] In Chan's earlier work, *Spiritual Theology*, he sought to examine the nature of the Christian life in relation to a "broader" theological framework. He recognizes that a separation has often been made between "doctrine" and "living unto God" (i.e., between systematic theology and praxis). In response to this, he sets out to express "theological studies concerning the principles and practices of the Christian life."[80] While still desiring to

---

76. Chan, "Spiritual Practices."

77. "New Directions," 236. Others have also attempted a more convergent approach. For example, see Webber, *Worship Old and New*; Cocksworth, *Holding Together*; Smith, *Evangelical, Sacramental & Pentecostal*.

78. Chan, "New Directions." Notable contemporary works on spiritual disciplines have been Foster, *Celebration of Discipline*; Willard, *Spirit of the Disciplines*; Whitney, *Disciplines within the Church*; *Disciplines for the Christian Life*; Tan and Gregg, *Disciplines of the Holy Spirit*; Peterson, *Long Obedience*; Calhoun, *Spiritual Disciplines Handbook*; Mathis, *Habits of Grace*. For an evaluation of the concept of spiritual disciplines, see Carson, "Spiritual Disciplines."

79. Chan, "Spiritual Practices."

80. Chan, *Spiritual Theology*, 16.

hold an "evangelical" commitment, he also seeks to explore a "broader" understanding by being more ecumenical in his trajectory.

Chan divides this work into two sections, the first part looking at theological principles, and the second examining spiritual practice. The disconnected explorations into "doctrine" and "praxis" suggest that he has not fully understood the proper relationship between the two. In the first half of his book, he seeks to relate a rather select list of Christian doctrines (theology proper, harmatiology, soteriology, and ecclesiology) to the Christian life. In the second half, Chan focuses solely on practical issues. In doing so, the theological formulations outlined in the earlier chapters all but disappear. Although he seeks to connect these two parts, he is unable to truly bridge the gap because experiential practice is not wholly understood in relation to his doctrinal categories. In like manner, he is unable to fully contextualize his propositional theology in terms of its relevance to the experiential dimensions of everyday life.[81]

In Chan's subsequent work, *Liturgical Theology,* he points to the need for self-identified evangelicals to shift away from simply advocating a "broader" series of personal disciplines, toward the more central need for ecclesial practices and liturgical structure. Chan believes that the ecclesiology and liturgy within evangelicalism is weak, and so sets out what he understands to be a "richer" and more liturgical ecclesiology that is to be embraced in all its forms. In doing so, he focuses on the need for transformation to occur through the integration of theology and liturgy, with an emphasis on a communal setting.

Chan speaks of the effects of liturgical worship in forming persons into a "community of character," placing focus on "Word" and "sacrament" as the primary source of spiritual nourishment.[82] Chan makes a distinction between personal practices and communal liturgical practices, with the latter understood as being able to form persons in ways that individualistic means cannot.[83] He attests to the mystery of divine action in the liturgy, recognizing that this changes persons, not because they have made a conscious effort to be shaped by it, but because it has an inherent power to transform.[84] His belief is that "over time this pervading 'Spirit' of the liturgy will have its

---

81. There are other studies more helpful in delineating the proper relation between the concerns of theology and spirituality. For example, see McIntosh, *Mystical Theology*; Sheldrake, *Spirituality and Theology*; Coe, "Spiritual Theology"; Peters, "On Spiritual Theology"; Graham, "Spiritual Formation"; Kapic, "Systematic Theology"; Jones, *Practicing Christian Doctrine*; Johnson, *Theology as Discipleship*.

82. Chan, *Liturgical Theology*, 55.

83. Ibid., 91.

84. Ibid.

unseen effect on individual members and form them into members of the body of Christ."[85] Such an understanding appears to affirm a principal role for passivity, rather than placing the central focus on an active response to the preaching of the Word.

In this book, Chan has sought to move focus away from an individualistic form of spirituality. He emphasizes the importance of gathered practices within an ecclesial setting as a means of participation in the redemptive story. As a result, he does not leave room for the lived worship of the "scattered church"; because all is tied in so closely with centralized liturgical acts or practices.[86] The "participation in doctrine" is recognized as being present in the "performance" of the centralized liturgy; the church being seen as needing to "act out"—rather than solely focus on—an assent to doctrinal propositions. Chan believes that the heart of ecclesial practice is the common liturgy, and concentrates on the need for participation in centralized church activities. Given that performance is centered in specific acts and a particular location, he does not wholly affirm the sacredness and importance of the everyday narrative for transformation. Though Chan brings an important dimension of the Christian life to the fore, he places too much focus on it as being the solution.

Chan has started with the premise that "evangelical spirituality" expresses distinct characteristics. He sees the "evangelical tradition" as being deficient because it is understood to demonstrate a particular form that is limited in its specific emphasis and bias. Consequently, to be "complete," self-identified evangelicals are seen as needing to converge with the "common heritage." In taking this approach, he looks away from a rational-linguistic center as being the principal means of enabling integration and formation, believing it to be insufficient. Rather than taking the lead from the biblical text itself—with the biblical gospel remaining at the very core—Chan looks toward the broader tradition and shared ecclesial practices. Consequently, authority, theology, and transformation are seen to rest more on lived experience.

Ultimately, Chan's belief that convergence will somehow solve the transformation problem is misguided because there is an assumed "wisdom" of collective ecclesial traditions above Scripture itself. He understands the central problem as being the overt focus on "evangelical doctrine," and does not see a series of propositional truths grounded in the biblical text as

---

85. Ibid., 92.

86. In *Desiring the Kingdom*, James K. A. Smith emphasizes the worship of the "scattered church," attempting to frame everyday life within more liturgical terms. This work relies heavily on the Eastern Orthodox tradition, being a reinterpretation of Schmemann, *For the Life of the World*.

being sufficient to facilitate a transformed life amongst believers. Therefore, he proposes a "broader" approach where the individual believer is set within the church and the wider Christian tradition and called to participate in the "performance" of shared practices. The two principal works of Chan mentioned attempt to bring together doctrine and praxis in different ways, but do so without moving toward a cohesive and fully integral approach. Though Chan's ideas and suggestions promise more breadth and depth to spirituality, they remain highly fragmented. Attempts such as this to move toward prescribed solutions to the "transformation problem"—by shifting away from a rational-linguistic center—can only result in disillusionment and perpetual searching.

Michael Horton

In recent years, an important contributor to the conversation from a "confessional" position has been Michael Horton. As a Reformed theologian, Horton has sought to ground the understanding and lived experience of the Christian life within a theological framework that is both biblical and systematic, rather than taking his lead from ecumenical tradition or the social sciences. Horton has written extensively on the Christian life, while also maintaining a focus on Christian doctrine. Most notably, he has produced a significant volume on systematic theology, *The Christian Faith,* in which he attempts to find ways of integrating doctrine and life through the interconnected categories of "drama, dogma, doxology, and discipleship."

Horton supposes that a solid belief structure is a prerequisite to a transformed experience in the life of the believer. Therefore, he places emphasis on the need for persons to be taught propositional doctrine. Horton does not see the problem as being that Christians are not living their doctrine, but rather that they *are* living their doctrine—and that it is a human-centered one. He does not see any value in approaches to Christian formation that focus on pragmatism but instead concentrates on the indispensability of doctrine. For Horton, doctrine stems from a need to verbally communicate the nature of the redemptive drama in history, for the purpose of worship and a transformed life. Without doctrine, sustainable transformation—in any authentic sense—is not seen to be possible.

Some of Horton's writings have drawn attention to problems within the contemporary "evangelical world"—particularly by highlighting the anti-theological bias, which he understands to be the driving factor behind the lack of seriousness amongst self-identified evangelicals. In his book *Christless Christianity,* Horton points out the absence of the biblical gospel within so-called "evangelicalism," showing that much of the focus is human-centered rather than Christ-centered. He points out the problem with self-styled approaches to spirituality that are characterized by subjective experience. Such are understood to overly exhibit pragmatism, moralism, and anti-intellectualism.

In his book *In the Face of God,* Horton critiques a "spirituality" that is rooted in personal subjectivity, in particular where the focus is on a so-called "personal relationship" with God that is not solidly grounded in a response to the biblical gospel. Horton reacts against approaches to spirituality that begin with private and subjective experiences, and/or those primarily praxis based or rooted in humanistic moralism. He highlights the problems that arise, especially where there is seen to be preoccupation with an "inward experience," over and above faith in objective logocentric revelation (i.e., Christ and Scripture). Horton understands these approaches to be—at best—futile human-centered attempts to be saved and transformed apart from the knowledge of God in Christ. He is especially critical of persons seeking after immediate transformation, through some "direct" gnostic encounter.[87] Horton also has a problem with the concept of subjective inner guidance, because the authority here is seen to stem from the individual, namely, their reason, will, feelings, and desires, rather than originating from an authority that is outside and above them.

In response to the "transformation problem," Horton simply points toward the biblical gospel. Of the books he has written on the nature of the gospel, most notable is *The Gospel-Driven Life.*[88] Horton highlights the redemptive drama of God that has occurred within history. He directs believers back to the ground of salvation and only means of ongoing sanctification—the objective historical salvific work of Christ. Horton points to the affirmation of a rational-linguistic approach. He expresses that the need is for persons to come to faith in a transcendent God—to be taken out of themselves through hearing a Word from God that is external to them—namely, the biblical gospel and the Scriptures. It is only in this encounter with externality that persons are understood to be able to experience any authentic change.

Horton does not simply focus on the communication of the historical drama of God, but also on how persons are to live now in God's unfolding drama from a position of union with the risen Christ. He believes that the

---

87. Some studies on the Christian life have focused on the need for an experiential encounter with God, and/or on the importance of the affections. For example, see Rognlien, *Experiential Worship*; Hotz and Mathews, *Shaping the Christian Life*; Webber, *Divine Embrace*; Davis, *Worship, Meditation and Communion.*

88. See also Horton, *Putting Amazing Back into Grace.*

Christian life is about persons living in the light of Christ's death and resurrection through personal faith, rather than relying on their subjective inclinations. As well as an emphasis on the biblical gospel, Horton also focuses on the correct use of the law in his work *The Law of Perfect Freedom*. He recognizes the proper designated role for indicatives and imperatives, maintaining the right delineation between "gospel"—being the announcement of what God has done—and "law"—being the expression of what persons are to do.

Regarding the Christian life, Horton's approach is more ecclesial than individualistic, emphasizing the importance of the "means of grace" for individuals within the worshipping community.[89] His focus remains on the gathered context, rather than highlighting the means of formation in a broader context.[90] In *The Gospel Commission*, Horton points to the need for the transformational message of the gospel to be received through the church, over and above the possibility of ecclesial action "transforming the world." He also critiques the misguided ecclesial focus on the possibility of "cultural transformation" in a subsequent book *Ordinary*.

Horton has pointed out the ignorance of the biblical gospel within much of the so-called evangelical church. He provides a necessary critique of the reliance on spiritual disciplines as a means of spiritual growth, and on the narcissistic "feeling-centered" experiences that have become normative across much of the contemporary church. Horton may be correct in his evaluation of the superficiality across "evangelicalism," and in his criticism of attempts to reform spirituality based upon anything other than the biblical gospel. However, he often underplays the proper place and value of personal "spiritual practices" and the principal place of the affections.[91]

Horton has not sought to construct a broad and holistic understanding of transformational theology. His comprehensive work on systematic theology is specifically orientated toward the importance of doctrinal truth as the central means of discipleship, rather than chiefly being orientated toward praxis and the full scope of the Christian life. Horton has constructed a theology around the classic parameters of a Reformed theological framework and provided shorter, more popular works that separately address issues

---

89. See Horton, *A Better Way*.

90. For an approach that focuses on formational potential within the everyday narrative, see Ford, *Shape of Living*; *Drama of Living*.

91. Horton's understanding here appears to stand in contrast to James K. A. Smith, who challenges the centrality of the rational faculties in the transformative process in, *You Are What You Love*, Smith argues that persons are primarily driven and shaped by what they love. He suggests that formation is most able to occur when persons begin by reshaping their desires and affections, rather than their rational processes.

relating to the Christian life. It is fair to state that the focal point for his understanding of the Christian life is not transformation, for this is not seen as being required to authenticate the truth of the gospel. Although Horton focuses on the biblical gospel and advocates serious Christian living, he remains sober regarding the actual possibility of radical transformation in this present age—instead, warning against unrealistic expectations of change.

1.6 THE WAY FORWARD

A review of representative contemporary works reveals the ongoing concern amongst self-identified evangelicals over the need for evidential change as a mark of authenticity. The sample of literature discussed has included a variety of different perspectives regarding the renewal of Christian formation, and drawn out various methodologies that reflect the contemporary landscape. Although there have been many attempts to explore a proper understanding of Christian formation, there remains the need to comprehensively outline a common, coherent, broad, integrated, and distinctly Christian vision of transformational theology.

Various approaches could be taken when attempting to provide an original integrated theological model of Christian formation. In this book, the premise is that the "transformation problem" is not resolved where there is a division between "theology" (here denoting propositional doctrine and belief structure) and "spirituality" (indicating lived faith, experience, and praxis). Consequently, it is seen to be necessary to take an approach that examines the interface between doctrine and life, one that involves a blend of theological and practical insight. Therefore, the constructed synthesis will be doctrinal, in that it will be forged within the discipline of systematic theology, as well as being practical—containing a theology of the Christian life.

In this book, the foundation for a reconstruction of transformational theology will occur as a result of engaging with two influential Christian thinkers, J. I. Packer and Maximus Confessor. Packer is being put forward as an example figure within the contemporary church who has intentionally sought to integrate the concerns of theology and spirituality. His thought will be examined as an initial basis for pursuing a proto-evangelical approach to Christian formation. There are many reasons for selecting Packer as a central subject. He is a well-known figure who has had a lasting and significant influence on the modern evangelical scene, especially amongst more Reformed groups. Although Packer spent much of his life as a systematic theologian, he has also demonstrated a strong concern for spirituality in his writings and sought to do theology "for the sake of the people of God," rather than just for the academic community.

To determine the breadth of Packer's approach, he is being brought into dialogue with a Patristic Father. Maximus Confessor has been selected because he is a significant figure from another tradition who has sought a broad and holistic approach by integrating theology and lived faith. In keeping with the Eastern Christian tradition, Maximus provides a comprehensive synthesis between the concerns of theology and spirituality. He is an example of an early church theologian who sought to bring together a broad array of insights and ideas into an integrated vision—without contradiction.

Both Packer and Maximus share the common characteristic of being pedagogical in their approach, both using forms of catechesis, albeit in a different sense.[92] Both of them express their distinct view of Christian formation and point toward the possibility of a comprehensive and integral approach. An examination of these two "theologians of the Christian life" will take place over the course of the next three chapters, in order to provide a solid basis for the later development of a proto-evangelical model of transformational theology.

Chapter 2 will involve an examination of Packer's thought. His approach will be put forward as being one that is grounded in a rational-linguistic center. There will be an examination of the way Packer seeks to integrate the concerns of theology and spirituality in order to explore how he points toward a truly all-encompassing approach to Christian formation.

In Chapter 3, the focus will shift to examining the thought of Maximus. This will involve exploring an alternative theology of the Christian life that is built around a different logocentric method from that of Packer. Maximus's thought will be presented as a means of exposure to a comprehensive and integrated vision of Christian formation, challenging Packer's approach.

Chapter 4 will involve further analysis and dialogue based on the approaches of Packer and Maximus explored in previous chapters. Here, it will be determined what is suitable for a holistic re-reading of transformational

---

92. In *Desiring the Kingdom*, James K. A. Smith reacts against a pedagogical approach, where the primary need and starting point for formation is a transfer of cognitive information. In doing so, he allows a false dichotomy, separating the "renewing of the mind" from the formation of the whole person. He also overlooks the fact that rational-linguistic pedagogy was core to the discipleship method of Jesus, who—as an itinerant rabbi—used it to invoke *understanding* in the hearers that would lead to a response affecting the whole person (see Matt 5–7; 11:1; 13:10–23; Luke 24:45; John 8:42–47; 13–17). Jesus also instructed his disciples to make disciples by teaching others to observe all that he had taught them (see Matt 28:18). For an examination of Jesus's educational methods, see Collinson, *Making Disciples*.

theology, while defending a perspective grounded in a rational-linguistic center. The further engagement with both thinkers will involve looking at the extent of their ability to provide an integral system of Christian formation. The insights derived here will form the basis upon which to outline an original proto-evangelical synthesis.

The climax of the book will occur in chapters 5 and 6. These chapters will outline a proto-evangelical model of transformational theology that is grounded in a rational-linguistic center. This will be done in reference to the discussion and conclusions expressed in Chapter 4. The construction of a new theological synthesis will occur in two integrated parts. Broadly speaking, the first part will represent the concerns of theology, and the second part the concerns of spirituality. Together these two chapters will point toward the possibility of developing a cohesive, integrated, broad, effectual and distinctly Christian vision.

Chapter 5 will involve developing an original theological framework within which an understanding of the Christian life will be located. This integrated propositional model will be seen to provide a proper context within which to incorporate the scope and diversity of Christian formation while describing the common elements and underlying principles.

In Chapter 6, there will be a construction of the second part of a proto-evangelical model. This will involve explaining how fundamental areas of the Christian life can be held together in a cohesive way within the context of the framework provided in Chapter 5. There will be a demonstration of how a propositional understanding of transformational theory relates to lived experience and practice—removing any false dichotomy between the concerns of theology and spirituality.

Finally, Chapter 7 will offer brief conclusions that can be drawn from the model that is developed in chapters 5 and 6.

Chapter 2

The "Systematic Spirituality" of J. I. Packer

2.1 INTRODUCTION

EXAMINING J. I. PACKER's theology of the Christian life will provide a starting point for exploring an integrated, comprehensive, cohesive, broad, and balanced understanding of Christian formation. This chapter will focus on the contours of Packer's thought. Given that he has authored and edited a vast amount of scholarly and popular material, it is beyond the scope of this study to attempt an in-depth analysis of his theology.[1] However, a wide range of primary sources will be used, especially material that aids toward expressing his thought as a whole and understanding his theology of the Christian life.[2]

   1. Payne, *Theology of the Christian Life*, 3.
   2. In this book, use is made of works which provide the closest synopsis of his thought—namely, *Concise Theology* and *18 Words*—along with the vast array of academic articles Packer has written which are published in his four-volume *Collected Shorter Works*—specifically, the articles related to soteriology, the Christian life, and theological method. To explore Packer's understanding of the Christian life, the main popular works consulted in this book are *Knowing God, Rediscovering Holiness,* and *Knowing Christianity*. Despite Packer's huge influence and literary output, there have been very few secondary studies on his thought. The most significant publication at present is *The Theology of the Christian Life in J. I. Packer's Thought* by Don Payne, which is a revised PhD thesis. Apart from this research, there has been little scholarship examining Packer's understanding of the Christian life. Sam Storms has set out a more concise and popular treatment in his book *Packer on the Christian Life*.

Given that Packer is regarded as one of the most significant and influential English-speaking "evangelical" thinkers of the twentieth century, the value of examining his thought is self-evident. Alister McGrath says that Packer has "made landmark contributions to the evangelical discussion of the theology of Scripture and the theological basis of evangelicalism . . . perhaps most importantly, he has demonstrated the inextricable link between theology and spirituality."[3] After spending years teaching on historical and systematic theology Packer conceded:

> I should have known all along I was writing spirituality, for the Puritan passion for application got into my blood quite early; I have always conceived theology, ethics, and apologetics as truth for people, and have never felt free to leave unapplied any truth that I taught, whether orally or on paper, and to speak of the application of truth to life is to look at life as itself a relationship with God; and when one does that, one is talking spirituality.[4]

Packer refers to the union between systematic theology and spiritual theology—or between theology and spirituality—as "systematic spirituality."[5] While theology is seen to involve that which is thought and understood about God, spirituality is understood to consist of the experience of acquired knowledge—in terms of a lived relationship with God, and the application of biblical truth. His understanding is that both theology and spirituality are wholly interdependent.[6] Taking his lead from the English Puritans, Packer's belief is that spirituality has its origins in the application of theology. Consequently, he understands that "bad theology" will simply lead to "bad spirituality."[7] On the basis that true spirituality is understood to involve the application of truth to life, Packer highlights the problems of any form of spirituality that is not grounded in Scripture, and criticizes the lack of a theological framework in many forms of spirituality:

---

3. McGrath, "Importance of Tradition," 159. Although Packer uses the term "spirituality," he prefers the term "spiritual theology" as it denotes the application of systematic theology rather than a separate discipline that is different from theology, see McGrath, *Know and Serve God*, 257.

4. Packer, *Serving People of God*, 306.

5. Ibid., 314.

6. Ibid.

7. McGrath, *Know and Serve God*, 56. Alister McGrath states: "Packer's vision is strongly integrative, in that he sees theology as offering both a foundation and coherence to Christian thinking and living. As those who have immersed themselves in Packer's writing will know, he considers that the Puritan vision of the Christian life offers exactly such an integrative vision" (Ibid., 287).

> Spirituality books are written that contain no application of Scripture, just as theological tomes are written that contain no application of truth to life. As I want to see theological study done as an aspect and means of our relating to God, so I want to see spirituality studied within an evaluative theological frame.[8]

As well as following the scholasticism of Princetonian Calvinism, Packer has been strongly influenced by the Puritans—who, he says—helped him to see that "all theology is also spirituality."[9] Packer has sought to recover the Puritan vision, which places a strong focus on the affections as well as the intellect.[10] He would affirm that a response to God needs to involve the whole person, including cognitive, affective, volitional, and embodied domains of human experience. Packer's way of being both rigorously academic and highly pragmatic may explain some of his popularity and impact. In the midst of the fragmentation within the "evangelical world," he has sought to bring unity in the understanding of doctrine and lived faith, promoting commonality in *both* orthodoxy and orthopraxy.

Packer is particularly well-known for a defense of—what he understands to be—"doctrinal orthodoxy" within the stream of the "Great Tradition." Although he stands firmly within the "Evangelical Anglican" tradition, his enemy is not ecumenism; but rather that which he sees as diluting and weakening the faith—namely, heterodoxy and liberalism. One of the ways Packer has sought to bring ecclesial unity is through the affirmation and defense of orthodox doctrinal beliefs.[11] He describes himself as a "catechist" who is looking to "transmit truth" that will enable persons to mature in Christ. Consequently, he not only focuses on the affirmation of beliefs that

---

8. Packer, *Serving People of God*, 314.

9. Packer, *Quest for Godliness*, 15. McGrath observes that "his [Packer's] vision of the interrelatedness and interdependence of theological orthodoxy, liturgy, personal conversion and spiritual nurture, congregational structures and social witness . . . had its origins in the Puritan vision" (*Know and Serve God*, 56).

10. Ibid., 57.

11. Packer's passion for doctrinal unity in the church is demonstrated in his work with Thomas Oden called *One Faith*. In holding to biblical authority and orthodox doctrine, Packer's consistent aim has been to seek unity and renewal within the Anglican Communion and to work toward ecumenism with people of other denominations by promoting "Great Tradition" Christianity. His understanding of ecumenism is reflected in his essay "On from Orr." As well as being involved in *Catholics and Evangelicals Together*, Packer has demonstrated an interest in Eastern Orthodoxy. In 1997 he taught a course on Eastern Orthodoxy and Evangelicalism with Bradley Nassif at Regent College, Vancouver. He also wrote the foreword to a book, which compared these two traditions; see Stamoolis, *Eastern Orthodoxy and Evangelicalism*.

he understands to express biblical orthodoxy but also on presenting truths that will lead to persons living a transformed life.

The next section of this chapter will briefly set out Packer's prolegomena to demonstrate how his thought is grounded in a rational-linguistic center. Following that, there will be a synopsis of various significant areas of Packer's theology—which will provide the groundwork for his understanding of the Christian life. This will involve marking out important elements of his dogmatic thought relating to the doctrine of God, anthropology, Christology, and soteriology. This all acts as a backdrop—in preparation for the final extended section at the end of the chapter that focuses on the implications of Packer's theological system on the Christian life.

2.2 PROLEGOMENA

Packer's theologizing wholly depends upon the certainty of God having already revealed himself in Scripture. Rational-linguistic truths derived from the biblical text are seen as the only means through which theology can be constructed. Packer's belief in the importance of attempting to set out a theological synthesis stems from the understanding that there is an inherent unity in what the whole of Scripture teaches. His desire to express propositional truths is demonstrated in *Concise Theology*, where he conveys what he sees as the "permanent essentials of Christianity," both in terms of a belief system and way of living.[12] Being a prominent "catechist," he believes that Christian formation begins with the need for the rational-linguistic instruction of these truths.[13]

Packer draws a clear distinction between "knowledge by description"—referring to knowledge *about* something—and "knowledge by acquaintance"—in terms of "direct" contact with that reality.[14] In Packer's writings it is evident that he desires to help his readers to experience God more deeply. He does this by teaching truths about the character and nature of God as revealed in Scripture. His belief is that having a rational understanding of God—through the inerrant Scriptures—is a prerequisite to a personal knowledge of God. This is not an end in itself. He states: "While

12. Packer, *Concise Theology*, xiii. In *Growing in Christ*, Packer sets out a clear catechetical approach that includes laying out both indicatives and imperatives.

13. This is demonstrated in Packer and Parrett, *Grounded in the Gospel*.

14. Packer, *Knowing Christianity*, 15. Packer affirms that "Christians know—that is are consciously and cognitively related to—the personal mind and power that is behind everything; and this knowledge is itself a personal relationship, knowledge-in-union, and knowledge-in-fellowship, a precious reality of experience for which 'eternal life' is the proper name" (Ibid., 12).

God's linguistic mind-to-mind self-disclosure in and through biblical testimony is meant to be grasped intellectually, his revelatory action is not complete until he comes to be personally known in a responsive relationship."[15] Nevertheless, as a starting point Packer places foremost attention on rational-linguistic revelation, and believes that—by necessity—God communicates to persons through human language in propositional form:

> He discloses himself by telling us about himself. His revelation is personal just because it is propositional; for it is precisely by making true statements about himself to us that God makes himself known to us, and if he did not speak in this way we could never know him at all. To affirm, as some do, that man can discover and know God without God speaking to him is really to deny that God is personal. Persons cannot be known unless in some way they speak to reveal themselves.[16]

Although Packer fully acknowledges the theological difficulties of speaking about an ineffable God beyond human grasp, he firmly believes that human language can be used to speak intelligibly of God—because God has spoken intelligibly of himself through it.[17] Packer also points out that Scripture itself speaks of God in a variety of human ways. Although he recognizes the limitations in the human capacity to understand God and to contain God's fullness, his acknowledgment of God as "mystery" does not mean he sees a sense of uncertainty in being able to come to true knowledge of God through rational propositions.[18]

Clearly, Packer's approach upholds God's immanence in revealing himself both objectively and rationally—and God's transcendence—in that he exceeds the grasp of created intelligence and maintains divine infinitude. He states, "our Creator is bound to surpass our comprehension. Though our knowledge of him may be true as far as it goes, it will necessarily be

---

15. Packer, "Revelation," 621. Packer describes the dimensions of the knowledge of God as "intellectual (knowing the truth about God; Deut 7:9; Ps 100:3); volitional (trusting, obeying, and worshipping God in terms of that truth); and moral (practicing justice and love: Jer 22:16; 1 John 4:7–8)" (*Concise Theology*, 20).

16. Packer, *18 Words*, 20.

17. Packer affirms: "The fact that God's self-disclosure is couched linguistically in the same personal terms in which we talk about ourselves and is therefore intelligible to us does not mean that God must have misrepresented himself in what he said. What it means, rather, is that in our personhood and in our capacity to give and receive verbal communication, we are less unlike God than we perhaps thought" (*Honouring Written Word*, 39).

18. Packer, "God the Image-Maker," 31.

incomplete."[19] Packer also speaks of "a unique kind of knowledge which, though real, is not full; it is knowledge of what is discernible within a circle of light against the background of a larger darkness, it is, in short, knowledge of a mystery, the mystery of the living God at work."[20] Elsewhere, he affirms a similar line of thought:

> As creatures, we are unable fully to comprehend either the being or the actions of the Creator. As it would be wrong, however, to suppose ourselves to know everything about God (and so in effect to imprison him in the box of our own limited notion of him), so it would be wrong to doubt whether our concept constitutes real knowledge of him. Part of the significance of our creation in God's image is that we are able both to know about him and to know him relationally in a true if limited sense of 'know'; and what God tells us in Scripture about himself is true as far as it goes.[21]

Ultimately, Packer understands rational-linguistic truths derived from Scripture as being a necessary and sufficient means of coming to a true knowledge of God. Therefore, when laying out propositions, he rejects the need for dialectical language involving affirmation and negation.[22] Packer's understanding is that "by trying to hold these two self-contradictory positions together, modern theology has condemned itself to an endless sequence of arbitrary oscillations between affirming and denying the trustworthiness of human speculations and biblical assertions respectively."[23]

Packer has described his theological system as being "historic and classic mainstream" and maintains that he has always sought to integrate historic evangelical convictions with classic orthodoxy.[24] He says: "I theologize out of what I see as the authentic biblical and creedal mainstream of Christian identity, the 'confessional' and liturgical 'Great Tradition' that the church on earth has characteristically maintained from the start."[25] In *One Faith*, Packer sets out to outline an "evangelical consensus" that claims continuity with what has always been believed by faithful Christians through

---

19. Packer, *Meeting God*, 7.
20. Packer, *Celebrating Saving Work*, 88.
21. Packer, *Concise Theology*, 45.
22. Packer recognizes this as being different from the dialectic between hidden and revealed knowledge, which is congruent with the dialectic between divine transcendence and immanence.
23. Packer, *Honouring Written Word*, 79–80.
24. Packer, *Concise Theology*, xiii.
25. Packer, "On from Orr," 155.

history.²⁶ For Packer, evangelicalism is not understood as simply being a return to the doctrinal declarations of the Reformation. Rather, it is seen as a renewal movement within Christian orthodoxy that seeks unity around biblical truths and the historic ecumenical creeds of the church.²⁷

Packer sees the authority of Scripture as the true foundation upon which doctrinal beliefs should be upheld and defended. It is assumed that in order to think true thoughts, persons are reliant upon God revealing truth to them through his written Word. Any other means of theologizing is seen as rejecting the self-authenticating divine disclosure in Scripture, replacing it with rationalism, subjective experience, pluralism, and relativism. Clearly, the upholding of biblical authority is, for Packer, essential to the possibility of both orthodoxy and orthopraxy:

> I see biblical authority as methodologically the most basic of theological issues. And I have fought for it, not just for the sake of 'confessional' orthodoxy or theological certainty or evangelical integrity or epistemological sanity or to counter dehumanizing irrationalisms, though all those concerns have entered into what I have done. But my affirmation and defence of Holy Scripture has been first and foremost for the sake of pastoral and evangelistic ministry, genuine godliness, the maturing of the church, and spiritual revival. By these things, the glory of God and the good of human beings are most truly advanced, and they simply are not found where the Bible does not have its proper place in Christians' lives.[28]

Packer's concern to uphold Scripture as being primary among all sources of religious authority is consistently evident in his writings. He sees the whole biblical text as being infallible and inerrant—totally true and entirely trustworthy—representing God's self-authenticating witness of himself.[29]

---

26. Packer and Oden, *One Faith*, 165.

27. Ibid., 164. In his essay, "On from Orr," Packer attempts to provide a model for convergent orthodoxy based on the work of James Orr.

28. Packer, *Truth & Power*, 76. Don Payne observes that the authority and inerrancy of Scripture are fundamental to Packer's understanding of piety, and affirms that the importance of Scripture for Packer cannot be overstated (*Theology of the Christian Life*, 244).

29. Different perspectives on inerrancy are reflected upon in Merrick and Garrett, *Five Views*. Packer's attempt to uphold the authority of Scripture has led him to adopt what he describes as the orthodox position of the historic church (i.e., that the Bible is wholly true and trustworthy in all it affirms because God is the author). Packer holds to what he sees as an "original" form of inerrancy, rather than its modern, literalistic counterpart. Though he recognizes the problems associated with the term, he maintains its present usefulness in light of modern attacks on the truthfulness of all Scripture.

Packer affirms: "Scripture expresses and mediates the authority of God, which means, formally, his right to be believed when he speaks and obeyed when he commands."[30] This strong emphasis on biblical authority remains the absolute basis for Packer's propositional theologizing:

> The first fact to be reckoned with, so I maintain, is the reality of the self-revealed, self-revealing God who in and through the Scriptures has spoken and still speaks to make himself known, and all accounts of the content and method of systematic theology that fail to do justice to this fact are to be rejected.[31]

Although Packer theologizes on the basis of the absolute authority of Scripture, he recognizes the fundamental importance of tradition in being able to challenge any private interpretation.[32] Tradition is not seen by him as being an original or authoritative source like Scripture, but rather as a tool required to lead the church toward a more accurate understanding of Scripture.[33] He recognizes that self-identified evangelicals must engage with—and learn from—other traditions to be able to continually challenge and correct their own. Alister McGrath affirms that Packer has sought to engage properly—both positively and critically—with tradition, in a manner that "opens the way to proper interpretation and theological reflection."[34] Packer maintains the understanding that though it is necessary to learn from past interpretations, all must be challenged by a continual return to the biblical text. He also holds to the primary assumption that—by definition—authoritative revelation, if true, must authenticate itself apart from any human witness. Given that Packer sees Scripture to be the final authority, all else is—by necessity—required to be subordinate. Ultimately, Packer's appeal to church and tradition is for the purpose of safeguarding and correctly receiving the

---

Kevin Vanhoozer points out Packer's attempt to distinguish between original inerrancy that focuses on the authorial intent and "mistaken uses and applications of rationalist inerrancy"—which are more about the interpreter's presuppositions than about hearing what God is saying in the text ("Response to R. Albert Mohler Jr.," 75).

30. Packer, "Scripture," 627–28.

31. Packer, *Serving People of God*, 311. Packer states: "The Christian principle of biblical authority means, on the one hand, that God purposes to direct the belief and behaviour of his people through the revealed truth set forth in Holy Scripture; on the other hand it means that all our ideas about God should be measured, tested, and where necessary corrected and enlarged, by reference to biblical teaching" (*Concise Theology*, 16).

32. McGrath and Lewis, *Doing Theology*, 163. See also McGrath, "Great Tradition."

33. See Lints, *Fabric of Theology*, 84, 86.

34. McGrath, "Great Tradition," 26.

written revelation of God.[35] Anything other than submission to objective divine revelation is seen as a movement toward "liberalism"—the subverting of divine authority.

2.3 THE NATURE OF GOD

The starting point for exploring Packer's thought is to consider his view of the nature of God. Packer recognizes that the basis for a proper understanding of both anthropology and the Christian life is a correct view of who God is. Given that human ontology is perceived to rest wholly upon divine ontology, the divine nature is seen as the beginning and end of understanding the *imago Dei* and Christian living.[36]

Packer does not hesitate to use propositional language when talking about the nature of God. He seeks to speak about God in the way that Scripture itself speaks about God. For example, he makes reference to "incommunicable attributes," which denote God's distinctiveness over and above creation in absolute freedom and independence (i.e., self-sufficiency, self-existence, omnipotence, and so forth), in contrast to God's "communicable attributes"—"the aspects of his moral character which are manifested in his words and deeds—his holiness, his love and mercy, his truthfulness, his faithfulness, his goodness, his patience, his justice."[37] In being created in the image of God, humanity is seen as being required to reflect these moral attributes. Packer recognizes *holiness* as being the core dimension of God's character. On one occasion he states that "every facet of God's nature and every aspect of his character may properly be spoken of as holy, just because it is his."[38] The summons is then for humanity to practice holiness that matches God's own.[39]

Another attribute of God that Packer highlights is *love*.[40] He declares: "God is love. That is, giving out of goodwill, for the recipient's benefit, is the abiding quality both of ongoing relationships within the Godhead and of

---

35. See Packer, "Comfort of Conservatism."

36. Packer appeals for a trinitarian view of the Christian life (*Serving People of God*, 259–61). His understanding of the nature of God, which includes an emphasis on God's holiness, and recognition of some form of subordination within triune activity (particularly reference to the "obedience of the Son") influences the rest of his thought.

37. Packer, *Knowing God*, 19.

38. Packer, *Concise Theology*, 38.

39. Ibid., 39.

40. Packer, *Knowing God*, 132–44; *Concise Theology*, 40–41.

God's primary outgoings in creation and to his creatures."[41] This shared love is understood to provide the shape for trinitarian ontology.[42] Packer recognizes that the members of the Trinity "interpenetrate, relate in mutual love, and co-operate in all divine actions."[43] Packer believes that God's purpose is to enlarge his "circle of eternal love and joy."[44] He sees reciprocal triune love as having clear implications for human experience. Packer states: "Our love relationship to the persons of the Godhead is thus to be modeled on a love relationship within the Godhead itself," and upholds that human relations are to correspond in nature with the fellowship of mutual honor and love within the Trinity.[45] In speaking of the "endless life of the Triune God as one of mutual affection and honor," he affirms that the need is for humanity to participate and glorify God by "sharing the joyful give-and-take of this divine life according to their own creaturely mode."[46]

Despite upholding the importance of some form of social trinitarianism—in terms of the divine patterns of giving-receiving—Packer does not fully develop a social understanding of the Trinity, nor make it central to his theological system. Instead, he focuses more on the distinct roles of Father, Son, and Spirit as revealed in Scripture, with the understanding that all three persons are working together, in everything.[47] In doing so, Packer suggests some form of subservience in the triune economy—particularly within salvation history—where he draws out the subordinate and functional roles.[48]

Ultimately, Packer believes that God has revealed himself in order that humanity may know him personally, not simply know what he is like. He states: "It is true that revelation is essentially self-disclosure on God's part and that its goal is to make men 'know the Lord,' in personal fellowship with a personal God."[49] Moreover, the absolute connection that he sees between divine self-revelation and human formation means there is the innate pos-

---

41. Packer, "God the Image-Maker," 35.

42. Packer, *Rediscovering Holiness*, 45.

43. Packer, "God," 275. Packer states: "The three persons of the Godhead are individuated in relation to each other without ever being separated from each other; they are consciously three while yet ontologically as well as co-operatively one" ("God the Image-Maker," 33).

44. Packer, *Celebrating Saving Work*, 15.

45. Packer, *Growing in Christ*, 228.

46. Packer, *Concise Theology*, 40. Packer affirms that "the essence of the Christian life is involvement in the relational life of the Triune Godhead" (*Serving People of God*, 260).

47. Packer, "Reflection and Response," 179–80.

48. Packer, *Knowing God*, 75.

49. Packer, *18 Words*, 19.

sibility of persons gradually coming to reveal the divine likeness. Humanity is understood as being able to both know and reveal divine knowledge—so being called to demonstrate the moral characteristics of its Maker.

2.4 CREATION AND REDEMPTION

2.4.1 God in Creation

Packer recognizes that God's speech-act formed the universe in order to reveal God's own existence, power, and glory. The work of God outwards in creation is seen as being the demonstration of his own personhood. He states: "God was revealing himself. He was showing his 'eternal power and deity' (Rom 1:20) as Maker and Master, and with that his character and his ways with men . . . so that he might be acknowledged and worshipped for all that he is and does and gives."[50] Packer sees knowledge of God revealed in creation as "general revelation" that points human beings toward a relationship with their Creator.[51] He affirms that this "form of revelation is given everywhere, to all men, through the ordinary experience of being alive in God's world."[52] This is believed to be distinct from the "special revelation" of God's saving grace in Christ.[53]

Packer understands God's self-revelation as bringing forth creatures in God's own image, for the purpose of revealing his glory.[54] He suggests that the self-revealing God forms humanity in congruence with his own *ad intra* revelation. Being created in the image of God would mean that the structural nature of human beings can only be understood in relation to the actual nature of the divine being. It also means that humanity is challenged to reflect God's holiness, love, rationality, and creativity—imitating that which is revealed by God himself.[55] Packer says, "as humans, we may reflect and reproduce at our own creaturely level the holy ways of God, and thus act as his direct representatives on earth. This is what humans are made to do, and in one sense we are human only to the extent that we are doing it."[56]

---

50. Ibid., 22.
51. Packer, *Freedom & Authority*, 37.
52. Packer, *18 Words*, 24.
53. Packer, "Revelation," 622.
54. Packer, *God's Plans for You*, 26–34.
55. Don Payne observes that Packer "uses God's communicable attributes as the logical connection between holiness and the *imago Dei*. The *imago Dei* is essentially these attributes expressed in the context of relationship with God and other people" (*Theology of the Christian Life*, 83).
56. Packer, *Concise Theology*, 61.

The focus of Packer's anthropology is characterized by the themes of "rationality," "righteousness," and "relationship."[57] Packer declares that we bear the divine image "of which rationality, relationality, and the capacity for that righteousness which consists of receiving and responding to God's revelation are the basic formal elements. We are able to know God, because as thinking, feeling, relating, loving beings we are to that extent like him."[58] The distinct characteristics that Packer highlights in his anthropology can be seen to have a direct impact on his vision of the Christian life.

Packer's starting point is the understanding that human beings are created with the capacity to know God rationally. Because the God whose image human beings bear is seen as being rational, he understands the *imago Dei* as being closely related to rationality.[59] God is seen as seeking to communicate to humanity in an intelligible way through rational-linguistic truth because of the rational nature that human beings share with God.[60] He says: "Man could not know, love, or serve God without this endowment of reason with which to apprehend him."[61] In being created in God's image, humans are understood to be given the faculties necessary to be able to comprehend and respond to God's inerrant law so that they may come to demonstrate this image of God more.[62] The rational nature of the *imago Dei* that Packer describes is believed to form the basis for a person's ability to walk in true righteousness. Humanity is recognized as being inherently subject to God's rational self-communication, and under the authority of God's law—being created to do God's will and to express his moral image.[63] In reference to Packer's view, Don Payne states: "All human responsibility

---

57. This is first put forward in Payne, *Theology of the Christian Life*, 200.

58. Packer, "God the Image-Maker," 49.

59. Payne, *Theology of the Christian Life*, 186. Given that all human form is created to image God, it is problematic if any specific human faculties (e.g., rationality) are too closely associated with the image of God itself. The language that Scripture employs to describe human physicality suggests a complexity of inner-outer faculties that—though distinct—interact as a whole, and—as Packer argues—are all animated in some way by the immaterial soul. For Packer, central to the human person are the inner faculties—specifically, the rational faculties—which he believes are to be leading.

60. Packer, *Honouring Written Word*, 27.

61. Packer, *Man's Sake*, 13.

62. Packer, *Honouring Written Word*, 27, 39. Packer says that human beings "proceed on the basis that both a sense of God and a language in which to converse with him were given to men as ingredients in, or perhaps preconditions of, the divine image from the start (Ibid., 38).

63. Packer, *Man's Sake*, 15; *Knowing God*, 127–28.

to law is but an outgrowth of the innate accountability to God's law that is embedded in the *imago Dei*."[64]

Furthermore, Packer understands the mind as being the foundation for conscience—which is a pivotal instrument that provides moral discernment. He recognizes the universal awareness of God, not only through creation but also "by the spontaneous self-judgments of conscience."[65] Packer affirms that "revelation is mediated through the voice of conscience, which speaks as God's monitor, telling every man something, at least, of the demands of his law."[66] His understanding is that the conscience speaks as a detached, independent voice (not our own) and recognizes it as the writing of God's laws on every human heart.[67]

Humanity is seen as being required to respond appropriately to God's self-revelation both in the created world and the law of conscience. The right response to God is that which leads creatures toward reflecting the glory and image of their Creator. Packer states: "We can only achieve full humanness in and through worship of the God whose image we bear."[68] He describes worship as the "due response of rational creatures to the self-revelation of their Creator. It is an honoring and glorifying of God by gratefully offering back to him all the good gifts, and all the knowledge of his greatness and graciousness, that he has given."[69]

Packer also understands rationality as the prerequisite for relational knowledge. He states that God has "made each human individual in his own image so that he might communicate cognitively with us, mind-to-mind in order that it might be heart-to-heart, for everlasting communion in joy and love."[70] The ground of this image is seen by Packer as relational, there being an inherent relationship with God with whom persons are created to live, so that they may worship and obey: "To this end, he makes himself known to us. He enters into communication with a view to communion."[71] In turn, Packer also wholly affirms the relational nature of humanity in a wider sense. He states: "Life is relationships and we can only live fully human lives in fellowship with other people."[72] Although Packer's understanding of the

---

64. Payne, *Theology of the Christian Life*, 89.
65. Packer, "Revelation," 622.
66. Packer, *18 Words*, 25.
67. Packer, *Concise Theology*, 82–83.
68. Packer and Howard, *Christianity*, 148.
69. Packer, *Concise Theology*, 84.
70. Packer, "God the Image-Maker," 50.
71. Packer, *Freedom & Authority*, 37.
72. Packer, *Man's Sake*, 19.

imago Dei is essentially integrated, relationality appears to take a secondary position to rationality and righteousness. Despite Packer's attempts to qualify himself, he appears to define the *imago Dei* individualistically as the role of community is restricted.[73]

A further characteristic of Packer's anthropology is that he affirms the dichotomy of persons consisting of a soul (or spirit) and body, of a "material body animated by an immaterial personal self."[74] The body is not seen as being part of the *imago Dei*, but is seen as being necessary to fulfilling it materially. He states: "The embodiment of the soul is integral to God's design for mankind. Through the body . . . we are to experience our environment, enjoy and control things around us, and relate to other people."[75] Because Packer's concern is to reflect how humanity relates to the communicable attributes of the divine nature, he does not describe an "incarnational" understanding of the human person. Instead, he sees the incarnation of Christ as being implicit in creation, and only explicit by the coming of Christ "as the true image of God in his humanity as well as in his divinity."[76]

As well as describing the God-given nature of human beings, Packer also depicts the state of humanity standing opposed to divine design. He speaks of the inclinations of humanity toward disobedience—seeing this as the rejection of divine authority, where persons seek freedom from the absolute truth of divine self-revelation.[77] He states: "Sin may be comprehensively defined as lack of conformity to the law of God in act, habit, attitude, outlook, disposition, motivation, and mode of existence."[78] In rejecting divine self-revelation, creatures are seen as seeking to "play God" by being self-sufficient and autonomous beings.[79]

Packer believes that the awareness of God's reality "is inescapable and universal, and comes through to everyone, although everywhere it gets falsified, to a greater or lesser degree, through the way it is processed in all minds and hearts."[80] He understands that knowledge of God is clearly evident in creation; but is being suppressed and distorted through expressions of idolatry and immorality. Given that Packer highlights rationality in the *imago Dei*, he focuses on the effect that sin has on the faculties of

---

73. Payne, *Theology of the Christian Life*, 202.
74. Packer, *Concise Theology*, 74.
75. Ibid., 63–64.
76. Ibid., 62.
77. Packer, *Freedom & Authority*, 18–23.
78. Packer, *Concise Theology*, 70.
79. Packer, "Christian and God's World," 91; Packer and Howard, *Christianity*, 26.
80. Packer and Nystrom, *Praying*, 53.

reason, in impairing the ability of persons to be able to come to a deeper understanding of the mind of God, which leads to an inability to obey the law of God. Packer also speaks of the conditioning and searing the conscience, and of a person's failure to fully apprehend "general revelation," so that there is confusion over moral decisions.[81]

Packer understands the perverse implications of disobedience. He affirms: "All our life at every point is being lived unnaturally if God is not at the center, and if his praise and glory . . . is not the supreme concern throughout."[82] He recognizes that when persons decline to worship God, they seek after false gods—rather than becoming humbly subject to God's self-revelation—something else takes its place. Packer affirms that "it is impossible to worship nothing; as humans, we are worshipping creatures, and if we do not worship the God who made us, we shall inevitably worship someone or something else."[83]

Given the inherent connection between God's self-revelation and the human image, a person's denial of divine knowledge is seen as being a denial of their humanity.[84] Although created in the image of God, the worship of something else obscures God's glory so that persons are "living lives that are qualitatively subhuman."[85] Packer sees the rejection of God as marring God's image and having an absolute effect on human personhood.[86] He holds to the belief that God's image cannot be lost in humanity, only distorted and perverted. However, his ongoing focus on the prevalence of indwelling sin underlines his belief in the total depravity of human nature stemming from original sin, and the ever-present possibility of "deformation."

2.4.2 God in Christ

Packer sees the Christian life as being wholly defined by God's redemptive self-disclosure in Christ. Given the insufficiency of "general revelation," humanity is understood to require "special revelation" to truly know God's character and obey his law. Packer states that human beings "have received

---

81. Packer, *18 Words*, 26; *Concise Theology*, 83.

82. Packer, *Man's Sake*, 21. Packer has described the Christian life in wholly theocentric terms, recognizing our purpose as being for God's glory, not our own. The Christian life, therefore, is characterized by self-denial with total reorientation toward God-centered living.

83. Packer and Howard, *Christianity*, 146.

84. In *Christianity: The New Humanism*, Packer makes it clear that any attempts to express our humanity outside of God are unnatural—and ultimately destructive.

85. Packer, *Rediscovering Holiness*, 26.

86. Packer, *18 Words*, 73.

'special revelation.' This is the supernatural saving revelation from God, that is set forth in Scripture and was embodied in Christ and is now proclaimed as the gospel of God."[87] He portrays the incarnation of Christ in linguistic manner—Jesus being seen as the supreme expression of God's verbal revelation.[88]

Packer recognizes Christ as the begotten Son of the Father—being revealed as a perfect expression of the divine image.[89] He states that Jesus "revealed the Father, not only by what he said, but by what he was, and what he did; for he, as the image of the Father, and all the many-sided fullness of the character of the invisible God was made visible in his incarnate life."[90] Packer affirms the Chalcedonian view of Christ.[91] In speaking of the interrelation between divinity and humanity in the person of Christ he states:

> Our Lord Jesus is both God for man and man for God; he is God's incarnate Son, fully divine and fully human. We know him as both the mediator of divine grace and the model of human godliness. And what is human godliness, the godliness that is true holiness, as seen in Jesus? It is simply human life lived as the Creator intended—in other words, it is perfect and ideal humanness, an existence in which the elements of the human person are completely united in a totally God-honoring and nature-fulfilling way.[92]

Packer believes that God's self-revelation in Christ expresses the fullness of what it means to be human—fulfilling the *imago Dei*. Christ is seen to demonstrate the pattern of life that God's people must follow in order to adopt a truly human way of living.[93] He states: "Christ's life displayed human dignity to the full, for he worshiped and served God the Father to the full."[94] Christ is understood to be fulfilling the moral dimension of the *imago Dei* by conforming to God's law in perfect obedience and submission, seeking to do the will of the Father.[95] Packer affirms: "Jesus was the law incarnate, he was also love incarnate, and following his way of self-giving is holiness in its purest

---

87. Packer and Nystrom, *Praying*, 54.
88. Packer, *God Has Spoken*, 46, 61.
89. Packer, *Growing in Christ*, 43–44; *18 Words*, 109; *Concise Theology*, 90.
90. Packer, *18 Words*, 21.
91. Packer, *Growing in Christ*, 44–45; *Concise Theology*, 91.
92. Packer, *Rediscovering Holiness*, 25.
93. Packer, *Man's Sake*, 24; Packer and Howard, *Christianity*, 41.
94. Ibid., 155.
95. Packer, *Freedom & Authority*, 25–26.

and most perfect expression."[96] In every sense, Christ's life is understood to express the exemplar response of human beings to God.

Packer gives particular attention to Christ's own rational-linguistic communication. Although he recognizes the importance of imitating Christ's example of obedience in the scheme of discipleship, Christ's primary method of discipleship is understood to occur through teaching. Packer observes that Christ declared the words of God based upon the authority of the Father:[97] "The Lord Jesus Christ fulfilled the ministry of a prophet, inasmuch as he spoke those words, and those only, which the Father had given him to speak (John 7:6; 8:28; 12:49f.; Heb 2:3f.)."[98] Given the premise of divine authority behind Christ's teaching, his words provide the basis through which persons are to live in obedience to God.

Although Packer knows that the incarnation provides the exemplar model for human personhood—in terms of Christ's example of obedience—it does not assume a primary epistemological function in his thought. Instead, the incarnation is only seen as being redemptive in that Christ's obedience to the Father demonstrates his sinlessness in fulfilling the law—to the point of death on the cross. His understanding of how the elect relate to the incarnation is in terms of imitating Christ's life, rather than expressing the need for an experiential and ontological participation. In being both truly God and truly man, Christ is acknowledged by Packer as the only mediator between God and humanity, with Christ's atonement being the necessary substitutionary work that enables reconciliation with God and eternal salvation. Though Christ's earthly example is seen as providing a model to follow, it is the path of Christ's death and resurrection that is understood as being the destiny for the elect.

Packer gives due weight to the reality that the risen and exalted Christ is the mediator of the new covenant, and forerunner of a new humanity. However, he does not appear to give the resurrection the same attention that he gives to the atonement. Central to Packer's soteriology is the notion of "penal substitution," where forensic justice is understood as being at the center of an orthodox interpretation of the atonement. Packer recognizes Christ's atoning act of obedience to the Father on behalf of humanity as being the climax of a perfect life. He highlights the legal aspects of the atonement—the act of propitiation being seen to be at the very heart of the gospel.[99] Packer's understanding is that legal guilt for sin under the

---

96. Packer, *Keep in Step*, 94.
97. Packer, *Freedom & Authority*, 32.
98. Packer, *18 Words*, 21.
99. Packer, *Knowing God*, 201–24.

law demands atonement. Given that human beings are perceived as being unable in their own efforts to mirror God's holiness, substitutionary sacrifice is acknowledged as being required from one who is sinless under the law. Packer states: "He was the substitution for us, paying the penalty incurred by our moral failure and disobedience."[100] Elsewhere, he affirms: "Atonement means making amends, blotting out the offense, and giving satisfaction for wrong done; thus reconciling to oneself the alienated other and restoring the disrupted relationship."[101] Packer's penal emphasis means that his understanding of the atonement points to Christ's sacrifice as, first and foremost, an intra-triune act of self-revelation done on behalf of humanity, an act which would allow human beings to be able to participate more fully in the divine life.

Packer recognizes the need for Christ to be the center of any theological system. He affirms: "The Christian consensus has always been that, as Scripture is the proper source from which theology should be derived, so Christology—that is our knowledge of the person, place, and work of Christ—is the true hub around which the wheel of theology must revolve."[102] Though Christ is clearly central in Packer's thought, it could be conceived that he places Scripture before Christ in his theological schema.[103] Don Payne points out Packer's emphasis on the propositional character of God's revelation in Scripture over the incarnation.[104] Given that Christ is seen as having a secondary epistemological function, the means of knowledge is placed before the object of knowledge.[105] Packer does speak of Scripture in "incarnational" language, in terms of seeing it reveal the same divine and human natures as Christ.[106] However, it could be argued that he does not sufficiently demonstrate how Christology and bibliology integrate within the process of formation itself.

2.5 UNION WITH CHRIST

Packer recognizes that the fulfillment of God's self-revelation in Christ occurs in his self-giving death, and his resurrection—where the eschatological image for the elect is revealed. A definitive response to the propositional

100. Packer, *Knowing Christianity*, 77.
101. Packer, *Concise Theology*, 118.
102. Packer, *Celebrating Saving Work*, 46.
103. Payne, *Theology of the Christian Life*, 223.
104. Ibid., 222.
105. Ibid., 223.
106. Packer, *Honouring Written Word*, 169; *Serving People of God*, 187.

gospel allows union with the risen Christ (and right standing with the Father to become *the* present reality). In this regard, Packer highlights three soteriological categories: *justification, regeneration,* and *adoption.*

Of primary importance to Packer is the understanding that identification with Christ's death and resurrection leads to being justified before God. He describes justification as involving "pardon and acceptance by God," with persons being declared righteous.[107] As a judicial act, the atonement is understood to be the means by which the righteousness of God may be imputed to persons, in accord with Christ's righteousness. Packer sees the justification of the elect through faith as being a once and for all act of eschatological judgment brought into the present.[108]

Packer does not simply view reconciliation with God in terms of a legal standing. Union with the risen Christ is understood to involve sharing in Christ's sonship and entering into a loving relationship with the Father. Packer highlights the importance of regeneration—which is perceived as the initial work of the Spirit occurring as a result of a person's identification with Christ's death and resurrection. He links the concept of regeneration with adoption—the basis for growth in sonship being a result of the regenerative work of the Spirit.[109] Packer believes that adoption into God's family is *the* climatic identity of persons who have been restored into relationship with God.[110] In summary, adoption is understood to occur as a result of a judicial change in the standing of the elect, who have been brought into reconciled relationship with the Father, after being regenerated and justified in Christ.

According to Packer, having an understanding of a definite and positional union with Christ is fundamental for a person's walk of holiness. The salvific work of Christ, the regenerative work of the Spirit, and personal righteous standing before God together form the absolute basis and ground of the Christian life.[111] A person's present relation to God is always linked back to the definitive predestined standing of the elect in Christ—which is the ground of holy living. Packer states: "The context of sanctification is justification by faith through Christ . . . The basis of sanctification is union with Christ in his death and resurrection."[112] The act of justification is understood as being an act of sanctification, of setting a person apart to God

---

107. Packer, *Knowing Christianity*, 84; *18 Words*, 135.
108. Packer, *Celebrating Saving Work*, 138.
109. Packer, "Justification," 644; *Concise Theology*, 136, 46.
110. Packer, *Concise Theology*, 145.
111. Packer, *Serving People of God*, 284–85.
112. Packer, *God's Plans for You*, 133–34.

for holy living. He affirms: "The root meaning of the word [sanctification] is relational, or as some say, positional: To sanctify, or consecrate, is to set something or someone apart for God, either in general and inclusive terms or for some specific purpose, and to have it, or him, or her, accepted by God for the end in view."[113]

Packer also portrays sanctification as a lifelong transformational process, leading to persons being more conformed to the likeness of the Son.[114] The outworking of the redemptive work of Christ is understood to be a present reality in the life of the believer who continues to respond to Christ in repentance and faith. The death-resurrection dialectic then becomes the formational paradigm that the elect participate in.[115] Packer does not define the exact way in which the work of Christ is outworked in the process of sanctification.[116] In broad terms, identification with Christ's death and resurrection is demonstrated through "mortification" and "vivification," through a present sharing in his dying, and ultimately in his risen life:[117]

> God unites the individual to the risen Lord in such a way that the dispositional drives of Christ's perfect human character—the inner urgings, that is, to honour, adore, love, obey, serve, and please God, and to benefit others for both their sake and his sake—are now reproduced at the motivational centre of that individual's being. And they are reproduced, in face of the contrary egocentric cravings of fallen nature, in a dominant way, so that the Christian, though still troubled and tormented by the urgings of indwelling sin, is no longer ruled by those urgings in the way that was true before.[118]

Packer understands new life in Christ as being distinctly characterized by the interrelation between love and holiness—holiness being grounded in a love relationship.[119] He points to love for God and humanity as being the fulfillment of the law. Packer states: "The heart of holiness is the spirit of love."[120] In grounding holiness in regeneration and adoption, he goes on to use the sonship motif to express the basic relationship between God and

---

113. Packer, Ibid., 127.
114. Packer, Ibid., 128. *Knowing Christianity*, 90.
115. Packer, *Keep in Step*, 136.
116. Payne, *Theology of the Christian Life*, 162.
117. Packer, *Serving People of God*, 264–66.
118. Ibid., 259.
119. Packer, *Rediscovering Holiness*, 162–64.
120. Ibid., 87.

the elect.[121] Packer recognizes that the requirement here is for persons to mature as children of God, growing in obedience to the Father by growing in a relationship of love. This kind of relationship is grounded in the giving and receiving of the triune life, which according to Packer is "the structural shape of the Christian's fellowship with God; this, in essence, is the Christian life."[122]

Packer's soteriology is characterized by a clear distinction between the modes of "past," "present," and "future" salvation, and places an emphasis upon the latter two categories being subordinate to the initial definitive position of *being* saved.[123] There is a tension between his affirmation of both the present and future dimensions of transformation. As well as the current state of lived consecration to God being seen in relation to an initiated union, it is also seen in relation to a future consummated union with Christ, with the emphasis in this present age being on the need for perseverance.[124] The destiny of the elect is understood to involve the final realization of a person's identification with the death and resurrection of Christ (i.e., physical death followed by the resurrection of the body—one that is created in the image of the risen Christ).[125] The future revelation of Christ's coming is recognized as being the final catalyst for these events.[126]

Packer understands the future transformational process to involve "glorification." He affirms: "Glorification (so-called because it is a manifesting of God in our lives, 2 Cor 3:18) is the scriptural name for God's completion of what he began when he regenerated us, namely, our moral and spiritual reconstruction so as to be perfectly and permanently conformed to Christ."[127] This is the eschatological consummation of the sanctification process.[128]

---

121. Packer, *Knowing God*, 225–60.

122. Packer, *18 Words*, 186. Packer states: "Of the relationship of giving and taking that exists between Christians and the first two persons of the Trinity, we can only speak briefly here. Suffice it to say that it is a two-sided relationship, in which both the divine and human participants are active. God's fellowship with men covers all that the Father and the Son have done, and do, and will do, in order to share their glory with us sinners. Our fellowship with God covers all the giving to him and taking from him that we do in order to express our faith and repentance" (Ibid.).

123. Packer, *Rediscovering Holiness*, 43–44.

124. Packer, *Concise Theology*, 205–06.

125. Ibid., 109–10, 214–16.

126. Packer, *18 Words*, 27.

127. Packer, *Concise Theology*, 215.

128. Ibid., 148.

2.6 LIVING IN CHRIST

2.6.1 Divine Initiation

Packer recognizes that the present process of transformation toward Christ-likeness is dependent on a co-operative human response to the divine initiative. It is a process determined chiefly by a supernatural work of God. He states: "Sanctification is not natural morality but supernatural conformity to the moral and spiritual likeness of Jesus Christ."[129] Packer's understanding of divine initiation is that God has already fully revealed himself to humanity in Christ's redemptive activity and in Scripture so that persons know what it is to be conformed to God's will, and are given the power to do so. Change then begins with a response to the biblical gospel and the Holy Spirit—who mediates the power of the risen Christ.

Packer understands that God has acted to make known his mind and will through the biblical record, inviting persons into a relationship. He affirms: "The Scriptures are God showing us himself: God communicating to us who he is and what he has done so that in the response of faith we may truly know him and live our lives in fellowship with him."[130] Elsewhere, he states "God sends his word to us in the character of both information and invitation. It comes to woo us as well as to instruct us; it not merely puts us in the picture of what God has done and is doing, but also calls us into personal communion with the loving Lord himself."[131] Packer recognizes that the purpose of Scripture is to bring persons closer to Christ. He affirms: "Only when your reading of the written Word feeds into your relationship with the living Word (Jesus) does the Bible operate as the channel of light and life that God means it to be."[132]

Furthermore, Packer recognizes that persons were created to live under God's authority and that "the only way we come under that authority and stay under it is by submitting in faith and obedience to what is in the Bible."[133] The possibility of holiness is seen to be dependent upon the absolute authority and inerrancy of Scripture—and upon a person's ability to understand and adhere to it. Packer perceives that precise knowledge of God's will—and subsequent obedience to it—are only possible on the assumption that God is able to accurately communicate his will to the rational faculties through the biblical text. If Scripture is not authoritative and true

---

129. Packer, *God's Plans for You*, 134.
130. Packer, *Knowing Christianity*, 22.
131. Packer, *Knowing God*, 123.
132. Packer, *Rediscovering Holiness*, 41.
133. Packer, *Freedom & Authority*, 49.

in *all* its parts—and consequently not trustworthy—then there are plain implications in the life of the believer—for Scripture would not be a wholly reliable ground for faith and obedience. Arguably, any error that is communicated can only beget error, rather than enabling the truth-filled (and transformed) life that all Christians are called to live.[134]

Packer does not see divine guidance as primarily occurring in the present "revelation" of the Spirit. Instead, he affirms the importance of the Spirit's role in conjunction with what has already been objectively revealed in Scripture. In the scheme of salvation, Packer understands the use of Scripture as being wholly bound up with the work of the Spirit. He states: "The Scripture brings no life save as the Spirit uses it, and the Spirit brings no life save as he applies the Word of God, the truth of the gospel, the testimony of Jesus to our hearts."[135] The possibility of persons being able to perceive, and apply, God's rational-linguistic communication, is seen to depend upon the Spirit enabling the illumination of truth to the mind. Packer affirms that the "continuing reality of revelation through each believer's life occurs under the enlightening ministry of the Holy Spirit, who interprets to us the contents of Scripture; however these are met."[136] Because the human mind is recognized as being fallen, the possibility of objective truth being made known and understood to the mind through the process of rationalistic exegesis is believed to depend on the Spirit's work.[137] The role of the Spirit is seen as being to mediate rational knowledge through the biblical text, rather than revealing the will of God apart from a witness to Christ and Scripture.[138]

In the context of a co-operative relationship with God, the elect are understood to be provided with grace—through the Spirit—to walk in God's revealed will. Packer acknowledges the work of the Spirit in mediating the life of God to persons as a result of Christ's atonement. The power of the Spirit poured out on the elect is recognized as the primary agent of change, bringing the fruit of Christlikeness.[139] The "Spirit of Christ" is understood to indwell believers in order to work in their lives. Packer states: "Christ and his Spirit empower them to put sinful habits to death and bring forth

---

134. For a discussion on the various views of inerrancy, see Merrick and Garrett.

135. Packer, *Serving People of God*, 182.

136. Packer, "Scripture," 629.

137. Payne, *Theology of the Christian Life*, 213–14; Packer, *18 Words*, 26.

138. Packer, *Keep in Step*, 57; *Concise Theology*, 135. Don Payne believes that Packer understands the Spirit's primary purpose as being to illuminate the text for application, while interpretation is seen as being more reliant on the rational faculties (*Theology of the Christian Life*, 259).

139. Packer, *Rediscovering Holiness*, 193, 206–09.

in them new behavioral patterns that constitute the Spirit's 'fruit' (Rom 8:9–13; 2 Cor 3:18; Gal 5:22–26)."[140] Consequently, he recognizes that there is a need for persons to fully depend on the power of the Holy Spirit. Packer affirms that it is the Spirit who "transforms their characters progressively into Christ's moral and spiritual likeness by instilling new desires for God and godliness that issues in new patterns of behavior."[141]

2.6.2 Human Response: Co-operation with God

In his writings, Packer is clear in pointing out the differences between monergism and synergism. The definitive work of regeneration is understood to be *monergistic*. Packer's understanding aligns firmly with a Reformed perspective where regeneration is seen as occurring in persons through the work of God alone, rather than involving any of their own work. This could lead some to the conclusion that a person's rejection of God stems from the absence of divine activity. Definitive salvation, as a legal act, is recognized as being determined by a more passive (rather than active) response to God. It is understood to be wholly dependent on trust and reliance upon Christ's substitutionary work, while "works" are only seen to be a product of this identification. Packer believes that saving faith becomes "a moral dynamic of unparalleled power in the believer's life. The proof that a man's faith is real is precisely this—that it makes him work."[142]

Sanctification is portrayed as being *synergistic*: involving both divine action and human effort. In regard to present formation, Packer affirms: "God is labouring in and with us to make us into the most glorious of all his works, namely, worshippers in the image and likeness of Jesus Christ."[143] Packer understands sanctification as being an ongoing co-operative process, where God initiates and persons are to respond. He says that it is "a gift (that is one side: God working in us to renew and transform us) and a task (the task of obedience, righteousness, and pleasing God). And we must never so stress either of the two sides that we lose sight of the other."[144] Elsewhere, he states: "God's method of sanctification is neither activism (self-reliant activity) nor apathy (God-reliant passivity), but God-dependent effort."[145]

---

140. Ibid., 51.
141. Packer, "Holy Spirit," 446.
142. Packer, *18 Words*, 131.
143. Packer and Howard, *Christianity*, 155.
144. Packer, *Serving People of God*, 320.
145. Packer, *Concise Theology*, 148.

This is not to say that Packer is advocating that the process of sanctification is dependent partly upon grace and partly upon works, but rather that it is wholly dependent upon both.[146] Packer's understanding of the relation between God and humanity here is characterized by some kind of reciprocity, in terms of the expression of a proper tension between faith and works in the process of ongoing sanctification, with persons needing to co-operate with what God has first initiated.

Packer rejects more passive "introspective" approaches to sanctification that do not take human responsibility seriously, in favor of a more active approach that takes a lead from Puritanism. He holds to the belief that the experience of growing in holiness is one of conflict.[147] Human responsibility is understood as involving the need for constant "mortification" (i.e., persons putting sin to death in themselves).[148] He does not believe that fighting against sin should simply occur through a passive reliance on the Spirit, but should instead require continual effort, discipline, and perseverance. He states: "The form that sanctification takes is the conflict with the indwelling sin that constantly assaults us. The conflict, which is lifelong, involves both resistance to sin's assaults and the counterattack of 'mortification,' whereby we seek to drain the life out of this troublesome enemy."[149] Packer places a strong focus on human effort in terms of a person responding to God's work within them: "It is true that we could not mortify sin by our own unaided efforts, but it is no less true that the Spirit will not mortify sin in us without our co-operation."[150] In a broader sense, this understanding may infer that the process of forming right thoughts (or beliefs), right feelings, and right actions would not occur in persons without them co-operating in some way (i.e., nothing is "forced" upon them). Packer's affirmation of synergism here stands in direct tension with his belief in monergistic regeneration.

In respect to ongoing formation, Packer underlines the importance of persons responding in repentance and faith to what is revealed in Scripture. Knowledge of God in Scripture is seen to lead to self-examination; revealing personal sin, and showing the path that persons need to take.[151] Packer declares that the fundamental need is for continual *repentance*, as a

---

146. Packer recognizes two fundamental errors (i.e., "legalism" and "antinomianism") that challenge the imperative of obeying the will of God, in the power of the Holy Spirit (*Rediscovering Holiness*, 88). For a more detailed discussion, see Barrs, *Delighting in the Law*; Jones, *Antinomianism*; Ferguson, *Whole Christ*.

147. Packer, *Keep in Step*, 91–92.

148. Packer, *Rediscovering Holiness*, 98.

149. Packer, *God's Plans for You*, 134.

150. Packer, *18 Words*, 179.

151. Packer, *God's Plans for You*, 139–40; Packer and Nystrom, *Praying*, 120–46.

response to the "God-knowledge" and "self-knowledge" that comes through the biblical text.[152] He believes that repentance "means changing one's mind so that one's view, values, goals, and ways are changed, and one's whole life is lived differently. The change is radical, both inwardly and outwardly; mind and judgment, will and affections, behaviour and lifestyle, motives and purposes, are all involved."[153] *Faith* is seen to be the other necessary response to God's authoritative revelation. Packer understands that "the word faith in ordinary speech covers both credence of propositions ('beliefs') and confidence in persons or things."[154] He believes that "faith weans us from all self-sufficiency, self-reliance, and self-absorption."[155] It involves resting upon the certainty of divine self-revelation as truth, of trusting in God and what he has said.[156]

Packer sees the Christian life as being primarily about obedience to the law of God. The elect are understood to enter into Christ's subordinate relation to the Father—expressing a need to respond in ongoing obedience to in order to fulfill the *imago Dei*. Given that God has already spoken and revealed himself personally through his written Word, Packer focuses on the need for a positive response—to apply what the text is saying. He recognizes the importance of the Scriptures being received, read, heard, meditated on, and obeyed in both private life and public worship.[157] Packer affirms: "Godliness means responding to God's revelation in trust and obedience, faith and worship, prayer and praise, submission and service. Life must be seen and lived in the light of God's Word."[158] All praxis for Packer stems from some kind of response to scriptural instruction—it simply involves the application of Scripture to life by being obedient to what God says. Packer states:

> Man's responsibility to his Maker is, indeed, the fundamental fact of his life, and it can never be taken too seriously. God made us as responsible moral agents, and he will not treat us as anything less. His Word addresses each of us individually, and each of us is responsible for the way in which he responds—for his attention or inattention, his belief or unbelief, his obedience or disobedience. We cannot evade responsibility for our reaction

---

152. Packer, *Rediscovering Holiness*, 123–24.
153. Packer, *Concise Theology*, 141.
154. Packer, "Faith," 432.
155. Packer, *God's Plans for You*, 146.
156. Packer, *18 Words*, 126–28.
157. Packer, *Under God's Word*, 95; *Honouring Written Word*, 151–52.
158. Packer, *Knowing God*, 18.

to God's revelation. We live under his law. We must answer to him for our lives.[159]

2.6.3 Human Response: Rational Primacy

Given that Packer sees Scripture as being able to mediate the will of God to the mind, he supposes that a proper response to God begins with rational engagement (i.e., applying the mind to appropriate the correct interpretation and understanding of Scripture).[160] In regard to Packer's approach, Don Payne observes: "The mind emerges as the 'gatekeeper' for the other faculties, without which holiness, the heart of the *imago Dei*, cannot be realised."[161] A person's ability to understand and respond to God's inerrant rational communication is seen to be grounded upon a specific view of the *imago Dei*. Obedience to the rational communication of God's law in Scripture is assumed by Packer to be the means of enabling the restoration of God's image in humanity. This starts with the need for understanding truths through means of reception to rational-linguistic communication, followed by applying them to life. Given that Packer places cognitive understanding before the affections there is the suggestion that the way in which persons are to approach the text is divided (i.e., being wholly rational, rather than the whole self involved).

The usefulness of Packer's approach rests wholly on the mind being able to accurately receive truth (and objective knowledge of God) through the right interpretation of the Scriptures. Although he speaks in absolute terms about the importance of coming to an existential knowledge of God through acquaintance, he appears suspicious of personal subjective experience. Given that the intellect is seen as the sole means of receiving instruction from God, it is understood by Packer to be more trustworthy than the emotions. In taking this line, he could be accused of isolating the operation of the rational faculties, so that reason alone remains a sufficiently reliable way of being able to discern the will of God. Because the rational faculties have direct access to Scripture, they are seen as being the best safeguard of orthodoxy and objectivity. It may be construed that the need for rational-linguistic truth to be communicated to the mind—for the purpose of an accurate understanding—occurs at the expense of the whole person. However, Packer is suggesting that God is *only* able to address the whole

---

159. Packer, *Evangelism*, 33.
160. Packer, *Under God's Word*, 19–36.
161. Payne, *Theology of the Christian Life*, 214.

self—and invoke a holistic response—via the prerequisite gateway of the rational faculties.

Packer highlights the need to rightly interpret the biblical text through grammatical-historical exegesis. He believes that persons need to seek the correct interpretation of Scripture in terms of finding its original (and objective) meaning so that they can understand and reapply the truth to their lives.[162] He says: "The interpreter's task is to draw from Scripture and apply to thought and life today that body of universal truths about God, humanity, and their mutual relations that the texts yield."[163] Based on the premise that Scripture is both divine and human in nature, a proper interpretation is understood to involve both the work of the interpreter and the work of the Holy Spirit. Packer does not see the process of understanding the text as being a solely intellectual exercise, but as requiring the illumination of the Spirit.[164] However, he appears to focus primarily on the work of the Spirit in the process of application rather than interpretation.

Packer's approach to using Scripture could be conceived as being individualistic, as well as rationalistic.[165] In terms of the process of biblical interpretation, the individual-social dialectic does not appear as being equal and reciprocal. Despite Packer strongly advocating the need to draw upon ecclesial tradition as a necessary tool of self-critique, the proper usage of a grammatical-historical method of interpretation may ultimately be understood to rely on the expertise of individual interpreters with the requisite skills. Indeed, he appears to speak of revelation primarily within the context of a "personal relationship" with God, the ground of such a relationship—in the first instance—being distinctly mind-to-mind between God and the individual.

Packer does not separate a person's understanding of God through Scripture from their knowledge of God through prayer, or from knowledge of God applied.[166] Although at times he appears to take an overly cerebral approach to Christian living, he always underlines the danger of persons having a rational knowledge about God without knowing God personally.[167] Alister McGrath upholds that Packer's concern is that "knowing true notions about God" and "knowing the true God himself" go together.[168] In

162. Packer, *Celebrating Saving Work*, 95.
163. Packer, "Scripture," 630.
164. Packer, *Under God's Word*, 29–31.
165. Payne, *Theology of the Christian Life*, 233–34.
166. Packer, *Knowing God*, 20–22, 39.
167. Ibid., 25–27.
168. McGrath, *Know and Serve God*, 259–60.

speaking of how the Puritans sought to counter arid intellectualism, Packer insists "conceptual knowledge kills if one does not move on from knowing notions to knowing the realities to which they refer—in this case, from knowing about God to relational acquaintance with God."[169] In *Knowing God*, he states:

> Our aim in studying the Godhead must be to know God himself better. Our concern must be to enlarge our acquaintance, not simply with the doctrine of God's attributes, but with the living God whose attributes they are. As he is the subject of our study, and our helper in it, so he must himself be the end of it. We must seek, in studying God, to be led to God. It was for this purpose that revelation was given, and it is to this use that we must put it.[170]

Though Packer fully recognizes that there is an absolute need for persons to move beyond knowing about God to a deep acquaintance with God, his approach to getting there could appear as rather rigid and mechanical. The method that Packer proposes for moving from "head knowledge" to "heart knowledge" involves discursive meditation on rational-linguistic truth in Scripture. He states: "How can we turn our knowledge *about* God into knowledge *of* God? The rule for doing this is demanding, but simple. It is that we turn each truth that we learn *about* God into a matter for meditation *before* God, leading to prayer and praise *to* God."[171] Rather than seeing progression toward a more contemplative awareness of God, discursive biblical meditation is portrayed as the only true imperative.[172] The use of meditation, in terms of rumination and listening to God, is seen as a means of preparation for conversation with God and the contemplating of God's greatness:[173] "In meditation the whole man is involved in deep and prayerful thought on the true meaning and bearing of a particular Bible passage, on its revelation of God and his ways with men, and on its application to our own life."[174]

In a passing reference to *Lectio Divina*, Packer affirms the stage of *contemplatio*—referring to it as meaning "peaceful rest" and "waiting in silence with hopeful expectation."[175] However, he does not place primary

---

169. Packer, *Quest for Godliness*, 32.
170. Packer, *Knowing God*, 21–22.
171. Ibid., 22.
172. Packer, *Quest for Godliness*, 13.
173. Packer, *Knowing Christianity*, 103–04; Packer and Nystrom, *Praying*, 68–95.
174. Packer, *Under God's Word*, 100–01.
175. Packer and Nystrom, *Praying*, 90–91.

importance on the need for a form of "direct" meditation on God himself. Consequently, acts of contemplation are not encouraged or seen as a central (or necessary) means of fostering Christian formation.[176] The primary discursive activity that leads to formation is understood to occur as a result of Scripture mediating the knowledge of God to the mind. Therefore, Packer focuses on advocating thoughts about God, rather than promoting any form of non-conceptual meditation.[177] He states:

> Meditation is the activity of calling to mind, and thinking over, and dwelling on, and applying to oneself, the various things that one knows about the works and ways and purposes and promises of God. It is an activity of holy thought, consciously performed in the presence of God, under the eye of God, by the help of God, as a means of communion with God. Its purpose is to clear one's mental and spiritual vision of God and to let his truth make its full and proper impact on one's mind and heart.[178]

Packer recognizes the fundamental importance of seeking regular fellowship with God as a "means of grace."[179] Rather than focusing on "direct" contemplation as a response to God, he points toward the need for a more active (and verbal) response to God in reaction to the biblical text. He states: "God's Word comes to us so that we may speak our word to him."[180] He consistently offers a view of prayer as a personal and dynamic encounter, which primarily involves verbal communication.[181] Packer implies that the same way God created human beings in his image to communicate with them through language, he also created them to respond back to him verbally—through praise, confession, petition, intercession, and thanksgiving.[182]

Packer affirms the criticality of inner dispositions (such as faith and affection) toward God and for the core of a person to be engaged. However, in his central scheme of thought, he does not give attention to the need for a sustained inner "act" as a principal means of deepening personal knowledge of God. Moreover, he appears to avoid any discussion of existential communion with God, and rejects more mystical forms of prayer because

---

176. Ibid., 65, 73–74.
177. Ibid., 65.
178. Packer, *Knowing God*, 22.
179. Packer, *Knowing Christianity*, 94.
180. Packer, *Under God's Word*, 96.
181. Packer, *Concise Theology*, 162–64.
182. Packer, "Path of Prayer," 57; *Knowing Christianity*, 98; *Honouring Written Word*, 44.

of their apparent passive nature and the danger of "quietism."[183] Given his concern to place objective (and rational) truth at the beginning of his system, subjective experience of God through the Spirit becomes a secondary concern, and within the central process of formation, he does not see any "gatekeeper" function for the a-rational faculties.

Packer remains reluctant to understand "direct" forms of "religious experience," or "experiences of the Spirit," as being central to spiritual growth. The position he takes may be a reaction to expressions of anti-rational experientialism in the church.[184] Given that Packer sees rational knowledge through Scripture as being more verifiable than "knowledge-through-love," he moves away from speaking about his own personal communion with God in subjective language.[185] For example, in reference to God's love, Packer prefers to speak about loving acts of God recorded in Scripture rather than about a subjective personal experience of God's love. His view of divine guidance also focuses more on a rational understanding tied to propositional instruction in Scripture, so that inner inclinations—desires, affections, emotions—and the possibility of inner promptings of the Spirit, are ultimately subservient to the rational faculties.

Rather than recognizing the central need for persons to experience some mystical or contemplative awareness of God—in terms of a "knowledge-through-love"—Packer's primary practical concern in epistemological terms is for a deepened knowledge of God through the experience of obeying biblical imperatives in daily life. Foremost attention remains on rational-linguistic knowledge and the need for *obedience*, while experiential "knowledge-through-love" remains wholly subordinate.

2.6.4 Growth in Community

Given that Packer has an anthropology characterized by individuality and subordination, it could be assumed that he offers an approach to the Christian life that is primarily individualistic.[186] Packer does appear to give priority to the individual within the scheme of "definitive salvation"—for the church is not seen as the ground of personal salvation. Although individual salvation is central to his understanding of justification, on numerous occasions he points toward the importance of community within the process of

---

183. Packer, "Path of Prayer," 58–59.
184. Packer, *Rediscovering Holiness*, 155.
185. Packer, "Path of Prayer," 56.
186. Payne, *Theology of the Christian Life*, 2, 202.

The "Systematic Spirituality" of J. I. Packer 65

sanctification.[187] For example, Packer acknowledges that holiness does not come through a state of isolation and solitude—it is seen to involve relationships and love.[188] Though he may sometimes appear to place emphasis on autonomous growth through the nurturing of personal discipline and obedience, he warns against the dangers of individualism.[189] Packer also places importance on ecclesial membership and the life of the church for spiritual growth—the gathered community being seen as an essential resource for personal holiness. Though he recognizes the centrality of ecclesial life, the underlying dynamic that he expresses between individual and social dimensions appears to weaken the latter. Despite his qualifying statements about the importance of church life in the process of sanctification, it remains secondary.

Packer is keen to demonstrate the absolute distinctiveness of Christian fellowship.[190] He recognizes that the ground of this fellowship is "special revelation." Packer supposes that Scripture is to provide the Christian community with its distinctiveness, understanding that it must be the basis for gathered fellowship. Moreover, his belief is that the fellowship that individuals have with God "is the source from which fellowship among Christians springs: and fellowship with God is the end to which Christian fellowship is a means."[191] As well as emphasizing how personal union with God brings about proper relations with others, Packer also sees ecclesial relations as being a catalyst for persons to be brought into deeper relationship with God.[192] He understands the purpose of such fellowship as being to lead persons toward God and to be a "means of grace" through which they can receive from God.[193] Packer states that "God has made us in such a way that our fellowship with himself is fed by our fellowship with fellow Christians, and requires to be so fed constantly for its own deepening and enrichment."[194]

Ultimately, ecclesial fellowship is understood as being for the purpose of revealing God to others and coming to a greater knowledge of him.[195]

---

187. Packer, *God's Plans for You*, 134, 48.
188. Packer, *Rediscovering Holiness*, 27–28.
189. Packer and Nystrom, *God's Will*, 140–42.
190. Packer, *18 Words*, 183–84.
191. Ibid., 185.
192. Ibid., 191. See also Packer and Howard, *Christianity*, 14.
193. Packer, *Serving People of God*, 15.
194. Packer, *18 Words*, 185.
195. Rather than emphasizing the place of relationships in the process that leads to holiness, Packer points out the interrelation between the love toward God and love toward one another. He states that "the outward life of loving one's neighbor and the inner life of loving one's God belong together, in such a sense that failure in either

Given that persons respond to God's will and express his holiness in the context of relationships, love is seen as being an expression of individual righteousness that stems from a "personal relationship" with God.[196] Indeed, Christian love is understood as being the central sign of the Christian life and an act of obedience to God.[197] Packer's belief in some form of subordination within the triune life—specifically within the "economic" Trinity—also affects his understanding of transformation within the life of the church. Given the obedience of the Son to the Father is seen as being the central model for the elect to follow, the substance of relationships is rooted in personal obedience to the law of God in Scripture. Subordinate rationalism is then exhibited in how the church (and world) fits into Packer's theological scheme of the Christian life—with personal holiness being achieved through obedience to the law in loving God and neighbor.[198]

Although Packer does not draw out a social trinitarian theology or make it central for the life of the church, he does see the ecclesial understanding of fellowship as being comparable to the "give-and-take" within the triune life, albeit through focusing on the gift of rational-linguistic communication.[199] Packer believes that earthly relations correspond with the fellowship of mutual honor and love in the triune life.[200] He states: "Christian fellowship is a family activity of God's sons. Like fellowship with the Father and the Son, it is a two-way traffic which involves giving and taking on both sides."[201] Elsewhere, he affirms: "God has called them [believers] into a relation of mutual love and service, of mutual listening and response, of asking, giving, taking, and sharing on both sides."[202]

Ultimately, giving and receiving are understood as being the substance of fellowship; where individuals give what they have received from God, and receive God's gifts through other persons.[203] Packer states: "fellowship means common participation in something either by giving what you have to the other person or receiving what he or she has. Give-and-take is the essence of fellowship, and give-and-take must be the way of fellowship in the

---

inescapably weakens the other" (*Rediscovering Holiness*, 89).

196. See Payne, *Theology of the Christian Life*, 202.
197. Packer, *Concise Theology*, 156–57.
198. Packer, *Rediscovering Holiness*, 162–63.
199. Packer, *Serving People of God*, 14.
200. Packer, *Celebrating Saving Work*, 15.
201. Packer, *18 Words*, 186.
202. Packer, *Growing in Christ*, 228.
203. Packer, *Knowing Christianity*, 120–24; *18 Words*, 184–85.

common life of the body of Christ."[204] Here, giving and receiving amounts to persons expressing the gifts of God toward one another for the purpose of drawing closer to God. Packer clearly recognizes the need for "every member ministry," involving gift-giving of all kinds, and the imitation of others.[205] He defines fellowship as

> seeking to share in what God has made known of himself to others, as a means to finding strength, refreshment, and instruction for one's own soul. In fellowship, one seeks to gain, as well as to give.... Thus, Christian fellowship is an expression of both love and humility. It springs from a desire to bring benefit to others, coupled with a sense of personal weakness and need. It has a double motive—the wish to help, and to be helped; to edify, and to be edified. It has a double aim—to do and to receive, good. It is a corporate seeking by Christian people to know God better through sharing with each other what, individually, they have learned of him already.[206]

Given that Packer is primarily interested in spiritual growth occurring through means of rational speech and comprehension, formation in a communal context is also seen to occur through rational-linguistic expression. In congruence with his wider theological scheme, Packer recognizes the importance of the mutual sharing of biblical truth, and a person's response to it. Because he places an emphasis on the communication of a rational message, proper receptivity and understanding become necessary for formation to occur. Packer does not focus on how knowledge of God is being revealed within the life of the church in a more integral sense, so "presence" and "act" are given less significance within the sanctification process. Ultimately, revealing the knowledge of God to others is primarily seen as an expression of Christian duty and witness, rather than as a formational means for both giver and receiver.

With regard to the gathered worship of the Christian community, the rational-linguistic emphasis is further demonstrated in a more formalized way, being seen in the value that Packer gives to *preaching*. He notes the New Testament emphasis on this particular "sacrament," and believes that use of Scripture should assume a central place in the life of the church, as in a person's daily devotions.[207] Packer states: "The purpose of preaching is to inform, persuade, and call forth an appropriate response to the God

---

204. Packer, *Serving People of God*, 13.
205. Packer, *Keep in Step*, 69–72, 153; Packer and Nystrom, *God's Will*, 163–79.
206. Packer, *18 Words*, 187.
207. Packer, *Under God's Word*, 64–71.

whose message and instruction are being delivered."[208] Any other elements of worship in corporate settings such as praise, prayer, and the ritual of communion are understood to occur as a response to God's self-revelation in Scripture.

Within a gathered church context, Packer sees an important place for the sacrament of communion. However, participating in the transforming presence of Christ through the act of communion is not assumed to have the same central position (or same formational value) as the "sacrament" of Scripture. Because of Packer's focus on rational-linguistic communication, he does not equally emphasize the qualities and specific function of speech, presence, and act in revealing knowledge of God. He could be more explicit in highlighting the purpose of immanent reflections of God in the life of the church through presence and act, rather than just focusing on the communication of Scripture.

As a "catechist," Packer emphasizes the importance of all forms of biblical instruction within an ecclesial setting. His interest is in the systematic teaching of truth about God and his dealings with the world so that persons might be able to receive truth that will form their mind and heart. Ultimately, he seeks to communicate that which engages the whole person, the "head, heart, and hands; doctrine, experience, and practice."[209] Packer fully understands that there is the need for holistic development, in terms of intellectual learning, worship, prayer, active obedience, and loving service.[210] On occasion, he does point to a broader understanding of Christian fellowship, recognizing the whole Christian duty toward self-gift in relationships. He states:

> The corporate aspect of Christian spirituality can be defined as practising mutual love and care in God's family on the basis that this is the life to which we are called and for which Christ equips us: each believer must be ready to lay down his or her life for Christ in others, and must be duly grateful when others lay down their lives and bear burdens for Christ in his or her own self.[211]

Nevertheless, with regard to the transmission of divine revelation in community, Packer's emphasis remains both rationalistic and linguistic. He believes that "Christian fellowship is seeking to share what God has made

---

208. Packer, *Honouring Written Word*, 253.
209. Packer and Parrett, *Grounded in the Gospel*, 30, 187–89.
210. Ibid., 117–36.
211. Packer, *Serving People of God*, 267.

known to us while letting others share with us what they know of him."[212] Elsewhere, Packer affirms that fellowship involves "first a sharing with our fellow believers the things that God has made known to us about himself, in hope that we may thus help them to know him better and so enrich their fellowship with him."[213] Ultimately, it appears that Packer's main emphasis in ecclesial life is for persons to grow in their understanding of Scripture through rational meditation and reflection, and to respond with verbal expression and active obedience.

2.6.5 Transformation in the World

Packer recognizes the church is to be a community of holiness that is different, but not separate from the world.[214] He understands that God's people are sent out as a scattered community—to witness to Christ and his kingdom, and to serve others. Packer states: "The universal church, and therefore every local congregation and every Christian in it, is sent into the world to fulfil a definite, defined task."[215] He believes that Christians are called to fully engage with society—not primarily for the cause of socio-political transformation—but as witnesses to the knowledge of God in Christ, inviting persons to respond in repentance and faith. He describes the two-fold task of mission within the categories of "proclamation" and "presence-act," but with a primary focus on the former:

> First and fundamentally, it is the work of worldwide witness, disciple-making and church-planting (Matt 24:14; 28:19–20; Mark 13:10; Luke 24:47–48). Jesus Christ is to be proclaimed everywhere as God incarnate, Lord, and Saviour; and God's authoritative invitation to find life through turning to Christ in repentance and faith (Matt 22:1–10; Luke 14:16–24) is to be delivered to all mankind. . . . [Secondly, it is that we are] . . . called to practice deeds of mercy and compassion, a thoroughgoing neighbour-love that responds unstintingly to all forms of human need as they present themselves (Luke 10:25–27; Rom 12:20–21).[216]

---

212. Packer, *Knowing Christianity*, 121.
213. Packer, *18 Words*, 186–87.
214. Packer, *Concise Theology*, 198–200.
215. Ibid., 189.
216. Ibid., 189–90.

The church is not only believed to be a community that witnesses to the knowledge of Christ through proclamation, but also to be one that demonstrates knowledge of Christ through presence, and acts of love. However, Packer does not see this kind of witness to those outside of the community of faith as having the same direct epistemological or redemptive value as rational-linguistic communication. He focuses on the transmission of the Word through verbal disclosure.[217] Packer believes that there is a necessary sharing of the propositional gospel (and subsequent understanding) before there can be any transformational response. Ultimately, the missional witness of the church and means of transformation in the world is only seen to occur through the proclamation of the Word directed at the mind rather than through an "integral witness" that also emphasizes presence and act.

As well as there being a call for Christians to witness to Christ, Packer also recognizes they are summoned to carry out a variety of vocational roles in society. He states that "Christians are called to fulfil the 'cultural mandate' that God gave to mankind at creation (Gen 1:28–30; Ps 8:6–8). Man was made to manage God's world, and this stewardship is part of the human vocation in Christ."[218] Packer believes that Christians become a "transforming cultural force" as they live out their callings in the world through all kinds of activities.[219] He affirms the mandate for positive involvement in the world as the vocation of the Christian and recognizes the need to fully engage in society in its fallen state, albeit in the light of the eternal.[220] However, Packer rejects any form of piety that may reduce the Christian faith to a sociopolitical scheme for "transforming" this present world.[221]

Although Packer understands the importance of societal work within the scheme of Christian mission, he does not portray it as a means through which Christian formation occurs. Indeed, Packer does not focus on how formation transpires in the Christian life as a result of engaging in any "ordinary" activity and interaction with the world. Although there is recognition that holiness is not something that can simply be worked out in solitude or detachment, he appears to make private and ecclesial space the environment for Christian formation, focusing on specific activities that occur in a particular context. Only this is understood to have formative value—bringing "special grace" that contributes toward persons becoming more

---

217. Packer, *Serving People of God*, 216; *Evangelism*, 34; *Concise Theology*, 199.
218. Packer, *Concise Theology*, 199.
219. Ibid., 199–200
220. Packer, *Knowing Christianity*, 143–44; Packer and Howard, *Christianity*, 177–80.
221. Packer, *Knowing Christianity*, 141–42.

like Christ. Packer repeatedly speaks of growth as being nurtured through specific "means of grace":

> The Holy Spirit works through means—through the objective 'means of grace,' namely, biblical truth, prayer, fellowship, worship, and the Lord's Supper, and with them through the subjective 'means of grace' whereby we open ourselves to change, namely, thinking, listening, questioning oneself, examining oneself, admonishing oneself, sharing what is in one's heart with others, and weighing any response they make.[222]

Rather than attempting to provide an exhaustive list of "spiritual disciplines" that may be beneficial for Christian growth, Packer focuses on select and limited means needed for Christian formation to occur. The lists he gives for this are not always the same, but there is consistent reference to central means being "Bible," "prayer," "worship," and "[ecclesial] fellowship."[223] These are understood as things that persons engage in to allow God to work in their lives and transform them.[224]

Given that sanctification is understood by Packer to be wholly reliant upon a personal response to "special revelation," a Christian's vocation in the world (and relation to the world) is not perceived as contributing to Christian formation. Rather, it is seen more as being an overflowing mission from within the community of faith, so that those who are outside may be drawn in. Given that any other environment, experience, or medium outside of the church is understood only to facilitate "common grace"—as opposed to redemptive action—Packer may be seen to limit the process of growing in holiness. It could be argued that a fully integral approach should be "inclusive," in terms of God being understood to work in a person's life through any means, while still acknowledging a special place for specific "means of grace." This would invoke further questions about the extent to which the work of "common grace"—given to all humanity—is present within the process of Christian formation.

Ultimately, Packer's understanding of the Christian life can be said to be "world-affirming" rather than "world-denying."[225] In recognizing physicality as a gift of God, he affirms the value of God-given pleasure in the body and insists on a proper integration of this into the life of godliness. However, this does not mean that the entirety of the human experience is seen as a permissible starting point in the formation process. Formation is

---

222. Packer, *Keep in Step*, 90.
223. Packer, *Serving People of God*, 290.
224. Packer, *Knowing Christianity*, 93.
225. Packer, "Christian and God's World," 93–94.

only understood to occur as a direct response to rational-linguistic speech. Consequently, relationships, and physicality are given a contextual, subordinate, and passive role rather than a proactive one that initiates personal holiness and formation. Packer's neglect of embodiment (and "outer" experience) in the process of formation is congruent with his anthropological emphasis.

2.7 CONCLUSION

The contours of J. I. Packer's thought point toward the possibility of an integrated, cohesive, broad, common, and balanced framework of transformational theology. He sees Christian formation as occurring as a result of responding to a sovereign God who has chosen to reveal himself. The special place that Packer gives to the function of rational-linguistic revelation (i.e., the communication of the Scriptures—of which the gospel of Christ is the center) is evident in the emphasis he places on the rational faculties and the need to understand and actively respond to biblical truth. Crucially, Packer sees Christian formation as only occurring where there has been the response of repentance and faith to the propositional gospel of Christ, leading to union with Christ.

Bibliology is clearly at the forefront of Packer's thought. He recognizes that the biblical text provides objective truth and carries the fullness of divine authority. The possibility of persons coming to orthodoxy and orthopraxy is understood to depend upon them being able to come to true knowledge of God through a grammatical-historical interpretation of Scripture. Packer's immediate concern is to express rational, propositional truths from the Bible, truths that he claims are consistent—and in continuity with—the biblical gospel and the stream of the "Great Tradition." He then focuses on the need for orderly instruction of such truths to the rational faculties—to invoke a broad response—so that formation can occur.[226]

Packer's theology has been outlined as a backdrop to understanding his view of the Christian life. Recognizing how he integrates the concerns of theology and spirituality (through holding together doctrine, communion with God, and applied knowledge) leads to an understanding how transformation is to occur. Packer affirms the importance of uniting the three dimensions of belief, experience, and practice, while also appealing for

---

226. Packer and Parrett, *Grounded in the Gospel*, 123. Packer's catechizing focuses on what leads to right beliefs, right actions, and deep communion with God—the need being to shape a person's mind with systematic instruction about prayer, moral behavior, and doctrinal beliefs.

balance between them.²²⁷ For formation to happen there needs to be cognitive understanding of biblical truth (i.e., an active response expressed first in rational engagement), followed by verbal forms of prayer and ongoing obedience.

As a whole, Packer's thought demonstrates the possibility of expressing a broad understanding that remains internally cohesive—not simply in terms of a theoretical framework—but also in terms of the Christian life. Although his core thought and praxis contain predominant characteristics, he endeavors to express a view of the Christian life that avoids dualistic tendencies. Packer has sought to provide an understanding that is not focused on extremes—such as anti-rational experientialism and dry intellectualism. He recognizes the dangers of imbalanced growth, where there may be a strong focus on either "rationalism," "experientialism," or "activism."²²⁸ Though he has not attempted to provide a comprehensive and integrated theological framework for Christian formation, he indicates the need for this and offers some helpful directives.

Ultimately, Packer points toward a proto-evangelical understanding—one that he sees as representing the mainstream Christian view.²²⁹ As well as presenting his view for self-identified evangelicals, he also offers it to the wider church, for the purpose of dialogue. He invites other traditions to examine his theological convictions, believing that what he sets out is within the mainstream orthodoxy of the early church and Reformers.²³⁰ However, Packer does not support ecumenical dialogue at the expense of abandoning orthodox Protestant doctrine. Being known for "collaboration without compromise," he engages outside of his tradition but does so on his own terms.²³¹

With this in mind, the next chapter will focus on the significant patristic figure of Maximus Confessor, whose alternative theology of the Christian life will be presented. This allows exposure to a broad and integrated vision of Christian formation from within another tradition to challenge the breadth and effectuality of Packer's thought.

227. Packer, *Rediscovering Holiness*, 57, 150–57.
228. Ibid., 154–56.
229. In regard to what faithful evangelicals claim, Packer believes that "far from being marginal in relation to the larger Christian world, they are in fact at its centre, upholding mainstream Christian faith in a way that is demonstrably more biblical than any alternative" ("Maintaining Evangelical Theology," 183). Packer sees evangelicalism as "true mainstream Christianity, in relation to which all forms of non-evangelicalism are sub-evangelical and eccentric" (Ibid., 186).
230. Packer and Oden, *One Faith*, 173.
231. McGrath, *Know and Serve God*, 288.

Chapter 3

The "Synthetic Vision" of Maximus Confessor

3.1 INTRODUCTION

THIS CHAPTER WILL EXAMINE the thought of Maximus Confessor. It will look at how the center of his system enables an alternative transformational vision that is broad and comprehensive in scope. Maximus's approach is vastly different from that of J. I. Packer because it is built around a different logocentric core—one that is not "rational-linguistic" in nature. The examination of Maximus's approach to Christian formation will involve observing how he provides a different means of integrating the concerns of theology and spirituality.

Maximus has assumed a mediatorial role as one of the last and most prolific minds of the Greek patristic era. In his writings he brought together various diverse ideas, fusing them into an original synthesis, bridging Christian traditions of East and West before the schism. He is recognized as someone who synthesized different concepts into an integrated system.[1] Crucially, he sought to seamlessly combine ascetical, mystical, dogmatic, and sacramental dimensions, expressing the importance of needing to bring things together—to integrate and remove divisions. Maximus's attempt to demonstrate an integrated and cohesive system arose from an "ecumenical"

---

1. Hans Urs von Balthasar called Maximus "the most daring systematician of his time" (*Cosmic Liturgy*, 29).

spirit, and a profound grasp of his heritage. In particular, he was influenced by the ascetical teachings of Evagrius Ponticus, Chalcedonian dogma, and Cappadocian thought. His work also acted as a corrective to elements of Origenist thought and Dionysian spirituality.

Maximus's main intention was to affirm already existing orthodox views rather than to provide originality in his thought. He endeavored to develop a comprehensive orthodox theological vision by embracing the testimony of Scripture and the "common opinion" of the church. His expressions of orthodoxy are based on the convergence of sources and traditions (i.e., apostolic authority, the church fathers, councils, creeds, liturgy, and Scripture). Although Maximus's theological method does not involve a sophisticated exegesis, he maintained a high view of Scripture and Scripture is central to his articulation of orthodoxy.

This chapter will explore some of the central ideas in Maximus's thought through the use of translated works and relevant secondary studies. Although none of his writings provide a systematic presentation of his theology as a whole, together they reflect a synthesis that is both comprehensive and coherent.[2] There have been a significant number of English editions of his works appearing in recent years, the most important to date are *Liber Ambiguorum* (The Ambigua or Difficulties), *Quaestiones et Dubia* (Questions and Doubts), *Capita de Caritate* (Four Centuries on Love), *Capita Theologiae et Oeconomiae* (Centuries on Knowledge), *Liber Asceticus* (The Ascetic Life), and *Mystagogia* (English edition given same title). An analysis of this material will provide insight into Maximus's overall theory and his understanding of the Christian life.[3]

This chapter will reveal the broad nature of Maximus's transformational theology. As with the previous chapter, there will be the setting forth of a theological framework in order to provide the proper grounding to explore the Christian life. The next section will begin by outlining the logocentric core of Maximus's thought. By exploring major themes in relation to this, it will be seen how his whole theological system is integrated. Toward the end of the chapter there will be a more specific focus on examining how

---

2. A full chronological list of his writings is given in Jankowiak and Booth, "Works of Maximus the Confessor."

3. There have been a significant number of secondary studies that focus on various aspects of Maximus's thought. Three of the big names in Maximian studies are Polycarp Sherwood, Hans Urs von Balthasar, and Lars Thunberg. There have also been some excellent studies done more recently, in particular, a series of short essays on Maximus appears in Allen and Neil, *Oxford Handbook*. Recent research on Maximus has been documented in Nichols, *Byzantine Gospel*; Louth, "Recent Research on St Maximus"; Lollar, "Maximian Thought."

Maximus integrates the concerns of theology and spirituality around his theological center.

3.2 CHRISTOLOGY AND INTEGRATION

3.2.1 Introduction

In this section, the unifying center of Maximus's theology will be outlined. Commentators have expressed differing views on what they believe the core of his theology is. Polycarp Sherwood has understood it to involve the uniting of all things in Christ. Hans Urs von Balthasar has described internal unity "without mixture" as being the center of Maximus's theological system—the Chalcedonian Definition being the key to unlocking the structural principle of reality.[4] Torstein Tollefsen recognizes Christology as being the heart of Maximus's cosmological system, but without any special reference to dialectic.[5] Melchisedec Törönen, on the other hand, portrays the relation between "union" and "distinction" as being the center of Maximus's theology, but does so without special reference to Christology.[6] Törönen sees the metaphysical principle of reality—based upon the notion of "whole and parts"—as conveying the overriding structure of Maximus's theology, being both the "law of being" and the "law of synthesis."

In this chapter, it is proposed that the center of Maximus's thought is the motif of *union and distinction in Christ*. This becomes the unifying theme for his whole system—the dialectical ontology in the person of Christ infiltrating all elements of his theology.[7] This center will be seen to provide cohesiveness across Maximus's thought. It will also be understood to offer the basis for integrating the concerns of theology and spirituality, and in doing so point toward a comprehensive vision of transformational theology.

An examination of Maximus's work reveals that he offers a way of integrating diverse ideas and concepts, rather than seeing them as opposing. The theological system he has put forward points to his intended goal of overcoming division and coming to wholeness. Maximus describes the basis for orthodoxy and synthesis in Christian theology as involving dialectical

---

4. Sherwood, *Maximus the Confessor*; Balthasar, *Cosmic Liturgy*.
5. Tollefsen, *Cosmology of St Maximus*.
6. See Törönen, *Union and Distinction*.
7. The term "dialectic" is understood as involving the interaction between juxtaposed elements (or truths) that seemingly appear to contradict and be in conflict. Each pole can be held together in paradoxical tension, being seen to affirm rather than oppose the other. This "both/and" position maintains union without confusion and so provides a way of overcoming dualism and false dichotomies.

ontology.⁸ He gives attention to the use of dialectical language in order to express union and differentiation in understanding both the Trinity and the person of Christ—in particular—through a specific usage of perichoretic language in the latter.⁹ Maximus sees union and difference as being interdependent, in terms of there being a simultaneous reality of "unity without confusion." Törönen has argued that this idea pervades various aspects of Maximus's thought, and that any synthesis of Maximus's work must be seen in the light of it.¹⁰

Although Maximus recognizes dialectical language as finding its source in the Trinity, he more specifically relates this language to the person of Christ. This becomes the overarching theme that unites all of his thought, both in terms of theology and practice—the incarnation of the Logos being the paradigm within a wider vision of reality. Ultimately, Maximus's whole system is dependent on his Christology—his method of synthesis being built around a christological paradigm. The hypostatic union is seen as being the key element in the metaphysical structure of reality; the central point from which all of creation draws its meaning and significance. The incarnation is not only recognized as a historical event. It is understood to continue to unveil the absolute significance of Christ's being in the structure and principles of the universe.

Maximus portrays God as purposing to integrate the fractures in the broken world—reconciling everything together through the incarnate Logos. Consequently, integration in Christ is the goal of Maximus's theology. In simple terms, he understands this goal as being accomplished through the divine and human union in Christ's person. Ultimately, Maximus presents every part of life as demonstrating a theandric dimension—so

---

8. Melchisedec Törönen has pointed out that the fundamental question in both trinitarian theology and Christology has been "how to reconcile simultaneous unity and difference" (*Union and Distinction*, 47).

9. Oliver Crisp notes that the concept of *perichoresis* was first used by Gregory Nazianzus and Maximus Confessor in relation to the hypostatic union in Christ. Later on, the concept was applied by John of Damascus to the nature of the triune life. The term has been used to denote interpenetration, without confusion, for the purpose of upholding both union and distinction. In contemporary theology it is most often used to describe the way the persons of the Triune God relate to each other, denoting a mutual indwelling and sharing in the lives of the other while allowing a distinct individual identity. Apart from being used in relation to Christ and the Trinity, it has also been applied more widely ("Problems with Perichoresis," 122). See Vishnevskaya, "Divinization and Spiritual Progress"; "Divinization as Perichoretic Embrace"; Gifford, *Perichoretic Salvation*.

10. Törönen, *Union and Distinction*, 1, 28–30.

uniting everything together within a theandrical system of divine-human reciprocity.[11]

Part of the originality of Maximus's vision is in how he brings the Chalcedonian faith into the development of a "natural theology," being an elaboration of a cosmological vision centered on the incarnation of Christ. His intense commitment to the Chalcedonian dialectic causes him to interpret all areas of the church's teaching in relation to it. Indeed, all aspects of Maximus's theology become viewed through a Christocentric lens of "Chalcedonian logic"—being transferred to his soteriology, cosmology, bibliology, ecclesiology, anthropology, and his understanding of the Christian life.

To summarize, it is proposed that the central idea found in Maximus's thought is synthesis through the usage of dialectical language of union and distinction in Christ (i.e., all is being integrated together through the divine-human dialectic). For Maximus, this motif provides a way of developing a unified and cohesive theology of the Christian life, as opposed to simply outlining a dogmatic series of separate doctrines that do not have a unifying center. He also uses this motif to express the means of transformation in the Christian life

3.2.2 Christ and the Trinity

Christian orthodoxy rests upon both trinitarian and christological ontology. Although Christology is most central to Maximus's system, it is important to recognize the relation between his understanding of the theandric and his trinitarian thought. Maximus adopts a view of the divine triad that appears to incorporate Chalcedonian Christology, as articulated by the Cappadocians. It can be assumed that the perichoretic dynamics—understood to be within the person of Christ—are, first and foremost, demonstrated in the Trinity, as per a Cappadocian definition. Although Maximus's concern is not to speak directly of *perichoresis* within the triune life, it is there by implication, given that the incarnation is seen to be grounded in the intra-triune life.

Maximus speaks of a dialectic of "monad and triad" to denote the union and difference between the divine persons. He describes the Triune God as "one God, one nature and three persons, unity of essence in three persons and consubstantial Trinity, of persons; Trinity in unity and unity in Trinity."[12] The relation between the divine persons is seen as involving a

---

11. Lars Thunberg notes that the term "theandric" is Maximus's "preferred expression of the divine-human reciprocity in action" (*Man and the Cosmos*, 72).

12. Confessor, "Mystagogy," 205.

"union without confusion," maintaining distinction without separation or division.[13] For Maximus, both oneness and threeness are a simultaneous reality. He believes that neither pole has "ontological priority" over the other as they are aspects of a single reality—what unites is seen to differentiate and what differentiates is seen to unite.[14]

Although Maximus does not fully develop his trinitarian thought, it clearly remains present behind his Christology. His neglect of a broader discussion or development in this area may be because of his focus on the apophatic nature of the triune life—in recognizing that God is beyond every human contemplation. Ultimately, Maximus understands the incarnation of Christ as being located within the trinitarian matrix—the sent Logos being an activity of the Trinity itself, revealing the triune life in created order.

3.2.3 The Two Natures of Christ

Maximus's understanding of the two natures of Christ is founded in the Chalcedonian faith. Two hundred years after the Council of Chalcedon, he was clearly wrestling with language to express the nature of the hypostatic union. Maximus sought to defend the Chalcedonian position that Christ was both truly divine and truly human against new heresies, and was most commonly known for his defense against Monothelitism, which stated that Christ possessed two natures but only one will.[15]

Maximus speaks of a dialectic in the person of Christ, in terms of union-distinction between the divine and human, as a single *hypostasis* in two natures, being both without separation and without confusion. He affirms: "[Christ] himself was the unconfused union. And this union admits no division between the two natures—of which he himself was the *hypostasis* . . . He was the true *hypostasis* of true natures united in an ineffable union. Acting in both of these natures in a manner suitable and consistent with each, he was shown forth as one truly preserving them unconfused."[16] Maximus's understanding is that there is the expression of a dialectical tension that allows it to be possible for there to be one *hypostasis* and two different natures in simultaneous union-distinction, yet without contradiction.

Maximus makes an important contribution to Christology by using perichoretic language to express the dialectic—maintaining the co-existent union-distinction relation between divinity and humanity, which is without

13. Ibid.
14. Confessor, "Ambigua 23–71," 115–19.
15. See Nichols, *Byzantine Gospel*, 95–102; Balthasar, *Cosmic Liturgy*, 260–63.
16. Confessor, "Ambigua 1–22," 29.

division or confusion. In respect to Maximus's usage of *perichoresis* to designate the co-inherence of the divine and human nature of the incarnate Logos, Janet Williams states:

> Through this notion of mutual penetration, thus, Maximus works through the implications of his Chalcedonian commitment so as to express not simply the identity of Christ, but the entirety of the relation between divinity and created being, initiated by the incarnation, expressed in the pouring of divine and creation into each another with loving self-abandonment, and completed in the eschaton.[17]

The language of *perichoresis* used by Maximus denotes interpenetration between divine and human natures, while each still remains distinct. He holds that it is a "peri-choresis," not a "meta-choresis," meaning that there is no change from one nature into the other. However, what he describes still involves a mutual exchange between the two, an interpenetration of essentially different natures, rather than simply involving a penetration of divine into human.[18] In describing a reciprocity that involves a mutual kenosis of both natures, he goes beyond predecessors who saw this as only being one way. The nature of this divine-human relation, expressed throughout Maximus's theological system, provides a basis for the goal of deification, as well as being the dynamic seen to be central to transformation.

3.2.4 Christ the Mediator

Before examining how the theandric dimension is present within other aspects of Maximus's thought, it is important to recognize that he sees the relationship between God and creation as being christological in nature. Maximus understands the relation between the two natures of Christ as the paradigm for the relation between God and created order. The Logos-Christ—being the mediator between the Trinity and creation—is seen as the means through which God is reconciled to humanity and the whole cosmos integrated.[19]

Maximus maintains that the dynamic of union-distinction filters into the relation between God and humanity. He points to a perichoretic structural union existing between them, in terms of God being intimately

---

17. Williams, "Pseudo-Dionysius and Maximus," 197. See also Confessor, "Ambigua 1–22," 55–57.
18. Vishnevskaya, "Divinization as Perichoretic Embrace," 132–33.
19. Confessor, "Ambigua 23–71," 103–21.

involved in his creation, alongside humanity penetrating into God. Elena Vishnevskaya believes that Maximus sees the perichoretic relation between God and humanity as being the same as the union in the person of Christ.[20] Maximus maintains reciprocity in this relation, expressing a mutual exchange of properties—congruent with the interpenetration of divine and human natures in Christ. In regard to Maximus's view, Vishnevskaya affirms that as the two natures "interpenetrate and exchange," similarly "God and the human being, the infinite and the finite, join in divinizing union."[21] Maximus sees the perichoretic relation between divine and human natures in the incarnate Word as defining the relation between the noetic and the material. The ongoing interpenetrative movement between God and humanity is believed to bring forth deification.[22]

Maximus recognizes the purpose of Christ's mediatorial role as being to bring created order into a place of unity-in-diversity. It is understood that underlying the multiplicity in the created world, is the single controlling intent of the Creator—the Logos made flesh. The Logos is perceived to be hidden behind all things, being the means through which persons participate in unity, while being revealed through all things in their own diversity.[23] For Maximus, nothing created properly exists in itself; it is instead marked by movement toward "broader" communion, all ultimately encompassed by the one divine Logos who is the source and end of creaturely existence.[24] Everything is seen to have its own Logos, and the totality of *logoi* are contained as a plurality in unity, in the Logos—the Word of God. This unity of all that exists in the Logos means there is to be a "providential return of the many to the One—as if to an all-powerful point of origin."[25]

Maximus sees participation in the incarnation of Christ as enabling humanity to partake in the triune life, albeit a life expressed in human physicality. Although the source of union-distinction is the Trinity, the medium through which this dynamic is expressed and given to humanity is the person of Christ. Maximus understands the Logos-Christ as enabling creation to manifest the union and division that is expressed within the triune life as it participates in the union-division demonstrated in Christ. Ultimately, the Logos himself is seen as being the principle and cause of all.[26] In describ-

20. Vishnevskaya, "Divinization as Perichoretic Embrace," 134.
21. Ibid.
22. Confessor, "Ambigua 1–22," 105–07, 221; "Ambigua 23–71," 109.
23. Confessor, "Ambigua 1–22," 95–105.
24. Ibid., 101–03.
25. Ibid., 101.
26. Ibid., 95.

ing Maximus's understanding here, Melchisedec Törönen affirms: "There is, therefore, a simultaneous union and distinction in the Logos himself, a simultaneous union and distinction which he communicates to the created order through the *logoi*."[27]

Maximus sees this dialectic as being present in both the structural nature and deification of humanity. The Logos procession in creation demonstrates the hypostatic union of divine and human natures and is the mediatory means by which God unites all to himself, while also uniting it within itself. Through the hypostatic union, humanity is seen as being able to fully participate in the divine nature, making deification possible. This means that, in Christ, persons are also understood to become mediators between God and the cosmos, reconciling divine and human elements in themselves.[28] Maximus sees the dialectical principle as being central in the ongoing process of integration and transformation.

3.3 ANTHROPOLOGY AND DEIFICATION

3.3.1 Introduction

Maximus's anthropology demonstrates an understanding that consistently points toward the central goal of deification. He positions human ontology wholly in relation to God, expressing an understanding of human life in respect to both Christ and the Trinity. Given that the triune life provides the ground for his Christology, it is important to firstly acknowledge how he relates trinitarian thought to the human person before looking at its christological nature. In being the source of all created reality, the Trinity is seen as a model for both human personhood and intra-creational realities. Thunberg affirms that the dialectic of unity and differentiation characterizes all that Maximus has to say about a person and their relationships, being something that filters down from his view of the Trinity.[29] Because human beings are inherently related to God, they are understood to reflect the unity and distinction in the likeness of the "monad and triad."[30] Therefore, the essence of Maximus's anthropology involves a clear dialectic—with God being made manifest in his creation as both union and difference. As already noted, Maximus affirms that the incarnation of Christ is the means through

---

27. Törönen, *Union and Distinction*, 135.
28. Confessor, "Mystagogy," 196–97; "Ambigua 23–71," 103–21.
29. Thunberg, *Microcosm and Mediator*, 404.
30. Confessor, "Ambigua 1–22," 321–23.

which humanity is able to participate in (and reflect) the triune life, albeit within physicality.

Ultimately, Maximus presents an anthropology that appears far more christological than trinitarian, hence his bipartite focus. He sees the theandric as the key to understanding everything in his anthropological system—the incarnation of Christ having absolute significance for human personhood. Maximus believes that an individual human being is a whole, a unity of both intelligible (soul) and sensible (body), clearly denoting their relation to both God and the physical world. He relates Christology to anthropology, in terms of demonstrating the relation between soul-body and divine-human parts. Not only does he use perichoretic language in his Christology (and imply it within the Trinity), he also applies it to the relation between soul and body, and to the process of deification—the mutual penetration of divine and human becoming the dialectic that all are to participate in.[31]

3.3.2 The Three Modes of Personhood

Maximus positions the bipartite self in relation to the triad of "original-middle-end"—three modes which are kept in a form of triune dialectic—being one, and yet three. In doing so, he fully integrates the protological, soteriological, and eschatological concerns of anthropology rather than seeing them as disconnected—the unifying dimension between them being the event of the incarnation. Maximus has demonstrated how the concrete historical expression of the incarnated Logos is worked out in the cosmos in relation to the modes of "being, well-being, and ever-being," the work of the Word in creation, incarnation, and deification, being seen to be both forming and re-forming. He sees this process as a positive development rather than a restoration of the original state.

The first "anthropological mode" is protological, relating to the original structure of creation. Maximus defines created order in a theandric sense—Christ being associated to creation by first principle. The principle of the Logos is understood to remain in created order, willing God's purpose, a purpose that is fully demonstrated by the historic incarnation of Christ. Given that the Logos within human personhood is seen to define the first principle and structure of human personhood, it is also perceived to define the present framework and end goal of human existence. In Maximus's system, movement is related to the idea of purpose and eschaton, for

---

31. Confessor, "Ambigua 23–71," 131.

"nothing that has come into being is its own proper end, in so far as it is not self-caused."[32]

Maximus describes how, through being created in the image of God, humanity reflects the tension of union and distinction that is present in the divine-human *hypostasis*. He speaks of the union between soul and body as exhibiting the perichoretic and hypostatic union in Christ—in structural terms—so demonstrating God's original purpose for his creatures. Maximus describes persons as "being united to God made flesh, like the soul united to the body, wholly interpenetrating it in an unconfused union."[33] He appears to indicate that the soul and body are co-existent in some way, each being mutually dependent upon the other.

Maximus also points out how lived expressions of human existence contradict the divine purpose for which human beings were made.[34] Though he understands human personhood as expressing unconfused union and differentiation at a structural level, he recognizes all relationships as being disjointed, the self being "divided" and in need of wholeness.[35] Moreover, he portrays a disrupted integration at all levels of human experience (i.e., in the "divine-human" relation, "intra-self" relation, and "intra-creational" relation). Such is seen to create a dualistic separation between the noetic and the material, demonstrated in an unhealthy relation to either one, rather than holding both together in tension. In particular, Maximus refers to the unhealthy attachment to the sensible, in which detachment is required before a healthy integration can occur.[36]

For Maximus, the two natures of Christ provide the pattern, not only for structural personhood but also for the Christian life—the principle of the Logos in creation defining God's intention for human existence. The structural nature of humanity is seen as being able to become fully expressed through a process of deification. Maximus understands the movement of the Logos becoming flesh as continually causing the divine and human to come together, both in the act of creation and recreation. Therefore, the Logos is seen to create and deify in the same way. Deification becomes the actualization of the Logos made flesh, the Logos sustaining and transforming that which is created.

---

32. Confessor, "Ambigua 1–22," 83.

33. Confessor, "Ambigua 23–71," 131. See also Törönen, *Union and Distinction*, 37–38.

34. Confessor, "Ambigua 23–71," 113–15.

35. Confessor, "Letter 2," 87.

36. Confessor, "Chapters on Love," 71.

Maximus understands the ground of salvation as being the incarnation of Christ—an ontological event believed to transform human personhood. He sees deification (*theosis*) as being the integration that occurs between Creator and creature, which is foreshadowed in the incarnation. This reconciliation between God and humanity—fully revealed in Christ—is understood to be demonstrated in the "intra-self" relation and "intra-creational" relation. The relation of humanity to the incarnation is believed to involve participation in the two natures of Christ. Persons are seen as needing to become more divine and human to be more like Christ. Therefore, Maximus's understanding of deification involves a subsequent humanization alongside divinization. He sees deification as involving a dialectic between the two poles, rather than one being absorbed in the other. The concept of *perichoresis* is seen to be demonstrated in the process of deification, the perichoretic relation between God and humanity denoting a union-distinction.[37]

Maximus's progressive redemptive scheme involves movement toward both union and distinction, and in doing so expresses a move toward wholeness and the integration of the self away from fragmentation.[38] This process of deification is believed to lead toward the proper integration of the two parts of the self, the noetic and the material. It is understood to involve gradually overcoming the duality that separates humanity from God as the self becomes integrated. The soul and body that were seen to be divided—at odds—are now being joined together into right relation, through the work of the Logos.[39]

Ultimately Maximus understands all aspects of human reality as being simultaneously integrated through Christ. As persons participate in the Logos and divine energies, they are seen to increasingly reflect union and distinction in themselves, in their relation to God, and their relation with the whole cosmos. Maximus recognizes the need for an integrated self—in right relation to God and creation—demonstrating both union and distinction, rather than there being a divided self drawn toward either the "passions" or the "spiritual" alone. He understands deification as involving a participation in the divine life and a revealing of this life in the world. It is therefore related to both parts of the self. Deification is believed to require an interaction of the whole self with the "sensible," being both a precondition and a result of union with God. Maximus sees the goal as being for the

---

37. See Vishnevskaya, "Divinization as Perichoretic Embrace." See also Confessor, "Chapters on Knowledge," 149.

38. Törönen, *Union and Distinction*, 183–95.

39. Confessor, "Questions and Doubts," 76.

whole person to be transformed as a result of movement between the two dimensions of the self.

The incarnation of Christ is understood to be fully demonstrated in relation to the consummation that occurs in the age to come. Maximus believes that humanity is created for some form of eschatological theandrism—to be conformed to Christ's image. Although this future state is seen as being distinct from this present age, it is also believed to be fully entwined with it. For Maximus, eschatological fulfillment is not something that is entirely separate from the original creation. He sees the end as being the same as the beginning, while also being distinctly different. It is the same, in the sense that God's will for created order is there from the start, being given by the Logos. Consequently, the future state is understood to be a fulfillment of God's original purpose for humanity, rather than being a state that bears no correlation to it or any continuity with this present age. Maximus does not see it as being a restoration of the original state, he sees the fullest demonstration of God's will as only becoming apparent at the eschaton.

Maximus maintains the soul-body dialectic when integrating the eschaton with original and present stages. The age to come is seen to involve a transformation of the soul and the resurrection of the body, while maintaining continuity with this present age. As with the previous two modes, the age to come is also understood to be brought about through the movement of the Logos. This is seen to determine a person's final state—together with the choices of the human will in this present age—which is in accord (or not) with the Creator's original purpose. Persons are understood to "determine themselves" either toward a good existence, or toward an existence that is against nature.

3.3.3 Humanity and the Cosmos

Maximus's transformational vision concerns the integration of all reality and the deification of the entire cosmos. He understands humanity's original mission in the world as being for individuals to unify all divisions in themselves. The entrance of sin is not seen to detract human beings from their original mission. Through the incarnation, they are understood to be given the renewed ability to carry it out.[40] By way of participating in Christ's own mediatorial role, persons are seen as being restored to their function as mediators for the salvation of the whole cosmos, bringing it to God and unifying it within itself—overcoming all divisions.[41]

40. Confessor, "Ambigua 23–71," 51–53.
41. Ibid., 103–05.

The "Synthetic Vision" of Maximus Confessor

Maximus believes that all of creation comes to its *logoi*—to its archetypes—through humanity. Together with human beings, the whole cosmos is seen to be able to move toward deification—all things "always drawing closer to their own predetermined principles."[42] The incarnation is understood as being the center of the integration that takes place, leading to the reconciliation of the division between Creator and creation.

Maximus supposes that this cosmic mission is derived from persons being a microcosm—being the image of the cosmos.[43] As a microcosm, human beings are understood to be recapitulating in themselves—in their soul and body—the elements of the entire world. The reintegration of the soul-body (the "intra-self" relation) is seen to be related to a person's own relation to God (the "divine-human" relation), to creation (the "intra-creational" relation), and to their ability to integrate both God and creation together. There is seen to be the need for reconciliation within persons while drawing all creation into union with God and with itself.[44] This reconciliation is only believed to occur when love is directed toward both God and created order.

3.4 BIBLIOLOGY, COSMOLOGY, AND ECCLESIOLOGY

Maximus links the theandric dimension to the cosmos and Scripture—relating the incarnation of Christ to both the "natural law" (creation) and the "written law" (Scripture).[45] As a result, he comes to describe three embodiments through which the reconciling power of God reaches out to humanity—Scripture, cosmos, and Christ.[46]

Maximus correlates creation and Scripture with the person of Christ in terms of them expressing knowledge as both "hidden and revealed." He applies a christological dialectic to the relation between apophatic and cataphatic functions in created order and Scripture. Alongside other ancient writers, such as Evagrius Ponticus and Anthony the Great, the physical universe and the biblical text are both understood to be vehicles of the Logos. Both are seen to contain the Logos in a physical medium, the cataphatic containing the apophatic Word behind it.[47] Maximus emphasizes the knowledge that is given beyond the mediation of the created world and

---

42. Ibid., 149.
43. Confessor, "Mystagogy," 196–97.
44. Confessor, "Ambigua 23–71," 103–05.
45. Confessor, "Ambigua 1–22," 191–203.
46. Confessor, "Ambigua 23–71," 63–65.
47. Confessor, "Ambigua 1–22," 191–203.

Scripture (i.e., unmediated knowledge of God acquired through contemplation or theoria).

In relating Scripture to the incarnation, Maximus gives it high value within the scheme of salvation.[48] He affirms the importance of a reading of Scripture that is "beyond the letter," rather than solely following a rationalistic reading of the text. Maximus draws attention to the Logos behind the surface of the text itself; the text being seen as the vehicle for the Logos to become flesh in persons. He understands Christ to be the unity and center of the Scriptures. At the same time, Scripture is believed to demonstrate diversity in its humanity.

Furthermore, the singular unifying Logos is understood to be hidden in the multiplicity of all "embodiments" of the Logos (i.e., in the *logoi* of creation and the *logoi* of the Holy Scripture). There is seen to be a dialectic between God's union with the cosmos and his distinction from it. The union-distinction between God and the cosmos are understood to be transferred to creation through the Logos. The Logos is seen to bring forth God's social image in creation—the *imago Trinitas*. Maximus understands God as being present in all things together and particular, the harmony and differentiation of the cosmos reflecting the Trinity.

Maximus recognizes all created order as expressing union and distinction through its relation to God, as part of God's purpose and will. Christ is seen as an archetype for union and distinction in the created world, where difference and unity condition each other (as they do in the person of Christ).[49] Everything is understood to find its unity in the Logos behind them without taking away from their diversity, all expressing unity without confusion.[50] The Logos behind created order (as *logoi*) becomes the individuating principle of human existence, as well as being that which unites all. Maximus highlights the ontological primacy of the Logos, which safeguards a diversity of natures in the person of Christ and the whole of created order. The Chalcedonian dialectic between unity and plurality is seen to offer a paradigm for a theology of divine embodiment that simultaneously serves as a christological legitimation of "natural theology."[51]

Although Maximus's ontology is more focused on cosmology than ecclesiology, his view of the church is congruent with the rest of his system. Maximus sees the church as expressing the image of the Triune God,

---

48. "Chapters on Knowledge," 159–60.
49. Confessor, "Ambigua 1–22," 309–11.
50. Ibid., 95–105.
51. Ibid.

of "whole and parts," both united and distinct.[52] However, the focus in his understanding of the gathered community is characteristically more christological in nature. Of central importance to Maximus is the presence of Christ in corporate worship. He points to the starting place for both theology and formation as being through "image," "act," and "participation." His Christocentric ecclesiology specifically focuses on the physical space of worship—nave, sanctuary, and altar—and the gathered community within. The church building is seen by Maximus as being an image (icon) of the christological unity of the visible and invisible world. This physical space and its liturgy are understood to be an image and symbol of the human person, in terms of both its unity and its divisions—of its active and passive faculties.[53] The gathering of the church within is seen as being an image of the visible-invisible world.[54] Through its relation to Christ, the gathering is also understood as being symbolic, contributing to the deification of humanity and the cosmos.[55]

In terms of the gathered liturgy, Maximus emphasizes various elements such as "the reading of the Scriptures," "the great entrance," "the creed," "the Sanctus," "the Lord's Prayer," and "the Sancta Sanctis." The reading of Scripture is understood by Maximus to be rooted in the communal gathering rather than an individualistic context. Although Scripture is seen as being a significant part of the gathering, the center of the service is the Eucharist. His understanding is that the Eucharist—like everything else—is grounded in the incarnation, the central goal being the formation of communicants into Christ.[56] Maximus believes the liturgy to be a symbol of the incarnational union, involving the movement of the cosmos and humanity toward the state of deification. There is a dynamic relation seen to occur between the symbol of communion and the symbolized, Christ being understood as the archetypal image. The deepening of the relation between divine and human is perceived as being the goal of the liturgical action—through means of Christ's transforming presence.

Maximus portrays the ecclesial gathering as being central to ecclesiological mission. In being related to the incarnation, the gathering of the church is seen as being a "sacrament," pointing toward the deification, not only of humanity but also of the whole cosmos. With the ecclesial gathering symbolizing the image of the human person, the central act of liturgy is

52. Confessor, "Mystagogy," 186–88.
53. Ibid., 189–90.
54. Ibid., 188–89.
55. Ibid., 206–13.
56. Ibid.

understood to represent the sacramental presence of Christ in the world and the lived narrative of the church. The sacramental gathering is also seen as being related to the integration of the apophatic and cataphatic dimensions of creation, which it also symbolizes. Ultimately, Maximus is concerned with the integration of all reality in congruence with the triune life and the deification of the entire cosmos.

3.5 INTEGRATING KNOWLEDGE AND PRAXIS

3.5.1 Introduction

In previous sections of this chapter, the theandric center of Maximus's thought has been shown to be present across his theological framework. This framework provides the necessary grounding through which to explore his understanding of the Christian life. The final section of this chapter will focus on how Maximus seeks to integrate the concerns of theology and spirituality—and in doing so, express a distinct and holistic view of Christian formation. This will further demonstrate how Maximus's christological approach is seen to lead toward an integrated understanding.

Maximus has made a substantial contribution to the integration of dogmatic theology with mystical and ascetical dimensions. His theological system does not consist of dogmatic thought separated from the Christian life. The "theological-mystical" tradition within which he stood provided a way of unifying dogma and lived faith. Maximus was influenced by both the ascetic and dogmatic tradition, and instinctively combined theological orthodoxy with a Byzantine theology of prayer. Theology and the spiritual life are seen to be indivisible—there being no separation between theology and prayer.

Maximus can be seen to present his dogmatic and ascetic theology as a coherent whole. His ascetical theology is grounded in a theological background, while his dogmatic theology can be seen as being filled in by his ascetic theology. Andrew Louth affirms that Maximus provides an orthodox dogmatic background to his ascetical theology, while his dogmatic theology presupposes ascetical formation.[57] Maximus's earlier writings focus more on the ascetic life, drawing on Byzantine monasticism going back to the desert fathers. His later, christologically focused works, provide a theological backdrop for his earlier more ascetic works. An example of this is seen in the theological reorientation that he gives to the Dionysian system of mystical theology. According to George Berthold, Maximus restates and reinterprets

---

57. Louth, *Maximus Confessor*, 43.

the Dionysian structure of theology and spirituality within a more orthodox framework.[58]

Maximus keeps the intellectual life integrated with the contemplative and ascetic life. In doing so, there is the suggestion that he denotes three clear distinctions. Firstly, *dogmatic thought*, in terms of expressing a doctrine within some kind of propositional system of Christian theology, a form of knowledge that is known and developed through the means of the senses and rational thought. Secondly, *mystical thought,* in terms of identifying a more contemplative knowledge of God, which is known and experienced beyond, but not necessarily apart, from rational thought. Thirdly, *praxis,* in terms of the experience of lived actions, behaviors, and virtues that persons perform. Maximus finds a way of integrating all three of these areas in his theological system—and does so in a way that is Christocentric in nature.

3.5.2 Forms of Divine Knowledge

Maximus uses the theandric motif to integrate forms of divine knowledge that relate to mystical and dogmatic dimensions. In terms of the knowledge of God, he allows a place for positive affirmations, while also holding to the apophatic. The incarnation is seen as being a demonstration of divine speech—the Logos being both hidden and revealed through physicality. Maximus understands God's ineffability as being disclosed in Christ, who is the ground of all that persons can know and say about God. This demonstrates the christological dialectic between two ways of doing theology (i.e., apophatic and cataphatic, hidden and revealed, speaking about God and not speaking about God).

Maximus relates the two ways of "divine knowing," namely, reason and contemplation, to human ontology—involving the "two parts of the soul."[59] He recognizes that the human mind is able to contemplate God beyond a "natural contemplation" that perceives God within physicality.[60] He sees a movement from thoughts—to the thought of God—to knowing God. However, like Pseudo-Dionysius, Maximus maintains that salvation involves a dialectic between two forms of knowledge. This is understood as being a direct participation in divine knowledge, through both contemplation and intermediaries—through both hidden and revealed means. Such is not seen as a complete movement away from a "lower" form of knowledge, but rather as involving a dialectic between the two. In following Dionysius, Maximus

58. Berthold, *Maximus Confessor*, 6–7.
59. Confessor, "Mystagogy," 190–195; "Ambigua 1–22," 163–65.
60. Confessor, "Chapters on Love," 47.

uses the language of affirmation and denial. While Dionysius sees the need to alternate between apophatic and cataphatic modes as a logical function of theological predication, Maximus specifically relates them to the intrinsic logic of the incarnation. It is not purely seen to be about modes of knowledge, but about the mode of being.

Maximus sees the ascetic life as involving an ongoing dialectical engagement between negation and affirmation, of unknowing and knowing. He points to the reality of persons coming to know God outside of God (i.e., as they are in themselves, as "embodied souls"). In seeking to integrate the two forms of divine knowledge that relate to the mystical and dogmatic dimensions, contemplation and reason, he seeks a "third way" between a person's ability to grasp God with their intellect, and a complete denial of their ability to know God. Maximus does not put the nature of God at the forefront of his system, nor speak about it in rational propositions. Indeed, there is seen to be no grasping of God conceptually. Instead, he speaks of a participatory knowledge, participation (*methexis*) that remains intellectual in character.[61] This becomes a way of relating God to the "two parts of the soul," for the purpose of transforming a person's way of knowing and being.

For Maximus, knowledge of God is not primarily seen to be arrived at through understanding, via rational-linguistic truth in Scripture. He does not see orthodoxy as simply being a set of beliefs that can be outlined in a dogmatic system; but rather as that which is to be fully lived in. Maximus believes that knowledge of God does not place ascendancy on intellectual comprehension, but instead, on experiential union through theoria. Consequently, deification is seen to necessitate experiential knowledge of God, involving "direct" encounter and communion at the deepest levels of human existence. Moreover, experiential knowledge of God is placed before scholastic thought rather than being subordinate to it.

3.5.3 Theoria and Praxis

Maximus stands within the Eastern Christian tradition of seeking to fully integrate knowledge of God and practice, so his expressions of divine knowledge are not seen as separate from the Christian life. He recognizes an inherent relation between theoria and praxis, the insistence of a union between them that involves a dialectical interplay between reflection and action.[62] In *Questions and Doubts,* Maximus attempts to teach about the ascetical life through engaging in a dialectic between theoria and praxis.

---

61. Ibid., 64.
62. Confessor, "Questions and Doubts," 111.

Here, the maintaining of discipline over the passions is understood to lead toward knowledge of God, while the pursuing of a virtuous life occurs by means of divine knowledge.

Maximus grounds his understanding of the Christian life in the incarnation of Christ, the Logos being the basis for both knowledge and praxis, demonstrating both divine and human elements. Christ's life is seen as a paradigm that persons need to follow, the practice of knowledge and virtue together being an expression of the integration occurring between the soul and body. There is understood to be the need for both engaging the heart toward God, and engaging the body in asceticism and forming virtues—the process of deification involving the interrelation between theoria and praxis.

Polycarp Sherwood has pointed out that the theoria-praxis dynamic is present in Maximus's understanding of love.[63] Maximus sees an interpenetration between contemplative knowledge of God and the active life. In correlation with this, he highlights the centrality of the relational exchange orientated toward both God and others.[64] This is a two-fold love seen to be based upon the two-fold nature being integrated in the self—namely, love for God (which he associates with soul) and love for others (which he associates with body). Maximus relates love to the theandric dimension of incarnation. The lived experience of a love of God and love of humanity is understood as being the demonstration of a continual incarnation between divine and human, with both being united in a person.

Maximus recognizes that spiritual progress is being achieved through the concurrent pursuit of theoria and praxis, through the love of God and the love of neighbor. It is only through expressing both that persons are seen to be able to move toward reflecting the divine image. A person's transformation (or deification) is understood to require a continual dialectic between the two, which is also a dialectic between the spiritual and physical. Such is seen in congruence with the ability of human beings to be mediators, reconciling God and the cosmos.

3.6 CONCLUSION

The purpose of this chapter has been to display Maximus Confessor's broad and integrated vision. On the whole he provides a vastly different theology of the Christian life than that of J. I. Packer. Rather than being grounded in a rational-linguistic center, Maximus's vision of transformation is unified

63. Sherwood, *Maximus the Confessor*, 91–97.
64. Confessor, "Letter 2," 90.

around the concept of *union-distinction in Christ,* the theandric dialectic holding everything together.

Examining Maximus's theological concerns provides the necessary backdrop to understanding his view of the Christian life. Maximus does not focus on building a dogmatic framework that is grounded in the unity of biblical teaching. Instead, he seeks to unify around christological ontology, with major elements of his theology being viewed through a Christocentric lens of "Chalcedonian logic." Maximus synthesizes, bringing together opposing elements through this christological dialectic. In particular, he makes a substantial contribution to the integration of dogmatic theology with mystical and ascetical dimensions. His vision demonstrates how the dynamic relationship between divine and human is central to how Christian formation occurs.

Given his constant reference to the theandric, the need for deification (or transformation) is implicitly grounded in Maximus's theological vision. The christological dialectic that has been described expresses a specific type of relation, one that is seen to both integrate and transform. In putting this at the center, Maximus keeps deification (the goal of the Christian life) at the fore throughout his thought. The dynamic relation between God and humanity that he describes is understood to be what deifies. Through the spoken Logos-Christ procession—the incarnation—all is seen to be able to become transformed and united, the Logos bringing a dialectic of union and distinction in every dimension.

Maximus makes it clear that it is through the incarnation that the life of the Trinity comes to be reflected in the deified human person. The Logos is seen to bring forth God's social image in creation, the *imago Trinitas*, expressing "whole and parts," union and distinction. Maximus's vision of transformation is that God is seeking to integrate the fractures in the broken world, reconciling everything together through the incarnation of his Son. This begins with reconciliation between God and humanity, which leads to affect the relation between soul and body, and the intra-creational relation—with God being more manifest in his creation as both union and difference.

Maximus's view of transformation is grounded in the concerns of theology and spirituality. His expressions of knowledge are not seen as being separate in any way from praxis. There is an insistence of a dialectical (union-distinction) interplay between knowing and doing, the incarnate Logos being understood as the basis for the relation between the two. He holds knowledge and praxis together as a demonstration of the integration between soul and body. In congruence with this, the process of deification is seen as requiring the interrelation between the two, including a demonstration of the two-fold love in the integrated person—namely—a love for God/theoria (soul), and a love for others/praxis (body). It is this approach that is understood to provide the basis for a proper view of how transformation occurs.

The next chapter will involve a comparative analysis between the perspectives of Packer and Maximus. This will enable further exploration into the scope and diversity of a Christian view of transformation, and an understanding of common characteristics in its nature and practice. As a result, the requirements of a proto-evangelical model will be determined, pointing toward the possibility of a cohesive, integrated, broad, effectual, and distinctly Christian vision of transformational theology.

Chapter 4

Dialogue and Analysis

4.1 INTRODUCTION

IN THE LAST TWO chapters, the perspectives of two "theologians of the Christian life" have been given as the starting point for developing a comprehensive proto-evangelical model of transformational theology. J. I. Packer's rational-linguistic approach has been brought into dialogue with the thought of a significant patristic figure concerned with defending Christian orthodoxy. Both Packer and Maximus offer ways of integrating the concerns of theology and spirituality, and subsequently present divergent expressions of how authentic transformation occurs. Each of them also point toward the need for a broad, integrated, and effectual approach to Christian formation.

In this chapter, there will be further analysis of the thought outlined in previous chapters and a critical conversation between the two theologians. While engaging with insights from Maximus's "comprehensive" vision, problems with areas of his thought will be expressed based upon a defense of a perspective grounded in a rational-linguistic center. As well as determining the principles required for a broad, diverse, and holistic reconstruction of transformational theology, the common characteristics of an approach grounded in rational-linguistic truth will also be established. This will provide a solid basis from which to outline an original proto-evangelical synthesis in chapters 5 and 6.

This chapter will explore various areas relevant to transformational theology in order to best examine the perspectives of Packer and Maximus within the same basic framework. The first part of the chapter will survey categories related to "framing" a model of transformational theology—looking at the means of properly integrating the concerns of theology and spirituality. Following this, there will be a critical conversation around foundational theological categories—namely, the Trinity, the person and work of Christ, and the nature of Scripture. These are at the center of a transformational theology. Next, there will be a discussion around three distinct "anthropological modes." Firstly, *transitional modes*—in reference to formational stages across the narrative of creation and redemption. Secondly, *relational modes*—which refer to a person's relationship with God, within themself, and with others. And lastly, *ecclesial modes*—which signify the context of the church as being both gathered and scattered. The chapter will end by looking at the dynamics between knowledge and transformation.

4.2 FRAMING TRANSFORMATION

4.2.1 Propositional Doctrine

The first categories to be looked at express the broad concerns of theology and spirituality. There are two "framing" categories that emerge from previous chapters—these are *propositional doctrine* and *lived experience*. In this section, the concerns of Packer and Maximus will be observed (as pertains to these two categories) to demonstrate that a transformational theology needs to fully integrate both.

To begin with, Packer and Maximus have different views on the value of propositional doctrine. Maximus is committed to apophatic theology so does not focus on propositions. In contrast, Packer has no sense of uncertainty about persons being able to come to true knowledge of God—but he acknowledges that they can only know and express it in part. He understands that God has chosen to reveal himself to his creatures in a way suitable for them—speaking through human language. Packer recognizes that human beings are created to know God within the limitations of physical mediums in order to come to a knowledge that transcends understanding. This is congruent with the creaturely need to uphold the transcendence and immanence of God, in recognition that each is mutually affirming of the other (in dialectic) rather than in conflict.

Moreover, Packer believes that God invites his people to believe and speak his words after him, rather than to negate, deny, or suppress them. Although he recognizes the difficulties in speaking about an ineffable God, he rejects the need for contradictory modes of affirmation and negation.[1] Instead, he understands that it is necessary to affirm fundamental propositions, and believes that a theological system can only be cohesive when it is fully grounded in what God has already revealed objectively through the Scriptures.

Packer points toward the need to utilize propositional truth to develop a broad and integrated framework of transformational theology, and makes it fundamental to the process of Christian formation itself.[2] He has sought to outline the necessary tenets of an orthodox Christian view, and to defend universal and unchanging beliefs of the historic church.[3] Packer takes the position that a coherent propositional system must be a prerequisite to all praxis. His stance is congruent with the Reformed tradition that has focused on the need to derive rational-linguistic truths from Scripture as the ground of a cohesive doctrinal system. This allows the possibility for doctrine to be able to exist (and be assented to) apart from the lived experience of transformation.

Packer believes that the process of Christian formation begins with the need to articulate and teach biblical truths about God. As a catechizer, the need to affirm rational-linguistic communication is at the heart of his understanding of doctrine, teaching, and formation. He recognizes how persons live is directly related to what they truly believe (i.e., beliefs are understood to drive practices). Consequently, his method of discipleship starts by deriving truths from Scripture in order to set out the permanent essentials of the Christian faith viewed as a belief system.[4] The possibility of an effectual transformational theology would then be seen to consist of a systematic and unified propositional framework in congruence with the internal coherence of the biblical text.

---

1. Packer, "God the Image-Maker," 31; *Honouring Written Word*, 39; *Meeting God*, 7.

2. Lewis, "Propositional Revelation," 272. It is important to make clear the distinction between *propositional truth* and *rational-linguistic communication*. Propositional truth involves assertions or proposals of true (rational-linguistic) statements understood to correspond with objective universal reality or fact, and the revealed mind of God on the subject, in accord with Scripture. It is associated with indicative statements, divine promises, doctrinal affirmations, and theological systems of thought. A proposition is only *one* form of rational-linguistic expression seen within the Scriptures. There are other forms of rational-linguistic communication that are not propositional in nature (e.g., law, narrative, poetry, and so forth).

3. Packer, "Reflection and Response," 179–81.

4. Packer, *Concise Theology*, xiii. For example, see "Reflection and Response," 178–81.

4.2.2 Lived Experience

The construction of an effectual transformational theology does not merely involve articulating an isolated propositional framework. Both Packer and Maximus understand the need for truth to be lived, rather than it only being known and affirmed. While Packer stands on the shoulders of Reformed dogmaticians in seeking to outline theological truths derived from Scripture into a structured form, Maximus's world is free from the systematic and analytical nature of post-reformation doctrinal categories. Therefore, he does not see systematic dogma as primary or needing to be articulated.

Although Maximus recognizes that persons approach God in a way that is intellectual in character, he does not principally seek to develop a body of doctrine outside of the experience of deification. Rather than starting with a system of belief and prerequisite understanding, he begins with a lived participation and experience of God—characterized by the presence of Christ—in the midst of community and sacrament. Maximus believes that the sole purpose of theologizing is for deification, and sees no possible separation between doctrinal understanding and the formation of the whole person.

While it is problematic to have a distinct system of propositional doctrine apart from a fully lived experience, it is equally difficult to speak in isolated terms about Christian experience and practice, as if it can be authenticated and sustained outside of a rational-linguistic framework. Rather than there being a disconnect between what is believed and what is lived, both praxis and experience have to be rooted in a robust propositional doctrine.[5] Within an effectual framework of transformational theology there is no false dichotomy between the concerns of theology and spirituality. To properly integrate theology and praxis, orthodox doctrine needs to be present in the practice itself—being lived within. Such understanding fully combines the concerns of theology and spirituality, and so points to means by which persons can be led toward ongoing formation into the image of Christ.

4.3 FOUNDATIONAL CATEGORIES

4.3.1 The Triune God

This section will look at the first series of theological themes that arise from previous chapters. It will examine four areas (referred to as "foundational

---

5. Packer, *Honouring Written Word*, 79–80.

categories") that are central to the process of developing a transformational theology. The four themes explored will be *the Triune God, the person of Christ, death and resurrection,* and *Holy Scripture.* The first two of these themes express the core dynamics that the latter two themes are grounded in.

The first foundational area is the life of the Triune God. The nature of the Trinity expressed by both Packer and Maximus influences their understanding of the Christian life. Although they each maintain a different emphasis, both hold to a view of the Trinity that is congruent with the early creeds of the church, and so affirm the central ontological paradox of the three-in-one. While neither Packer nor Maximus allow trinitarian dynamics to be a central integrating motif in their theologizing, insights can be drawn from their trinitarian thought that contribute toward an effectual transformational theology.

The need to grow in understanding the nature of God is of primary importance for Packer. He has sought to outline a view of God that is based upon propositions derived from Scripture. Packer's descriptions include describing God's moral attributes, which human beings are to know and imitate.[6] Packer also highlights the distinct roles of Father, Son, and Holy Spirit as revealed in the biblical text, and affirms some form of economic subordination—while upholding their ontological equality. He recognizes how individual roles in the Trinity play out in salvation history—particularly in the Son living in obedience to the will of the Father. This has ramifications for his understanding of the Christian life in terms of persons needing to live under divine authority by means of a mind-to-mind communication.

Given that Maximus holds strongly to a sense of knowledge that goes beyond rational understanding, he does not elaborate on trinitarian thought or the nature of God. Rather than making rational propositions about God, he points toward the need for persons to encounter God "as he is," beyond concepts. Though his christological ontology is made primary, a perichoretic understanding of the triune life (i.e., as "monad and triad") emphasizing equality and union-distinction is seen to be present by implication.[7] All this becomes central to Maximus's cosmology—an individual-social dialectic being placed at the very core of both human existence and the scheme of salvation.

Although Packer affirms some form of "social Trinity" when speaking of the dynamics of giving-receiving and interpenetration, he does not develop this as a central motif nor focus on drawing out an individual-social

---

6. Ibid., 169.
7. Confessor, "Mystagogy," 205.

dialectic. However, he understands the importance of the communal dynamics of mutual self-giving—dynamics needing to be centralized if self-transcendence is fundamental to transformation.

The trinitarian dynamics expressed by Packer and Maximus have implications for the nature of the Christian life. Given that anthropology and soteriology are wholly dependent upon the nature of God, an effectual transformational theology would require the ontological and epistemological dynamics within the triune life to be foundational to the nature and process of Christian formation. For example, a robust framework of transformational theology would need to recognize the importance of an individual-social dialectic, with the concept of *perichoresis* being related across all areas of thought.[8] At the same time, in recognition of the distinctive and individual roles within the Trinity, an effectual model would also need to incorporate the function of economic subordination that plays out in salvation history.[9]

4.3.2 The Person of Christ

The second foundational category needed to develop a transformational theology involves the person of Christ. Both Packer and Maximus explicitly defend Chalcedonian Christology and recognize its central importance. However, Maximus focuses more on exploring the specific dynamics between the two natures of Christ. He allows the ontology of the incarnation to become the integrating factor across his thought and permits it to assume a primary epistemological function.

Maximus has understood the hypostatic union as the key element in the metaphysical structure of all reality. Rather than formulating his system on the unity of Scripture, the spoken Logos-Christ is seen to take the central role at the ground of his scheme. He uses the christological dialectic of union-distinction as a basis for everything—allowing an ontology of mutual penetration between divine and human to infiltrate different elements of his thought. In doing so, he constructs a cosmological vision of Christian orthodoxy that is integrated around the implications of a Chalcedonian commitment.

---

8. The importance of *perichoresis* as a theological motif has been demonstrated in Gifford, *Perichoretic Salvation*; Twombly, *Perichoresis and Personhood*; Leithart, *Traces of the Trinity*.

9. Varied perspectives on subordination in the Trinity have been explored in Jowers and House, *New Evangelical Subordinationism*. Although complex interpretations may be sought, a plain reading of Scripture points to the ontological equality of Son with Father (in substance or essence), and functional (or economic) subordination, see John 14:28; 1 Cor 11:3; 15:28; Phil 2:6–11.

The starting point for Maximus's theology is the inherent unity in Christ—without any dichotomy. He sees everything as being held together as an integrated system around a clear theological center, eliminating all dualisms. In seeking to maintain a universal pattern, his approach becomes simplistic—overlooking the intricacies needed to accurately position an array of diverse theological categories around the same principle. More crucially, there are no biblical grounds for making the incarnation motif principal. Consequently, it cannot be the overarching salvific center or the core of an effectual transformational theology.

Rather than upholding a theandric emphasis, Packer affirms the importance of Christ's obedience to God's law—recognizing that Christ provided the model and example for humanity to follow. Christ is understood to reflect the express image of the Father and acknowledged as a perfect representation of a human being.[10] Packer recognizes him as God's redemptive self-disclosure who came to reconcile the elect to God for the life of obedience. He sees the redemptive function of the incarnation as wholly tied to the atonement (and the point of "double satisfaction") through which persons are united with the exalted Christ. In this sense, the unique personhood of Christ remains central to salvation, because it is the prerequisite to Christ's atonement being salvific. However, Packer does not see the incarnation as continuing to perform a principal ontological or epistemological function. Christ's revelatory role on earth is understood to be replaced by Scripture and the work of the Holy Spirit.

Maximus has used perichoretic language to describe the dialectic between the divine and human natures—involving mutual exchange and interpenetration. He applies this ontology in a variety of ways within his thought. He also uses these dynamics to denote an epistemology that portrays knowledge of God as being both hidden and revealed, going beyond rationality. Such understanding is in contrast to Packer, who allows the rational-linguistic function of Scripture to be foremost, rather than exploring an epistemology grounded in the incarnation.

Both Packer and Maximus agree that transformation is grounded in the divine-human encounter, and that in Christ this encounter is fully realized. Within an effectual transformational theology, the christological dialectic needs to be recognized as a central motif, especially as a means of exploring the nature of the divine-human relation as well as sacramentality.[11] However, while the Christian life is invariably centered on the person of

---

10. Packer, *Knowing God*, 19.

11. The term *sacrament* (and its cognates) means something "outward" (or material) that is endued with sacred meaning and significance beyond itself. A sacrament is often understood to be an intentional word, sign, act, symbol, or ritual conveying

Christ, it cannot be wholly based upon incarnational dynamics as Maximus assumes because there are no scriptural grounds for the incarnation to be the singular interpretive lens or something that humanity participate in. Packer understands the fundamental need is for the imitation of Christ—to follow his obedience to the law of God in order to reflect his image and likeness. Ultimately, an effectual transformational theology needs to see the divine-human relation as being characterized by both obedience and love—the latter being drawn out through exploring a perichoretic understanding.

4.3.3 Death and Resurrection

The third foundational category is the death and resurrection of Christ.[12] Christological differences between Packer and Maximus become more apparent when looking at how each portray Christ's salvific work. Because of the focus that Maximus gives to the person of Christ, the work of Christ becomes less dominant in his thought. Maximus believes that the ontology of Christ's person expresses the core of salvation—Christ's divine-human nature bringing reconciliation between God and man. Therefore, the atoning work of Christ is not placed at the forefront of his theology. This understanding is in clear contrast to Packer, who fully emphasizes the significance of the atonement with the person of Christ in the background.

Central to Packer's thought is the legal dimension of Christ's substitutionary atonement, which he sees as crucial to an orthodox soteriology. Such understanding has to remain within a proto-evangelical model of transformational theology. As well as recognizing the need for Christ to fulfill the law, Packer fully emphasizes the death of Christ as the central point of redemption. Although he rightly focuses on the atonement as the pinnacle of Christ's obedience to the Father, it becomes an exalted point of reference—far outweighing the attention he gives to the resurrection. Within an effectual transformational theology there is the need to emphasize the whole work of Christ—so his death needs to be held in dialectical relation to his resurrection.

This death-resurrection dialectic is most fully understood when grounded in the two aforementioned core dynamics—the person of Christ and the Trinity—being the link between them. The incarnation is part of the

---

something hidden, mysterious, and efficacious so that divine grace may be transmitted. In a broader sense, it can refer to God being known in embodied experience, in the life of the church and created order—all in some way pointing to a reality beyond the senses.

12. Packer, *Rediscovering Holiness*, 25.

redemptive story, being the basis for Christ giving himself as a substitute in obedience to the Father. Given Packer's emphasis on the "obedience of the Son," his focus remains on the atonement as a revelation of divine holiness. This is fully expressed in the relational self-gift of death-resurrection, where the Son gives up his life to the Father—and the Father gives life to his Son, through the Holy Spirit. Identification with Christ's death and resurrection then enables persons to enter into the formational self-giving dynamics within the Trinity.

Within an integrated model of transformational theology, the death-resurrection dialectic—the climatic Christo-triune expression—would be the central redemptive dynamic. Death-resurrection denotes the traits of self-transcendence, communion, and mutual self-gift. It also allows for perichoretic language in terms of union and distinction. All of this is core to transformation—expressing the loss of self and the receiving of new life. It is also the necessary unifying motif. The integration of all things occurs through union with Christ in his death and resurrection—not through his incarnation as Maximus suggests.

Ultimately, a suitable understanding of transformational theology needs to be rooted in the indicative of union with Christ's salvific work, and the imperative of following in Christ's obedience to the Father. Union with the exalted Christ acts as the basis for participation in divine sonship within the triune life. As a result, the elect remain grounded in Christ's law-fulfilling life and his death-resurrection.

4.3.4 Holy Scripture

The final foundational category concerns Holy Scripture. Both Packer and Maximus recognize that the use of the biblical text is fundamental in the Christian life. However, they differ in how they understand the nature of Scripture—which leads to contrasting views on the role it has.

Packer has sought to rigorously defend the inspiration and authority of the Bible. Given his belief that Scripture is the highest authority in the Christian life, anything other than submission to it is seen as disobedience to God. Maximus, on the other hand, seeks to defend an "orthodoxy" that is rooted in both the testimony of the biblical text and the "common opinion" of the church. He sees divine authority as being present in the convergence of sources and traditions, with all ultimately being under the authority of the church. Such methodology is not consistent with the belief that Scripture alone is the supreme authority, and only infallible rule of faith and practice.¹³ An effectual approach to transformational theology needs to uphold the ultimate authority of the biblical text, and place the same dependence upon the Scriptures as on the person of Christ.

Packer's understanding is that right beliefs and right practices are wholly dependent upon knowledge derived from God's self-revelation in the biblical text. He recognizes Scripture as being the only possible means through which a theology of the Christian life can be acquired, articulated, and practiced. Therefore, the cohesiveness and unity of Packer's system stems from strict adherence to the biblical canon. This commitment is characteristic of a "confessional" approach that seeks to uphold doctrinal unity based upon rational-linguistic truths derived from a grammatical-historical method of interpretation.¹⁴

Both Packer and Maximus accept Scripture as being divine-human in nature—with each adopting (what may be seen as) an "incarnational" perspective. Packer uses incarnational ontology to affirm the two-fold nature of Scripture, in terms of it being wholly inspired by God as well as truly human. As in Christ's person, there is seen to be a necessary paradox present rather than a false dichotomy or contradiction—in terms of its humanity being in conflict with divine inspiration. With this in mind, an incarnational view of Scripture would not merely be a helpful analogy, but be the way to fully affirm the inerrancy of Scripture, and the proper relation of Scripture to Christ.¹⁵

Maximus places a central emphasis on the christological nature of the biblical text. Scripture, like creation, is understood to function as a symbol of Christ.¹⁶ In relating the nature of Scripture to the incarnation, Maximus points toward its purpose as being to facilitate deification. He understands the incarnation as the basis for a bibliology that consists of "whole and parts." As with other areas of his thought, Maximus draws out the dialectical motif. Christ is seen as the unity and center of the Scriptures, while Scrip-

---

13. Kevin Vanhoozer affirms that the Protestant principle of *sola scriptura* "asserts the Bible's right of final say-so as concerns all matters of truth and right, faith and practice, thought and life" ("May We Go Beyond," 750). A historical study of *sola scriptura* is seen in Mathison, *Shape of Sola Scriptura*. See also Allen and Swain, *Reformed Catholicity*; Barrett, *God's Word Alone*.

14. Packer defines his understanding of the "Great Tradition" around what he perceives to be core doctrinal beliefs ("On from Orr," 156).

15. All generations have sought to defend the truthfulness, reliability, and faultless harmony of all of Scripture against cultural challenges. For a comprehensive defense of biblical authority and an examination of the full range of issues connected to it, see Carson, *Authority of the Christian Scriptures*. See also Beale, *Erosion of Inerrancy*; Gaffin and Lillback, *Thy Word Is Still Truth*.

16. Confessor, "Ambigua 23–71," 63–65.

ture is also understood to have its own multiplicity in its human form. This points to the function of Scripture as being to bring integration—which is in essence what Maximus understands deification as being about—to integrate on every level.

Packer has drawn out the rational nature of Scripture and allowed mind-to-mind communication to be foremost—which has implications for how it functions in enabling formation. Conversely, Maximus has sought to uphold a broad epistemology across his thought. Rather than placing a foundational emphasis on the need for Scripture to bring rational-linguistic truth (to be understood and applied), his focus goes beyond the rational text. Maximus expresses an epistemological role of Scripture that assumes a christological character through the hidden Logos.[17] Scripture is seen to demonstrate a hidden-revealed dialectic—which appeals to both the immanence and transcendence of God. His approach to understanding the biblical text suggests there is a need to engage with it in ways that are both rational and a-rational, moving toward an integral response and acquired knowledge of God through contemplation (i.e., theoria). An effectual re-reading of transformational theology needs to express a broad view of the nature of Scripture and how to engage with it. This means understanding the biblical text as "revelation" in the fullest sense of the word, while keeping a rational-linguistic function at the center.

Ultimately, a proper understanding of Scripture and how it functions in the Christian life must be within a framework that appeals to the nature of Christ and the triune life. The nature of Scripture can be integrated with the person of Christ, not solely for the purpose of defending biblical inerrancy (and upholding biblical authority) but so Scripture may be understood in its fullest sense. Although Maximus's understanding suggests a "holistic" view of Scripture (in terms of how it functions in the process of deification), he does not highlight the requirement for persons to live under the authority of Scripture—in the way Christ lived in obedience to the Father and placed himself under the Scriptures. Alongside this, there is a need for some kind of perichoretic dynamic to denote a dialogical engagement, because transformation occurs within the context of a divine-human relationship that is characterized by both subordination and *perichoresis*.

---

17. Confessor, "Ambigua 1–22," 191–203; "Ambigua 23–71," 63–65.

4.3.5 Summation

This section has explored the foundational categories within transformational theology.[18] Within the new model to be developed in chapters 5 and 6, these categories need to be held together in a suitable way. An integrated understanding of transformational theology depends especially on two core categories—the triune life and the person of Christ. These encapsulate the absolute center of Christian orthodoxy. There is a need for a theological framework that explores a proper understanding of the unfolding Triune dynamics within human life—recognizing that Christo-triune dynamics are to be both expressed and lived within.

Packer and Maximus rely on a specific theological center that is informed by their particular emphasis within Christo-Triune dynamics—this determines the nature of their thought. Packer has emphasized subordinate dynamics, which he sees as being especially present within the economic Trinity, playing out in salvation history. He understands the divine-human relation to denote humanity being in absolute subordination to God. This ties in with his central emphasis on bibliology—orthodoxy being rooted in the authority of Scripture and the subsequent need for obedience to God. Consequently, human categories of experience, tradition, and reason are seen as secondary (and in subjection) to God's objective communication of himself to humanity through Scripture. In contrast, Maximus has emphasized the perichoretic dynamics he understands to be present within the triune life. This brings him to use dialectical language of union and differentiation to express both the nature of the Trinity and the person of Christ, in particular, exploring a perichoretic Christology. Within an effectual approach to transformational theology there is a need to allow for the dynamics of both subordination and *perichoresis* to be expressed and lived within.

4.4 ANTHROPOLOGY AND TRANSFORMATION

4.4.1 Transitional Modes

The next theological categories to emerge are referred to as "anthropological modes." These have been divided into three distinct areas: *transitional modes*—meaning progressive stages that relate to the narrative of creation and redemption, *relational modes*—referring to a person's relationship with

---

18. All of these themes can be seen to express some form of dialectic—in terms of holding a tension between two paradoxical truths. For discussion on the importance of paradox, see Anderson, *Paradox in Christian Theology*.

God, within themself, and with others, and *ecclesial modes*—which concern the context of the church as both gathered and scattered. Within an effectual transformational theology, all these areas need to be grounded in the four foundational categories already discussed.

The first of three anthropological modes to be explored will be the "transitional modes." These denote the stages that occur in humanity from beginning to eschaton, and are typically thought to incorporate dynamics between "creation," "fall," "redemption," and "new creation." Within an effectual transformational theology there is a need for suitable relations between them and avoidance of any undue emphasis.

At a structural level, Maximus sees human beings as expressing an unconfused union and differentiation, while also recognizing present reality involves divisions that contradict the divine purpose in the original creation.[19] He also focuses on the relation that exists between the state of original creation and the soteriological category of deification. Rather than seeing any disconnect between creation and deification—in its progressive and final state—Maximus allows for integration between the three modes of "original-middle-end," uniting them around the event of the incarnation. In contrast, Packer recognizes the modes of creation and redemption as distinct while both grounded in the need for humanity to reflect God's image through obedience to his law. He understands sin as disobedience to the law of God—resulting in idolatry and the inability to reflect God's holiness.

The biblical narrative would suggest that there are distinct stages of the redemptive drama. Within the soteriological framework, Packer sees the salvific modes of "past-present-future" as being in loose correlation with the categories of justification, sanctification, and glorification. He understands salvation as being subordinate to the premise of initiation into a covenant relationship with God (i.e., justification by faith). He sees justification (and salvation) as a definitive legal position determined by identification with Christ—by faith alone. A proto-evangelical model of transformational theology needs to hold to the importance of justification as a central once-and-for-all divine act of final judgment brought into the present.[20]

Packer believes that the present redemptive center is the exalted Christ—who is the mediator of the new covenant and forerunner of a new humanity. He recognizes that union with Christ's substitutionary work leads to imputed righteousness and a position of right standing before the Father (i.e., being justified). Packer sees this legal act of reconciliation with the Father as leading to adoption, which places persons in relation to the

---

19. Confessor, "Letter 2," 87.
20. This understanding is put forward in Schreiner, *Faith Alone*, 153–157.

familial love of the Trinity. This position is seen to provide the context in which to live as set apart children of God. Consequently, Packer understands the absolute basis and possibility of a transformed life to be related back to the substitutionary work of Christ and the definitive legal standing of reconciliation with the Triune God. He does not affirm justification at the expense of sanctification, but instead, sees it as the ground from which ongoing formation can occur.

Conversely, Maximus understands the salvific center to be the incarnation of Christ—an ontological event believed to transform human personhood. A person's relation to the incarnation is understood to include participation in the fullness of the two natures of Christ, involving a humanization alongside a deification—there being a dialectic between the two poles. Because Maximus focuses on deification being grounded in the incarnation, he does not recognize the need for any legal position (i.e., being justified) for personal salvation.

Packer does not depict the incarnation as a suitable unifying center or an event to participate in, but rather, as being necessary for Christ to be able to obey the law of God. He sees the redemptive ground of union with the exalted Christ as being fulfilled in eschatological consummation. Such understanding is in recognition that persons are already pre-initiated into God's covenant community through identification with Christ. Packer describes future transformation as including glorification, with respect to involving the consummation of what began with regeneration. Maximus recognizes this future perfection as being part of the ongoing process of deification. He understands it to be in congruence with the fullness of the incarnation of Christ and points to some form of union and distinction between this present age and the one to come. Maximus sees the future state of humanity as being a fulfillment of God's will from the beginning—and in continuity with this present age.

Within an effectual transformational theology, there is a need to hold "transitional modes" together in the right way rather than see them as either too disconnected or too assimilated. It would be problematic if there were too much continuity or discontinuity, or if there was any unsuitable positioning between them. Maximus points to the incarnation as being the means of bringing union and distinction across modes of transition—Christ being the center uniting them with the same characteristics. The two natures of Christ are seen as providing the pattern, the movement of the Logos becoming flesh causing divine and human to come together, so creating and deifying in the same way. Maximus infers that these modes may be held together, with union and distinction between all—applying the same principles for continuity between "original-middle-end." He provides an example of a unified approach that is consistent and integrated.

However, an effectual approach to transformational theology cannot make the incarnation the pivotal center, because *the* redemptive locus is union with Christ. The call on God's people to increasingly reflect his image (from creation to new creation) can only truly occur through union with Christ's death-resurrection.[21] Although Packer recognizes that an imitation of Christ's obedient life is needed—he knows that this is only possible through living out of a definitive union with the exalted Christ.

4.4.2 Relational Mode I: Divine-Human

The next series of anthropological modes to be examined are being called "relational modes." These occur within the context of the theological categories already discussed. There are three different relational modes. Firstly, between God and humanity (the *divine-human* relation), secondly, within the human person (the *intra-self* relation), and lastly, between human beings (the *intra-human* relation). This section will look at exploring how Packer and Maximus see these three relationships.

The first (and primary) relational mode is the *divine-human* one. Packer speaks of humanity being created for relationship with God in order to worship and glorify him. In recognizing the essential relation of God to humanity, the summons is for persons to imitate God and reveal moral characteristics that match God's own. Packer does not set up this divine-human relation as being strictly christological in nature. What he does do is appeal to the relational life of the Trinity as a paradigm for the Christian life.[22] He believes that the relationships of love in the triune life—characterized by giving and receiving—provide the structural shape of the believer's fellowship with God.[23] Packer also emphasizes the sonship motif that expresses the basic relationship between God and the elect. Given that the

---

21. The phrase *union with Christ* refers to the believer's sharing in the life of Christ—in both his history and his eternity. Through faith, persons are identified with the objective death and resurrection of Christ in history, so that they may be united with the exalted Christ in eternity and adopted into the life of the Triune God. The fundamental importance of union with Christ as a redemptive motif has been demonstrated in a number of studies. See Burger, *Being in Christ*; Letham, *Union with Christ*; Gifford, *Perichoretic Salvation*; Beale, *New Testament Biblical Theology*; Campbell, *Paul and Union with Christ*; Macaskill, *Union with Christ*; Johnson, *One with Christ*; Peterson, *Salvation Applied by the Spirit*; Rankin, Union with Christ.

22. Packer, *Honouring Written Word*, 169.

23. Packer, *18 Words*, 186.

redeemed are seen to become children of God, the Christian life is understood to be about following in Christ's obedience to the Father—out of a familial relationship that is grounded in love.

For Maximus, it is the relationship between the two natures of Christ that is the paradigm for the relation between God and the created order. His understanding is that the incarnation enables the reconciliation of God and humanity—Christ being the eternal mediator based upon his own two-fold nature. A dialectic between union and distinction is seen as being expressed in the divine-human relation. This is understood to involve a structural perichoretic relation, characterized by a mutual exchange of properties between God and humanity, in congruence with the relation between the two natures of Christ. Maximus not only sees the incarnate Logos as the means through which God is intrinsically related to humanity, but also the means through which the divine-human relationship is fully realized in the process of deification. The continual dialectical and interpenetrative movement between God and human beings is seen as being what brings deification and a removal of all divisions.

Within an effectual transformational theology there is a need to express a proper relation between divine and human activity. Forms of human praxis can become "works" that are superfluous to the salvific work of Christ. Though Packer affirms that a definitive "positional salvation" is based upon a faith response to the propositional gospel (which corresponds with the salvific act of Christ) he does not apply the same principle to the ongoing process by which salvation becomes evidenced. Although Packer believes the definitive act of salvation is monergistic in terms of requiring divine action and passive response, he understands present transformation as being synergistic, involving a co-operative and active response. Packer has sought to set up a suitable divine-human tension in the process of sanctification. Rather than sanctification simply requiring a passive reliance on God, he believes it to concern a person's active response—"works" that are grounded in union with Christ's own salvific work.

For Maximus, the relation between divine and human activity is understood to be in correspondence with the incarnation of Christ. The self-giving action in the incarnation is seen to express divine grace, in terms of the divine will working through the movement of the Logos in the created world. Human co-operation with this involves the response of a person's will. Maximus understands the "two wills" as needing to co-operate in the same way that the two wills of Christ co-operate so that persons progress toward deification. He suggests this is a perichoretic relation, involving dialectical reciprocity in the dynamic between God and humanity. In contrast, Packer highlights the fact that persons are in a subordinate relationship to God that involves obedience to his law for the purpose of expressing holiness.

Ultimately, within an effectual transformational theology the divine-human relation needs to be grounded in Christo-Triune dynamics. This means that there is some form of perichoretic reciprocity between God and humanity, alongside dynamics that are wholly subordinate in nature.

4.4.3 Relational Mode II: Intra-Self

The second relational mode to be examined is the *intra-self* (i.e., involving relations between parts of the individual self). Packer and Maximus maintain a distinct emphasis in their understanding of human personhood. With regard to the inner faculties, Packer focuses on the rational part—the mind being placed over and above the a-rational faculties. This makes way for his primary emphasis on the need for mind-to-mind communication from God. Given that Packer affirms the priority of rationality in the first instance, he does not emphasize the possibility of persons being able to come to true knowledge of God through more a-rational means. Although personal knowledge of the Triune God is present to the elect through their union with Christ, it is understood by Packer to be wholly subject to the (rational) mediating function of Scripture.

In contrast, Maximus does not make such a clear separation between the role of the rational and a-rational faculties. He would understand persons as needing to know God with the heart (i.e., with both together). Maximus recognizes the soul as including both elements—as equals together without discrimination—a view that may seem more "holistic" and less hierarchical. However, instead of seeing the activity of the a-rational faculties as having a secondary function, he appears to give them more ascendancy.

Packer's central focus has been on humanity needing to reflect the moral characteristics of God—characteristics exemplified in the obedience of Christ. Consequently, he does not affirm a specifically "incarnational" understanding of the human person in his delineation of the soul-body relation. Nor does he recognize the incarnation as being a model for the Christian life. Instead, a person's present relation to the incarnation is seen to be there by means of Christ (the *imago Christi*) being the example persons are to imitate in order to fulfill the *imago Dei*. Although Packer recognizes the protological "embodiment" of the soul, he only sees the incarnation as being implicit in creation. His understanding of the inner-outer relation is principally hierarchical in terms of outer physicality being in subjection to rational faculties without the further addition of reciprocity. Rationality also becomes central to his understanding of the Christian life, being irreplaceable in the sanctification process. The Christian life is not seen as being so much about a transforming embodied experience, but more about obedience to rational-linguistic truth—for which outer physicality provides the context.

Maximus's anthropology is Christological—the theandric being seen as the key to understanding all in his anthropological system. In being created in God's image, persons are believed to reflect the tension of union and distinction in the divine-human *hypostasis*, in terms of being intelligible (soul) and sensible (body), expressing an integration that reflects God's incarnational pattern for humanity. In the same way, Christ's divinity is understood to permeate his human nature without mixing—the soul being seen as both united and distinct from the body—involving a perichoretic interpenetration and exchange. This would mean soul and body are mutually dependent upon the other, as opposed to simply being in hierarchical relation.

Although Maximus understands this as being present at a structural level, the starting position of human experience is seen to consist of divisions and a fragmentation of parts. He believes that participation in the perichoretic divine-human relationship leads toward deification that outworks the interpenetration already present between soul and body. This process is thought to bring the appropriate movement and integration between the two parts of the self, in congruence with a proper relation of the self to God and the sensible.

An effectual model of transformational theology needs to provide a proper understanding of how the individual self is integrated, without neglecting or overemphasizing the intellect, a-rational faculties, or outer physicality. It also needs to provide a framework that counters the dualistic separation between the inner (privatized worlds) and outer (everyday, shared, public worlds) which together shape human life. The process by which a person is formed must be seen to occur in an integrated way, the self interacting "perichoretically" in mutually and reciprocity, with inner-outer means acting together in dialectic. Such would prevent a solely hierarchical model of the human person.

4.4.4 Relational Mode III: Intra-Human

The final relational mode to be examined concerns *intra-human* relations. Packer expresses an anthropology characterized by rational individualism and piety. This appears to undermine the role that community has within the formation process. Rather than drawing out the individual-social dimension of the Trinity, he takes his lead from the relation between Father and Son—emphasizing the need for individual obedience. Packer defines the *imago Dei* individualistically—the focus being on a person's own relation to God. The emphasis on subordination and individualism in Packer's anthropology appears to weaken the need for equal reciprocation in human relations. As a result, his understanding of sanctification frequently comes across as being individualistic, with communal dynamics being subordinate.

Though Packer emphasizes the importance of ecclesial life, his primary focus is on the mind-to-mind communion between God and the individual. This is seen as the means through which persons are able to reflect God's image to others—love for others being the mark of individual righteousness. Packer sees the church as the context for Christian formation. Yet he clearly wants to safeguard personal salvation and growth through individual obedience to God, rather than understanding the church as providing any means of salvation.

Maximus's framework of union and distinction in creation could be seen to provide an appropriate context for holding together the individual-social dialectic in the process of formation. He recognizes that God's social image (the *imago Trinitas*) is brought forth in creation through the Logos. This means that the created world is believed to reflect the dialectic between "whole and parts," union and distinction being seen as mutually affirming. Maximus believes that created order expresses the triune image because the singular unifying Logos opens it to multiplicity. In this sense, he affirms an individual-social dialectic at a structural level.

Maximus understands deification to involve all divisions being unified through the incarnation. Consequently, he does not see the Christian life to be about the formation of the individual, but about the whole church growing to reflect the triune life within the context of physicality—so maintaining absolute individuality as well as full communion with others. Maximus portrays the Logos made flesh as demonstrating (and bringing forth) the union and distinction in creation—being derived from the nature of the triune life.[24] Persons are then seen to be able to express their individuality through their humanity while being united together through the divine Logos.

Packer would understand intra-triune dynamics as being expressed differently. Without drawing out the "social Trinity" as a central motif for the church, he sees their giving and receiving as the essence of Christian

---

24. Confessor, "Ambigua 1–22," 309–11.

fellowship.[25] Packer suggests that ecclesial giving-receiving involves expressing knowledge that each person has individually received from God—and receiving the same from others—so all may draw closer to God. Principally, he sees the divine gifts being expressed within the church as rational and verbal, so does not highlight the formational qualities of presence and act. In congruence with Packer's emphasis on the need for subordination to the spoken Word of God, his ecclesial focus is the formation in the receiver of mind-to-mind communication.

Ultimately, within an effectual re-reading of transformational theology, a true understanding of the Trinity needs to be reflected within ecclesial life. As well as expressing a broad epistemology (while recognizing the central function of rational-linguistic communication), ecclesial relationships require some form of perichoretic dynamic to allow a balanced understanding of the individual-social dialectic, while expressing the full nature of giving and receiving. While these communal dynamics are foundation to the process of formation, they remain subordinate to an individual's relationship to God.

4.4.5 Ecclesial Mode I: The Gathered Church

The last of the three anthropological modes to be examined concerns ecclesiological settings. This section will involve exploring the nature of formation that occurs within the two different ecclesial contexts—namely, as the church gathered and scattered. The context of the gathered church refers to an intentional time and place for corporate worship—which allows for specific "means of grace" to operate. The context of the scattered church refers to the narrative of God's people in daily societal roles where the call is for a broader worship response.

Packer recognizes the need for Scripture to be central within the gathered church context. He believes that (in the first instance) God needs to be made known in his church through the rational-linguistic communication of the biblical text.[26] The sharing of God's Word is seen as the primary means of formation in a collected setting. Acts of gathered worship, such as praise, prayer, and the ritual of communion are then understood as being a proper *response* to God's self-revelation.

As a "catechist," Packer's concern has been the systematic presentation of biblical truth for the purpose of engaging the whole person in intellectual

---

25. Packer, *Celebrating Saving Work*, 15; *18 Words*, 186.
26. Packer, *18 Words*, 186.

formation, worship toward God, and active service.[27] His rational-linguistic model of catechesis demonstrates a wholly different approach to formation from Maximus, who suggests a "broader" perspective. Packer believes that formation in community is only possible as a result of engaging with the spoken word of another—primarily with those in ecclesial teaching offices. The emphasis he gives to preaching is congruent with the emphasis given to subordination and scriptural authority—persons needing to be subject to divine authority through the spoken Word. This corresponds with his focus on the recipient being formed as a result of a submissive response to verbal revelation—beginning with humility and rational comprehension. By itself, this suggests an absence of reciprocity, rather than giver and receiver entering a mutual process of change.

Though Maximus incorporates the reading of Scripture into the communal gathering, the incarnation and presence of Christ are seen to be the center. The gathered church is then understood to be symbolic of Christ's presence, pointing toward the deification of the whole cosmos. While he sees trinitarian ontology as the ground of created order, christological ontology is related to the gathered church. His ecclesiology is chiefly centered around christological reflections on the building and the gathering within—which are seen as a symbolic image of the hypostatic union, the faculties of the human person, and the visible-invisible cosmos.[28] The Eucharist, where Christ's presence is symbolized, is understood to be at the heart of the ecclesial gathering. Here, participation in the enactment of the liturgy is believed to deepen the relation between God and humanity—bringing forth deification.

Given that Packer understands formation as primarily occurring through a response to rational-linguistic truth, knowledge of God expressed and revealed within the church through presence and act is seen as secondary and subordinate. Packer believes that the primary "sacrament" of the gathered community is the sharing of the rational word. Although he recognizes the absolute importance of participating in the sacrament of communion, Christ's transforming presence is not given a central place here. Packer's sacramental theology appears insufficient given his apparent neglect of presence-act. Because revealing the knowledge of God in community consists of more than rational speech, an effectual transformational theology needs to be explicit in acknowledging the centrality of Christ's presence within the gathered setting—recognizing the place and position of presence and act alongside speech, while still affirming that the latter is the

27. Ibid., 187.
28. Confessor, "Mystagogy," 186–95.

central catalyst for change. This helps to more fully convey how God uses holistic means to form lives.

4.4.6 Ecclesial Mode II: The Scattered Church

The other ecclesial mode to consider is the "scattered church." This concerns the lived experience of God's people outside of the gathered worship setting. Packer sees the central mission of the scattered church as involving the proclamation of the salvific gospel of Christ. Although he recognizes the need for believers to practice deeds of neighbor-love to those outside of the covenant community, a missional witness through presence and act is not understood as having the same direct epistemological or redemptive value as rational-linguistic communication. His missional focus remains solely on the verbal communication of the gospel and the need for a subordinate response, so that persons may be drawn into relationship with God and the life of the gathered community. With regard to the relation of the church to society, rational-linguistic truth is believed to have a distinct and irreplaceable function.

Packer recognizes that within a scattered context the focus can move away from the formation of individuals-in-community, toward the church seeking to "transform the world." The need for the scattered church to reflect Christ's glorious image to others (while inviting them to participate) can become replaced by the attempt to "redeem" societal structures, occurring outside of any salvific and ecclesial context. Packer has affirmed the need for Christians to be fully engaged in society, performing various roles, in order to have a positive influence. However, he has also offered a necessary corrective to those who would seek to make the central ecclesial focus the transformation of society through social action and cultural regeneration.

What Packer has not done is to draw out how everyday cultural roles and activities can become transformational for the subjects themselves. He makes no attempt to set up a framework for transformation that fully overcomes the sacred-secular divide often depicted across different contexts. Instead, he sees the possibility of formation as revolving around a gathered context where there is a specific liturgy, "spiritual disciplines," gathered fellowship, and anything else that may be designated a "means of grace." Rather than restricting the trajectory of transformation, an effectual transformational theology needs to be open to the understanding that persons are being formed in everything—albeit in different ways. While it is important to explore what is intentionally formational within the ecclesial gathering, this has to be held in appropriate relation to formation that occurs within the everyday narrative.

Maximus sees the gathered community as being a living witness to Christ for the transformation of both church and cosmos. The incarnational focus of the sacramental gathering is understood to be central to the integration of the cosmos—with mission being more about "presence" and "enactment." Maximus expresses an emphasis on *being* the church and inviting participation within the place of formation—the gathered ecclesial setting. Here, mission is primarily about human beings reconciling the entire cosmos to God, leading to the unification of the divisions that exist within the created world in congruence with the nature of the triune life and incarnation.[29] Maximus believes each person to be a microcosm recapitulating in themself the elements of the cosmos.[30] The Logos procession in creation is understood to express the hypostatic union—the means by which God unites all to himself and within itself. Because of the incarnation, humanity is seen as being able to participate in Christ's mediatorial role, fulfilling its original purpose of mediating between God and the cosmos. Reintegration is believed to occur within the individual in congruence with their relation to God and their ability to integrate the divisions in the created order.

Maximus has sought to make the ecclesial gathering symbolic of the integration within a person and in the cosmos.[31] He expresses the need to emphasize a richer, more sacramental gathering that is filled with meaning about the nature of humanity and the cosmos. As a result, there is no separation made between gathered and scattered modes—for one is contained in the other. Maximus suggests the gathered liturgy is tied together with anthropology and cosmology—the liturgy being what enacts the deification process. He also points to there being a dialectic between the gathered and scattered forms of liturgy. Such understanding would allow for both contexts to be a place of formation and witness—albeit in different ways.

An effectual transformational theology needs to hold both ecclesial settings in dialectical relation, in terms of the gathered context symbolizing what is to occur in the scattered context. Reciprocity is necessary between gathered-scattered modes, albeit the latter being subordinate in some way to the former. Both these modes have a specific function and are to be properly grounded in the theological categories already expressed.

---

29. Ibid., 196–97; "Ambigua 23–71," 103–19.
30. Confessor, "Mystagogy," 196–97.
31. Ibid., 196–97, 204–14.

4.5 KNOWLEDGE AND TRANSFORMATION

4.5.1 Introduction

The final group of categories to be discussed relate to the knowledge of God. In order to understand the relationship between knowledge and transformation there will be an analysis of three areas arising out of previous chapters—*rational knowledge, knowledge-in-union,* and *applied knowledge.* Both Packer and Maximus recognize that engaging with divine knowledge brings transformation, but they provide a different emphasis in how this occurs. This section of the chapter will demonstrate how they arrange the three categories differently. Contrasting of their thought within these three areas will lead to further insights for integrating the concerns of theology and spirituality.

In correspondence with the above categories, three distinct areas emerge in Packer's thought. Packer has spoken about achieving the right balance in the Christian life between "doctrine," "communion with God," and "practice"—and strives to integrate them.[32] In doing so, he demonstrates a specific way of bringing together the concerns of theology and spirituality, which leads to a particular understanding of how transformation takes place. Broadly speaking, Maximus has sought to explore the Christian life within the same three areas. He has attempted to integrate dogmatic theology with mystical and ascetical dimensions, holding the intellectual, contemplative, and ascetic life together without divisions.

4.5.2 Rational Knowledge

The first category to be explored is rational knowledge. Packer sees transformation as being grounded in an appropriate human response to rational-linguistic communication, on the basis that God has made himself known through his spoken Word. Packer's understanding has clear ramifications for how persons are to engage and respond to God. He emphasizes the need for the rational faculties to assume a foremost place in the formation process, the initial prerequisite being for the mind to correctly appropriate the Scriptures.[33] This suggests an overwhelming reliance on proper reception and comprehension in order for persons to be able to come to true knowledge of God, be obedient to his will, and be changed. Given Packer's

---

32. Packer, *Serving People of God,* 216; *Evangelism,* 34; *Rediscovering Holiness,* 57; *Concise Theology,* 199.

33. Packer and Parrett, *Grounded in the Gospel,* 123.

focus on the rational part of the self, he would appear to want to isolate the operation of the cognitive faculties from affections and emotions—which are to be made wholly subordinate.

Packer's understanding here affects his approach to biblical interpretation. He believes that there is first the need to fully apply the rational faculties to Scripture in order to determine the original objective meaning of the text and then reapply universal truths to one's own life.[34] His view is that objective knowledge of God through rational-linguistic truth needs to be accurately interpreted. Being able to rightly interpret Scripture through a grammatical-historical method is seen to rely heavily on the intellectual skill and expertise of the individual, and/or others with the appropriate ability. Although community and tradition are understood to become means of self-critique, biblical interpretation is sometimes portrayed as the responsibility of the individual interpreter as they purpose to live in obedience to God. In the name of "objectivity," the witness of the Spirit can become subordinate to a person's private interpretation. As well as the a-rational faculties being absent in the first instance, the illumination of the Spirit is also kept for the process of personal application rather than for the interpretation itself.

In contrast to Packer, Maximus focuses more on the action of the Logos as an activity indistinct from speech and presence. He does not start with the need for the rational faculties to rightly appropriate, understand, and receive truth. Instead, Maximus relates Scripture to the incarnation for the purpose of deification. He draws attention to the Logos behind the surface of the text itself; the text being seen to be the vehicle for the Logos to become flesh in human beings. Maximus does not position rational propositions at the forefront for persons to come to true knowledge of God. Consequently, comprehension through the rational faculties is not made a prerequisite to formation or seen as superior to the a-rational dispositions of the heart. Maximus speaks of a participatory form of mystical knowledge that remains intellectual in character, attempting to unify the task of the rational and a-rational faculties in coming to knowledge of God.[35]

Ultimately, an effectual understanding of transformational theology needs to allow rational-linguistic communication to remain a prerequisite, and give due weight to the importance of a grammatical-historical interpretation of Scripture in order for persons to be able to understand what God has said. At the same time, it must allow for an integral view of divine

---

34. Packer, *Celebrating Saving Work*, 95.
35. Confessor, "Chapters on Love," 64.

knowledge—to fully acknowledge the specific function and place of speech, presence, and act.

4.5.3 Knowledge-in-Union

The second form of knowledge to be discussed is that which occurs through personal experience and is more a-rational in nature. Although Packer places primary emphasis on the need for rational engagement with Scripture, he affirms that the purpose of coming to knowledge about God is to know God *personally*.[36] Packer speaks of a relationship with God involving both a mind-to-mind reality *and* knowledge by acquaintance. The process through which persons know God experientially is seen to rely heavily on the prerequisite rational and individualistic appropriation of Scripture.

Packer has suggested there is a need to meditate before God on the biblical text in order to move from head to heart knowledge.[37] Such would involve a heartfelt rumination on Scripture based upon already having an understanding of its objective meaning. This would enable persons to be led toward an appropriate verbal response to God and to right thoughts about God, rather than to non-conceptual contemplation on God.

Packer has always sought to lead persons toward experiencing God through understanding rational-linguistic truths. Consequently, he has often minimized the importance of knowledge of God derived outside of the rational appropriation of Scripture, being reluctant to focus on knowledge that comes from personal experience. This is evidenced by the absence of any attempted description of his own experiences of God.[38] He desires to hold to the certainty of objective truth revealed in Scripture, and so distrusts knowledge resulting from lived experience. Although the goal of Packer's method is to move toward knowing God personally, he does not portray personal experience as assuming any authoritative place in the Christian life. Experience is believed to remain secondary in the process of formation, being entirely subject to the rational knowledge derived from Scripture.

In making a more experiential "knowledge-through-love" secondary and subordinate to that which is known through the intellect, the way persons first approach God could appear divided (i.e., without affections involved). Indeed, Packer could appear to be setting up a false dichotomy between discursive rational acts and non-conceptual affective acts—between what allows for knowledge to be objective or subjective in nature.

---

36. Packer, "Scripture," 630; *Celebrating Saving Work*, 95.
37. Packer, *Knowing God*, 21–22.
38. Ibid., 22.

This reflects his anthropology—the emphasis being on the rational faculties, rather than the affections and emotions. All inner inclinations, desires, affections, and knowledge through the Spirit are made subservient to the rational faculties. Though the need to understand is believed to come before the need for inner affectivity, the rational faculties can be just as prone to subjective individualism as the a-rational faculties.

Maximus's approach to knowledge appears to be broader. He holds two forms of knowledge together in the person of Christ—"indirect knowing," being mediated through creation and Scripture—and "direct knowing," being unmediated through inner recollection (i.e., contemplation). Maximus has understood the process of deification to involve a dialectic between these forms of knowledge—knowing God in "natural contemplation," through physicality, and knowing him beyond any medium.[39] He speaks of an awareness of God that goes beyond the rational knowledge being revealed, while at the same time still holding to a rational element.[40] This indicates a "third way" for persons to know God—holding together both mystical and dogmatic dimensions. Maximus suggests the possibility of an experience of God beyond thoughts about him and without any prerequisite understanding. He attempts to keep the two parts of the "soul" together in how persons approach God, while trying to avoid placing the intellect above the a-rational faculties.[41]

Given Maximus's focus on the incarnation, he sees Christ's person and presence as being the center of a "personal relationship" with God rather than mind-to-mind communication. Maximus speaks about the reality of the immediate personal experience of God by virtue of the active presence of the Logos in creation. He appears to express the normality and necessity of some kind of mystical or existential encounter with God, a "direct" a-rational personal encounter at the deepest part of the self—something that Packer is more cautious about discussing. Maximus's understanding is that the central way to approach God is through faith and love, rather than beginning with comprehension. Consequently, he focuses on the value of contemplation (theoria), and love for God as a practice. In essence, he is speaking of an inner disposition of the heart toward God that involves pure faith.

---

39. Confessor, "Chapters on Love," 47.

40. Confessor, "Ambigua 1–22," 163–65.

41. It should be noted that Maximus and Packer use the term "soul" very differently. Maximus understands the soul to include the complex inner life and core of a person, while Packer refers to the soul as the immaterial part of a person that animates their physicality.

Although Packer places absolute value on faith toward God in the scheme of sanctification, he does not see forms of sustained inner disposition being able to lead to personal knowledge of God. Though the stirring of inner affections is clearly significant to Packer, he does not perceive formative value in any kind of inner receptivity. For Packer, faith toward God is understood as being a response to what has been revealed in the Scriptures, rather than some form of "contemplative" practice. He does not advocate any place for inner discursive acts of the heart on God, nor affirm the need to move from conceptual to non-conceptual rumination.

Packer understands the process through which sanctification occurs as involving active co-operation (i.e., concerning the "mortification" of sin). His focus on the need for active responsibility leads him away from placing any real value on forms of mystical or passive prayer—which he dismisses as "quietism."[42] Packer recognizes the importance of fellowship with God as a "means of grace."[43] His understanding of existential communion, as evidenced by his descriptions, rests largely upon verbal expressions toward God (e.g., prayer, praise, thanksgiving, and so forth), all in response to God's own verbal communication.[44] Though Packer focuses on cultivating affections in the Christian life as a result of rational comprehension, in the first instance the primary need is not seen to involve use of the a-rational faculties toward God. Packer's emphasis in communion with God remains on rational-linguistic dialogue—the chief need being for persons to hear God in the Scriptures and to verbally respond to him.

Maximus's epistemology would appear to present more scope in terms of seeking to rightly hold together the knowing of God in both mind and heart, as both hidden and revealed, rational and a-rational, transcendent and immanent. Although he attempts to draw out a broad understanding, his system comes to be less than fully integrated (or transforming) because rational-linguistic truth does not assume the primary role.

Ultimately, if knowledge acquired through wider means is integral to the triune life itself, then this would also be integral to life lived in relation to God. Divine-human communion does not merely involve mind-to-mind communication—there is also the need to focus on an inner disposition toward God. Instead of primarily appealing to the intellect, an effectual re-reading of transformational theology needs to allow for discursive acts of the a-rational faculties. Rather than simply maintaining a strong hierarchy between rational knowledge and a-rational knowledge, there needs

---

42. Packer, "Path of Prayer," 56.
43. Ibid., 58–59.
44. Packer, *Serving People of God*, 15.

4.5.4 Applied Knowledge

The final category relates to the application of knowledge. Packer's primary experiential concern is for persons to grow in their relationship with God as a result of obeying his commandments in Scripture. He focuses on the need to receive rational communication from God in order to live a life of holiness. For Packer, the application of knowledge is based upon the need to follow the example of Christ's obedience to the Father—expressing a subordinate law-fulfilling life. Therefore, the possibility of formation in the Christian life is understood to be dependent upon an individual's obedient response, based upon having rightly understood the Scriptures. Obedience to what God has spoken is seen to be from the place of union with Christ and through co-operating with the work of the indwelling Spirit.

Maximus seeks to integrate knowledge and praxis in an entirely different way. He does not understand knowledge of God as being separate from the lived Christian life. Instead, he sees a dialectical interplay between knowing and doing.[45] This is evident in Maximus's teaching on asceticism where there is a continual dialectic present between theoria and praxis. His understanding is that deification is to involve interpenetration between knowledge of God and praxis, the movement toward transformation requiring both together. Maximus maintains that the goal of deification is achieved through the integration of three different areas—the intellect, the affections, and outward actions—without making any primary. The ascetical life is seen to enable persons to grow in their knowledge of God, while knowledge of God is understood to help them maintain and pursue a virtuous life.

Maximus portrays Christ as the paradigm for the Christian life, in terms of the incarnation expressing the proper relation between knowledge and praxis. He believes the need for both knowledge and the practice of virtue is congruent with the integration of soul and body (e.g., the engagement of the inner faculties with God, and the engagement of outer faculties in ascetic practice). He sees the dynamics between theoria and praxis as being integrated in the self, as a result of love for God and love for others. As persons grow more to express a love of God and neighbor they are understood to demonstrate more integration in congruence with the incarnation. Therefore, deification is seen to involve the need for a dialectic between the

---

45. Confessor, "Questions and Doubts," 90, 111, 31, 36–37.

two. This "integrated" perspective would suggest a more dynamic and less mechanical understanding of Christian formation.

Within an effectual transformational theology, the three categories explored in this section need to be properly integrated. Packer integrates them by beginning with the need for systematic instruction of rational-linguistic truth—which is to be understood and lived so that formation can occur. He believes that transformation is only able to take place as persons actively respond to such communication, beginning with a cognitive understanding of Scripture, leading to communion with God in prayer and active obedience. Such a progression is seen to express a movement from knowing about God to knowing God—which is necessary for formation to occur. In contrast, Maximus appears to combine all concerns in congruence with a christological dialectic in order to express an integrated synthesis. Maximus's approach to formation is not simply based upon some kind of hierarchical procession from doctrinal truth to communion with God and praxis. Rather, he seeks to hold these three categories together in a way that involves more reciprocity. Ultimately, an effectual transformational theology would allow the central catalyst to be rational-linguistic knowledge, while also expressing an understanding of knowledge that is broad and all-encompassing. This would be done by grounding the three areas within the foundational categories expressed earlier.

4.6 CONCLUSION

The purpose of this chapter has been to ascertain requirements for an effectual model of transformational theology. Different areas of a distinctly Christian view of transformation have been looked at separately in order to examine its scope as well as its common characteristics. At the beginning of this book, it was proposed that the center and starting point of a proto-evangelical approach is rational-linguistic communication. The observations and conclusions expressed throughout this chapter point toward what is needed to outline a systematic model of Christian formation grounded in a rational-linguistic center.

Packer and Maximus display differences in how they integrate the concerns of theology and spirituality, and these lead to differences in how formation is seen to occur. The variances that transpire stem from the specific center that they each hold to. Both of them would agree that an integrated system of thought must be logocentric in terms of a central revelation of the Logos from God being the only basis for an orthodox and unified framework. The crucial difference is that Maximus focuses on unifying around the incarnation, while Packer grounds his theologizing in rational-linguistic communication, based on the unity of Scripture—of which the gospel is the center. Though Packer has not constructed a comprehensive and integral transformational theology, he provides substantial insights that would contribute toward it. At the core of his thought is a rigorous defense of Scriptural authority, and the recognition that Scripture provides a coherent worldview and absolute basis for the Christian life.

Maximus makes a significant contribution in attempting to integrate key concerns within a cohesive theological system—all being unified in the person of Christ. In holding to a dialectical divine-human relation across his theological system, Maximus can be seen to maintain the implicit need for transformation (or deification). However, his overarching motif is at times too simplistic and one-dimensional. There are also occasions when his approach conflicts with a method grounded in a rational-linguistic center. While Maximus strives to express a broad and coherent system, it is not all congruent with a grammatical-historical interpretation of Scripture. Although some of his concepts lend support toward the construction of a holistic model of transformational theology, there is a distinct problem with the central ground being the incarnation of Christ, rather than the exalted Lord.

Ultimately, an effectual re-reading of transformational theology needs to hold to a center that wholly integrates Christology with bibliology. Although the Scriptures are the present means to understand and participate in the fullness of the "theo-drama," they cannot be seen apart from their epistemological and ontological grounding in Christ. Transformational theology needs to be grounded in the Scriptures—the center of which is the biblical gospel.

In the next two chapters there will be systematic interaction between the separate theological categories expressed in this chapter. In demonstrating how all these categories can be held together appropriately, a proto-evangelical model of transformational theology will be outlined—and point toward the possibility of a distinctly Christian vision. In Chapter 5, a theoretical framework will be developed. Then, in Chapter 6, the nature of the Christian life will be examined within that framework. Together these two chapters will properly illustrate the integration of the concerns of theology and spirituality.

Chapter 5

Transformational Theology I—Theoretical Framework

5.1 INTRODUCTION

EXAMINING THE THOUGHT OF two "theologians of the Christian life" provides a solid basis for understanding what a "proto-evangelical" approach to transformational theology needs to incorporate. The next two chapters will outline a framework that points toward the possibility of a common, cohesive, integrated, broad, effectual, and distinctly Christian vision of transformation. This framework will illustrate the proper integration of the concerns of theology and spirituality—so holding together both propositional doctrine and lived experience. This chapter will provide a theoretical framework in which to locate an effectual understanding of the Christian life (to be outlined in the next chapter). In doing so, it presents the context in which to integrate common and diverse characteristics of a distinctly Christian view of transformation.

The starting point for formulating a broad, integrated, and effectual transformational theology is the rational-linguistic communication of the Scriptures—the center of which is the biblical gospel. God has communicated to humanity through his spoken Word. His self-revelation in Christ (and the Scriptures) exists as objectively true within human history, being *a priori* to any human experience (or human witness). The revealed Logos is not only the means of understanding the nature of the divine drama, but also the means of entering into it. As God's people grow in their knowledge of his rational-linguistic revelation—and appropriately respond—they can participate in the unfolding redemptive drama of God and increasingly come to reflect his likeness.

The last chapter concluded that an effectual transformational theology must be grounded in the epistemological and ontological dynamics of the Trinity. This chapter will outline the unfolding transformational drama of the triune life in human experience. Given that the Trinity is the *a priori* ground (and starting point of reference) for created order, human life is inescapably bound up in it. However, there can be no false transposing of trinitarian dynamics. These dynamics (as characterized by a subordinate-perichoretic dialectic) are not identical to any dimension of human existence because they are demonstrated within physicality *ad extra*.[1] They are most fully revealed in the person and work of Christ.

The first part of this chapter will lay the groundwork for an integrated transformational theology in three sections. Firstly, the focus will be on expressing the nature of the triune life. Secondly, anthropological implications will be looked at—in recognition that the nature of human personhood provides the ground for understanding the true nature of Christian formation. Thirdly, there will be an outline of the christological foundation required for an integral perspective. The latter part of the chapter will examine the present context for Christian formation on the basis of the groundwork provided in the first part of the chapter.

5.2 THE GROUND OF TRANSFORMATION

5.2.1 Trinitarian Dynamics

This first section looks at the life of the Trinity as the starting point for an integrated framework. The ontological and epistemological dynamics between Father, Son, and Holy Spirit are the foundation of an effectual transformational theology. The Triune God exists as an eternal, self-sufficient, and perfect being, expressing infinite and manifold perfections in his moral attributes—as the source and fullness of absolute life and reality. His *a priori* life determines the trajectory of human experience and the Christian life—and wholly exceeds it. Trinitarian dynamics are characterized by the inherent relation within one God in three persons—a dialectic between union and

---

1. This combines dynamics Packer and Maximus make central in their thought. For Packer, Christian formation involves complete submission to the law of God in Scripture in order to reflect the divine image. In contrast, Maximus's focus is on the unification of all things in Christ, with a perichoretic relation of union-distinction being demonstrated.

distinction, between commonality and individuality. Given the particularity and mutuality within the triune life, distinctive identities emerge from their reciprocal relations. These relations involve mutual self-revelation—where each person has absolute knowledge of the other, and so also reflects the glory of the other. The knowledge received and reflected includes rational-linguistic communication while going beyond it—it is grounded in loving presence and action.

The concept of *perichoresis*, which involves interpenetration, upholds the dialectical interchange between particularity and mutuality. It infers the unity of God without mixing and without separating—each person being taken out of themselves in order to be wholly in the other—while remaining distinct. The substance and cause of the union-distinction (that occurs through perichoretic dynamics) involve the mutual self-donation and receptivity of the other. This denotes an "exchange life," a self-emptying while receiving one another by virtue of an unwavering desire—and being filled, signifying that each person is loving and being loved by the other. As well as giving themselves to each other in their entirety, the divine persons are also the objects of each other's attention and devotion. These dynamics establish the nature of the triune life—the divine persons simultaneously affirming both individual identity and unity.

In being characterized by perichoretic relations, the divine being expresses both equality in nature and distinctive roles—without any conflict. Though co-equal, each person of the Trinity also demonstrates a difference in function (rather than in nature), their individual roles being readily manifested in economic terms within salvation history. The subordinate roles in the Triune God become expressed through the "sending" of the Son and Spirit—in particular, through the Son being subordinate to the will of God the Father. As well as being characterized by economic subordination, this revelatory action of "sending," denotes witnessing to another—not holding to their own authority, but glorying in another.

5.2.2 Anthropological Implications

The next section will look to outline an integrated understanding of human personhood. It will examine how the ontology and epistemology expressed within the Trinity (and exemplified in the person and work of Christ) provide the means for a cohesive anthropology and the necessary foundation for an integrated view of Christian formation.

God's relation to created order is grounded in his own nature and being. He is willing that his creatures know and reflect his character. His self-revelation, stemming from intra-triune activity, is extended outwards, to form and re-form created order in congruence with his own life. As the relations between Father, Son, and Spirit precede and unfold through history, they fully determine the nature of human existence. God draws humanity into his life to reflect intra-triune dynamics—albeit in a form suitable for creaturely existence (i.e., within the restrictions of human physicality). These dynamics of unity-in-diversity infiltrate a person's relation to God and, as a result, are to be demonstrated within them and in their relation to others. Given that human personhood—and all of human existence—is inescapably and universally grounded in the Trinity, it is also inherently related to the person of Christ.

God's will for humanity is two-fold. Firstly, it is bound up in the *imago Dei*. Human beings have been created in the image of God to worship and glorify their Maker. God reveals himself so that persons may know him, imitate him, and reveal characteristics that match his own. Although the elect are both created in God's image (and recreated in the image of Christ) they can only fully reflect this at the eschaton. Secondly, God's will is for the unification of all created things in himself. God's linguistic self-revelation has established the interconnected nature of the created order so that it structurally reflects the intra-triune life of union-distinction—albeit in creaturely form. All creation reveals the dialectic between "whole and parts," the union and distinction being a reflection of the triune image. This suggests an individual-social dialectic at a structural level, as a result of a singular unifying Logos in creation opening it to the multiplicity of its humanity. These dynamics only come to full fruition in the elect at the eschaton.

There are three different relationships where this is to be made evident—the *divine-human* relation (i.e., between God and humanity), the *intra-self* relation (i.e., between parts of the individual self), and the *intra-human* relation (i.e., between human beings). The first relational dimension is the *divine-human* one. The relationship between the two natures of Christ is in some way a paradigm for this, fulfilling what the created world can be. In creation, the divine-human relation is established through the revelation of the *a priori* Logos. The fullness of the archetypal union between God and created order is exemplified and fulfilled in Christ—the begotten Word made flesh. The relation between God and humanity is structurally perichoretic, involving a mutual exchange of properties (of equal reciprocity) in congruence with the interpenetration between the two natures of Christ. At the same time, humanity is in subjection to divinity.

Being in relation to God means being grounded in dynamics that are both perichoretic and subordinate in nature. However, the structural relation between God and humanity remains different from the triune life.

Although the divine-human relation expresses some form of *perichoresis*, that which is being reciprocated is not identical because human personhood is inherently dependent upon divine giftedness, while the Trinity is only reliant on its intra-relations—being the cause of its own being and communion. So while God remains wholly free and self-sufficient, human creatures derive their being from the divine life (the relation to him based upon necessity) while remaining distinct. God's kenotic *ad extra* activity brings forth the divine likeness in humanity—the *imago Dei* becoming the ground of the divine-human relation, and the intrinsic structure of human personhood. Nonetheless, though the divine-human relation is not to fully express trinitarian interpenetration; it cannot be anything other than perichoretic, for it is solely established upon (and sustained by) the divine movements.

The other intrinsic element of the divine-human relation is subordination. This is also unlike that which is demonstrated in the economic Trinity. The divine-human relation is grounded in the presupposition that God is wholly transcendent—over and above his creatures—so that all of human life is inherently under divine sovereignty. A subordinate relationship is established by God creating humanity in his image through his Word. On this basis, God is able to communicate rationally and objectively—so that human beings can grow in the knowledge of him and increasingly reflect his image in congruence with the divine law.

The second relational dimension to examine is the *intra-self*—referring to the connections between parts of the individual self. Humans consist of relations between the inner faculties and between inner and outer faculties. Varied language may be used to describe the intangible inner core of a person (e.g., mind, will, emotions, heart, and so forth) as distinct from outer physicality—though all parts are united. The whole person has to be understood as being integrated—with no neglecting or overemphasizing the intellect, a-rational faculties, or outer physicality. An individual reflects the tension of union and distinction, consisting of perichoretic interpenetration and exchange. The relation between rational and a-rational is perichoretic as well as subordinate. Reciprocity of some kind also exists within the inner-outer relation (i.e., between the inner self and outer physicality)—it cannot solely be understood as hierarchical. Although there is a need to speak about the ascendancy of the inner faculties over the outer faculties, it is also necessary to recognize the perichoretic relation—there being the mutual dependence between the two without contradiction in congruence with the divine-human dialectic. This would all set up a suitable understanding of the human person for the purpose of transformation.

The third relational dimension to mention is the *intra-human* relation—which concerns the interchange between human creatures. Trinitarian dynamics (affirming both mutuality and particularity) dictate and exceed the relations that are to exist between human beings. Humans are unique individuals formed and grounded in the same Logos. This denotes subordination to the same image-maker for the purpose of individual obedience and holiness. It also implies that persons are inherently interrelated to each other in their diversity. Human beings are created to reflect the character of God to one another—and to express the triune life in terms of a proper relation between individual and social dimensions. The dialectical relation between individuality and unity (which is inherent to human personhood) determines the nature by which individuals are to live and be formed. In essence, everything in creation contributes to the being of everything else, enabling distinctiveness and union without contradiction. The perichoretic nature of human relations wholly affirms uniqueness—the close relatedness never being to the detriment of particularity. Therefore, persons are able to become more themselves through their relation to others—their own "selfhood" becoming fully established.

Although the intra-triune notion of mutuality and particularity is transferable, union and distinction in creation cannot be expressed in the same way as other relations. While the Triune God is self-existent on the basis of its own intra-relations, human beings do not derive their being from their relation to each other. Though a person's central identity is dependent and bound up in their relation to God, common humanity binds persons together in a different way. Intra-human relations are brought forth to imitate intra-triune relations because they are a by-product of a (divine-human) relation where the primary focus is God's giftedness and human receptivity. The full realization of human personhood is dependent upon divine perichoretic movements being displayed within intra-human relations.

Human beings are continually being conformed to an image of some kind—for good or for ill. The possibility of Christian formation depends upon persons having true knowledge of God—which God has willed in objective rational-linguistic form. Since God makes himself known to all creatures in a way they can understand, they are accountable to live in accord with his will. Forms of "deformation" occur where there is suppression and rejection of the knowledge of God revealed in the divine Logos. Disobedience to the law of God demonstrates an inability to reflect God's image and leads to the construction of an illusory and distorted self that contradicts the divine structure present in the *imago Dei*. This rejection of divine authority (and the divine life) is a denial of one's own humanity. Any expressions of personhood that stem from a rejection of the "divine ground" would ultimately be a simulation of reality constructed apart from God.

Because of sin, the relations inherent to human existence do not express integration as they should. To begin with, when sin is demonstrated the created world is left to itself without any communion with an uncreated being.[2] In denying its inherent relation to God (and affirming its existence apart from God) individuals become subject to pursuing idols—causing corruption in all aspects of personhood.[3] When not seeking to be conformed to the likeness of God, human beings become conformed to the nature of their idols. Although humanity is called to engage "perichoretically" with created order, appropriate engagement ceases if persons are not grounded in their relationship with God (i.e., they come to engage with created order apart from God—without recognition of divine transcendence). Disconnection is also demonstrated in the nature of other relations not following their created order—present reality coming to express the fragmentation of parts and divisions at all levels. The distortion of the divine-human relation brings disorder and division within persons, and in their relation to the world.

5.2.3 Christology and Transformation

This next section will briefly outline the christological ground needed for an integrated and broad understanding of transformational theology. It will include looking at the nature of the incarnation of Christ, and his death and resurrection.

The giftedness demonstrated in God's proto-creative activity continues in his redemptive activity. He has revealed himself in human history—the kenotic humiliation of Christ being an overflow (*ad extra*) of the same self-giving dynamics present within the intra-triune (*ad intra*) life. Through the unconditional donation of the Logos, God has shown the fullness of his image within human flesh—the *imago Christi*—causing a hypostatic union of divine and human natures. This involves some form of perichoretic reciprocity between God and humanity—while at the same time the human element is subordinate to the divine. The perichoretic interpenetration in the person of Christ (i.e., one person in two natures) both integrates and differentiates. It provides a way of exploring union and distinction between God and humanity.

---

2. For a more detailed study of hamartiology, see Plantinga, *Breviary of Sin*; DeYoung, *Glittering Vices*; Morgan and Peterson, *Fallen*.

3. A discussion on the nature of idolatry in Scripture appears in Meadors, *Idolatry*; Beale, *Biblical Theology of Idolatry*; Lints, *Identity and Idolatry*.

The life of Christ is the sacramental manifestation of the triune life. Within salvation history, the relation of the Son to the Father denotes an expression of *perichoresis* alongside subordination. There was perichoretic mutual indwelling and self-giving, while at the same time, Christ's divinity was demonstrated in his law-fulfilling life, i.e., the obedient Son being subordinate to the Father. In doing so, Christ expressed a model for human life that God's people are called to imitate. As well as using rational-linguistic truth in the process of making disciples, he displayed the divine image as the exemplar expression of love and holiness.

Christ's salvific work demonstrates the full revelation of the triune life in human flesh—being the fullest expression of *perichoresis* and subordination. The death-resurrection dialectic can be understood in relation to both the Trinity and the person of Christ. Given that Christ expresses the fullness of both divinity and humanity in his person, he is able to become the representative and substitute for human beings through his salvific work. Christ lived in perfect submission to the Father—culminating in his sacrificial and substitutional death on the cross—before being resurrected to new life. The obedience of God the Son to the point of death was not just a demonstration of individual holiness under the law—it was a display of intra-triune love overflowing toward humanity. Christ's death and resurrection demonstrate intra-triune relations—the dialectical redemptive exchange between the Father and the Son (i.e., Christ giving himself to the Father—in his death—and the Father resurrecting him to new life through the power of the Spirit). As redemptive activity, this incorporates the intra-human relation—the God-man giving himself to both God and man, so that both may be reconciled together in him.

God's self-revelation in his Son expresses his perfect will for the elect and becomes *the* means through which he inaugurates a new humanity. Christ has been raised as the firstborn of a renewed creation, as the exalted Lord at the right hand of God the Father—the mediator between God and humanity. He now reveals the eschatological image of the new humanity and inaugurates the eternal heavenly worship. Through being united with Christ's death and resurrection the elect can share in the formational worship of the Triune God and fulfill their eternal destiny—to be recreated into the image of the risen Christ.

5.3 THE CONTEXT FOR TRANSFORMATION

5.3.1 Definitive Union with Christ

This next section will look at the present context in which transformation occurs. On the basis of God's salvific and regenerative work, the elect respond to the propositional gospel. Through being united with the exalted Christ, God's people are justified and take on a definitive standing before the Father—being reconciled to God as his adopted children. The initial need is to be identified with Christ's substitutionary death—which leads to imputed righteousness. Christ has become like humanity—acting as representative and substitute—while also revealing God's righteousness—which is to be received by his elect. This is the legal dimension of the atonement. However, the central focus of salvation is not justification alone. Being justified is simply the means of coming to be adopted in the Son and indwelt by the Holy Spirit.

Through union with the salvific work of Christ, the elect are initiated into covenantal union with the Triune God—sharing in the Son's eternal relationship with the Father, through the Spirit.[4] Being united with Christ means identifying with the redemptive dynamics of death-resurrection within the triune life—dynamics characterized by both subordination and *perichoresis*. Firstly, God's people are to reflect the divine nature through following in Christ's obedience to the Father to the point of death. Secondly, the redeemed come into the Son's communion with the Father while still retaining their particularity—the perichoretic relation between Christ and the believer (i.e., Christ in them and them in Christ) being inseparable from intra-triune relations. In identifying with Christ's death and resurrection, God's people have given their lives up (died with Christ) and received his life (been raised with Christ as new creations). The redeemed come to derive their eternal identity (i.e., "new self") from their relation to Christ, while also remaining separate—union-distinction being expressed.

The relation of the elect to the Triune God is both individual and corporate in nature. As a result of being united with the Trinity, the redeemed come into definitive relation to the communion of saints in heaven—being eternally inaugurated into God's new society. This does not mean salvation occurs *through* the church. Rather, through identification with the work of Christ individuals are saved and become *part of* the church. This ecclesial reconciliation is perichoretic in nature—it denotes a definitive union and distinction within the body of Christ—for individuals in Christ are in the

---

4. In *Life in the Trinity*, Donald Fairbairn brings attention to the central importance of the "life of the Son" for the Christian life.

family of God as well as being corporately indwelt by the Spirit of God. There is also a participation in trinitarian subordination, which is expressed in subordinate roles within the church—with Christ himself being the head.

The eschatological transformation of God's people is bound up in union with Christ's life, death, and resurrection. As the forerunner of the new creation, Jesus enacted the path for the elect to follow. His entrance from eternity to history—and exaltation in eternity inaugurates the already-not-yet (new) creation.[5] Furthermore, it is Christ's future revelation out of eternity into history that brings about the final consummation. On the basis of Christ's salvific work, definitive union with Christ becomes the source of present formation and assurance that the elect will come to reveal the glorified image of Christ in the age to come. This allows for proper relations across the transitional modes (i.e., the progressive stages across the redemptive narrative). Rather than point toward a linear "past-present-future" progression (e.g., justification, sanctification, and glorification), it allows for transitions to be held together in the right way so they are neither too disconnected (discontinuity) or assimilated (continuity).

5.3.2 The Nature and Position of Scripture

The following section will outline the nature and position of Scripture in the life of the church. God has already spoken forth his living Word—in his Son—embodied in human history. In like manner, God's written Word has been spoken forth and exists as a body of self-authenticating truth independent of human witness and interpretation. The Scriptures have been given to the covenant community to faithfully steward and communicate within the context of being united in Christ. They provide the sufficient means of facilitating worship of the Triune God (i.e., of participating in the ongoing theo-drama), which leads to the possibility of God's people being gradually formed into the image of Christ. Scripture has to be seen in relation to the ontology and epistemology of Christ and the Trinity, in terms of its nature and function. This allows a full perspective for how it is to be understood (and engaged with) in the life of the worshipping community.

Clear parallels may be drawn between the divine-human relation that is expressed in the incarnation and the nature of Scripture. Both demonstrate the Word of God as objective truth (in history) revealed in human form. The incarnation analogy can be used to affirm the nature of Scripture as being truly divine and truly human. Both Christ and Scripture are fully

---

5. In *New Testament Biblical Theology*, Gregory Beale brings into focus the full implications of the already-not-yet new creational reign of Christ.

true and (though in human form) not erring. Scripture reflects the divine-human nature—which is both subordinate and perichoretic in relation. The divine-human relation is not in conflict. The human will has become subject to the divine—each serving a particular function. Such understanding is an affirmation of Scripture's inherent unity-in-diversity, without contradiction—with a perichoretic relation between divine and human. Given that the whole biblical text is inspired by God, it is cohesive. It contains a unified narrative and a central message of the gospel of Christ—the climax of the story being the saving events of Christ's death and resurrection. At the same time, in being written through different human authors, the humanity of the biblical text is evident in its multiplicity and diversity.

The relation of God's people to Scripture is bound up in the nature of their union with Christ and the Triune God. The church is to be both fully under Scripture and also in perichoretic relation to it. Such understanding sets up the most appropriate context for formation to occur. As the written Word of God, the biblical text carries full divine authority. So submission to Scripture is submission to the Triune God.[6] The self-authenticating witness of the Triune God (demonstrated in the sending of the Son and Holy Spirit) affirms Scripture's authoritative position. The authority of Scripture is based upon it being inspired and inerrant (i.e., without error). The term *inerrancy* is bound up with convictions about Scripture's inspiration, reliability, authority, sufficiency, clarity, primacy—and ultimately convictions about the character of God. If the Bible—in the original autographs—is God-breathed in all its parts (verbatim down to the terminology and syntax) then it must all be true and trustworthy in what it affirms—for it is impossible for God to speak falsely (i.e., he cannot "err").[7] This would mean that as a whole it is coherent and without contradiction, reliable, and to be submitted to as the only clear rule and authority for Christian belief and conduct.

Scripture is given within the context of a lived relationship with the Triune God. When addressing humanity through the biblical text, God is not only concerned with mind-to-mind engagement. Scripture includes the

---

6. The principle of *sola scriptura* is grounded in the understanding that there is an external (and self-authenticating) written Word brought forth by the will of God in human history—the supreme authoritative text on all matters of doctrine and practice. A proper appropriation of the biblical text cannot happen apart from the "servants" of reason, tradition, and experience. However, these *only* express virtue and reliability to the extent that they are seen to submit to scriptural authority.

7. The need to affirm "original" or "classic" inerrancy (as opposed to a modern literalistic counterpart) is based on the understanding that all orthodox believers across the centuries have maintained a consistently high view of the nature of Scripture, and that the historic church has always recognized Scripture as the written Word of God, "wholly true, without error."

character of proposition, without being solely rational-linguistic in nature. The purpose of the biblical text is to enable persons to understand and know the triune life, and increasingly reflect it to others. Though a rational-linguistic understanding of Scripture is central, it does not lead to an experience or response that is solely rational, but to personal knowledge of God (through a lived union with Christ, by the Holy Spirit) that is beyond—yet congruent with—the witness of the biblical text.

5.3.3 Experiential Union with Christ: Living in the Trinity

The next two sections will look at the lived experience of union with Christ. As the climax of this chapter, it provides a setting for the applied understanding of Christian formation that will be explored in Chapter 6.

In being united to Christ, the elect are called into a relationship with God that involves divine initiation and human response. Although a person's definitive salvation is monergistic—based on the salvific work of Christ and subsequent regeneration of the Spirit—the process by which present formation takes place is synergistic. It involves a person's active response to divine self-revelation and the ongoing work of the indwelling Holy Spirit. Both divine action and human co-operation are to be in dialectical tension, because formation occurs by both grace and human effort. Although this is a perichoretic relation, there is also a need for subordination to divine action. Change becomes possible as persons co-operate with the divine activity through the submissive response of the human will.

Through being adopted in the Son, the redeemed participate in the redemptive heavenly worship, living within the subordinate-perichoretic dynamics of the triune life. Present union with the exalted Christ involves identifying with both his law-fulfilling life and his death-resurrection. This sets out the transformational path that God's people are called to follow. The relational life of the Trinity, of mutual self-gift (i.e., giving and receiving) suggests the structural shape of a person's fellowship with God.[8] This can be assimilated with the death-resurrection dialectic, which expresses a person's participation in the sufferings and glory of Christ. Such participation implies an "exchange life," where the believer gives up their life and receives their true self in Christ—while remaining themself. This requires the continual surrender of a person to God through "carrying their cross," being entwined with their ability to experience "new life." In doing so, the elect can be progressively transformed into the image of the one they are in communion with—while still retaining their particularity. As adopted

---

8. Packer, *18 Words*, 186.

children, they are also called to imitate Christ in his obedience to the will of the Father (fulfilling the law of God) by the power of the indwelling Spirit.

In this context, usage of the biblical text becomes the means of facilitating worship and authentic transformation. This necessitates participation insubordinate-perichoretic dynamics—the church being both fully under Scripture and in dialogical relation to it. Engaging in a perichoretic relation means dialoging with the text and being fully in it, in order to fully receive it. At the same time, a relation to Scripture is also wholly subordinate in nature. The people of God are called to follow Christ in his obedience to the law—in congruence with the biblical text.

5.3.4 Experiential Union with Christ: Personhood and Community

This section will briefly outline the present nature of "intra-self" relations (i.e., within the human person), and "intra-human" relations (i.e., relationships in the church)—all within the redemptive context. A proper understanding of *intra-self* relations (i.e., within the inner faculties, and between inner and outer faculties) is needed to not neglect or overemphasize the rational faculties, a-rational faculties, or outer physicality. In congruence with an integrated anthropology, the whole person interacts in the process of formation. To begin with, there is some form of subordination. Inner faculties have ascendancy over the outer faculties and all is subordinate to the intellect (i.e., rational processes lead to a whole-person response). The self also interacts "perichoretically" in mutuality and reciprocity. The relation between the mind and the affections involves an interpenetrative reciprocal element, not simply a subordinate one. This allows for a proper integration involving both union and distinction between parts. Given the interpenetration of inner and outer faculties, physicality is fully involved in the formation process. True formation encompasses the whole self in relation to everything. Persons become more integrated and formed through movements between both dimensions of the self as they relate to both God and creation in dialectic.

Within the context of lived union with Christ, there is also the need to express redeemed *intra-human* relations (i.e., within the church). The elect are called to participate in the heavenly worship within the triune life. This dictates the structure and substance of earthly worship, so that individuals increasingly reflect the image of Christ toward one another. As a result, they are to collectively reveal the image of the Trinity (i.e., the *imago Trinitas*) in sacramental form. Though the elect enter into union with Christ as individuals, the process by which formation occurs is a communal one.[9] It occurs where there is the right relationship between self and other. The church is to be characterized by union and distinction—a dialectic between both individuality and community. This means emphasizing both individual obedience to God and reciprocity in community (which is subordinate to their personal relationship with God).

This individual-social dialectic is realized through imitating the perichoretic nature of the Trinity. The triune life is to be expressed in ecclesial life through the presence of mutual giving and receiving.[10] Acts of gift-giving affirm the divine image in both giver and receiver. This kenotic activity enables persons to be in a state of receptivity—to receive the gifts of God from others. The sharing of divine gifts and reciprocation of perichoretic movements within community allows persons to be progressively formed so that they become both more distinct and united in relation to God and one another. Although rational-linguistic communication fulfills a specific function here, imitation of Christ involves the sharing of both his word (teaching) and image (lived example). True formation occurs through giving and receiving different expressions of divine knowledge—not only in ways that are rational and verbal; but also through presence and enactment. As persons grow in their knowledge of God, they can live as disciples and progressively come to express Christ's likeness toward others. Alongside perichoretic movements there is also the need for subordinate dynamics, which necessitates leadership in the church.[11]

Through participating in the redemptive activity of God (i.e., the death-resurrection of Christ) the church joins in the heavenly worship of the communion of saints. Earthly worship (both gathered and scattered) is subordinate to this. At the same time, worship that is scattered is subordinate to worship that is gathered, while both are in a reciprocal perichoretic relation. As a microcosm of the Christian life, the gathered context is to demonstrate how all of life is to be lived; symbolizing what is to occur in the scattered context.

---

9. The fundamental importance of community in Christian formation has been explored in Whitney, *Disciplines within the Church*; Samra, *Being Conformed to Christ*; Howard, *Progressive Sanctification*; Wilhoit, *Spiritual Formation*; Thompson, *Church According to Paul*.

10. For a detailed discussion of the "social Trinity" in relation to human personhood, see Grenz, *Social God*.

11. God-ordained expressions of authority and subordination are evident throughout Scripture. For example, these themes continually occur in the First Epistle of Peter. With regard to functional subordination in the Trinity, see John 14:28; 1 Cor 11:3; 15:28; Phil 2:6–11.

Although the transforming "means of grace" are to remain within the context of individual and corporate worship settings, divine grace remains present at all times. When vocational work is done as worship, everyday activities become redemptive for the subject—for they are being done toward God, for his glory. The "scattered worship" of the church in everyday life and activity within societal roles has the potential to form the subject. The central purpose for God's people in societal roles is to worship him—reflecting his glory throughout all creation (by displaying his characteristics) and inviting others to follow Christ. Although societal vocations provide God-given means for believers to fully engage in cultural preservation, this does not bring the redemptive transformation of society.[12]

Ecclesial mission also has correlation with the triune life. God's people demonstrate *exclusivity*—based upon the unique form of their intra-relations—and *inclusivity*—with respect to their missional outflowing life. The elect participate in the "sending" of God's Son—in mediating between God and created order. As they witness to Christ in speech, presence, and act those outside the community of God are drawn in. However, being reconciled with the Triune God—and being part of the covenant community—crucially depends on the propositional gospel being shared by the church to the world. True Christian formation can only occur when persons receive the gospel and come into covenantal relationship with God and the redeemed community. Therefore, priority needs to remain on the verbal communication of the gospel as the prerequisite to both salvation and transformation.

5.4 CONCLUSION

This chapter has presented the first part of a proto-evangelical model of transformational theology. It has outlined a propositional framework for a common, coherent, integrative, and broad approach, providing the context that will allow for the scope and diversity of a distinctly Christian view of transformation.

The starting point for this framework is the intra-triune life, which is characterized by both subordinate and perichoretic dynamics. This life has been fully disclosed in Christ, who came revealing the divine image in

---

12. An emphasis on societal transformation is most notable in the Neo-Kuyperian model of cultural engagement, see Dennison, "Dutch Neo-Calvinism"; Plantinga, *Engaging God's World*; Wolters, *Creation Regained*; Eglinton, "To Transform and to Transcend." In *Living in God's Two Kingdoms*, David VanDrunen critiques a view of Christianity and culture that focuses on the redemption of earthly society.

human flesh. Christ lived in subordination to the will of the Father, revealing his divinity on earth through his perfect law-fulfilling life. His obedience to the point of death was a demonstration of individual submission. The triune life of loving relationships has also been demonstrated, being characterized by perichoretic giving and receiving. The death-resurrection of Christ is the sacramental expression of trinitarian redemptive activity—the fullest manifestation of subordinate-perichoretic dynamics. Through living in union with the risen and exalted Christ, God's people share in the relationship the Son has with the Father, through the Spirit. In this present age, the elect are to participate in Christ's death and resurrection, as well as following the example of his law-fulfilling life in obedience to the Father—all through the power of the Holy Spirit. As a result, God's people can be formed more into the image of the risen Son.

In the next chapter, the second part of the proto-evangelical model will be outlined. The nature of the Christian life will be understood in relation to the propositional framework provided in this chapter, with attention moving toward how the conceptual dynamics can be fully lived and experienced. Together, these two chapters will represent a suitable integration of the concerns of theology and spirituality. In doing so, they express an integral understanding of a transformational theology.

Chapter 6

Transformational Theology II—Lived Experience

6.1 INTRODUCTION

THE TWO CONSTRUCTIVE CHAPTERS in this book set forth an understanding of transformational theology that is grounded in a rational-linguistic center. The last chapter provided an integrated, cohesive, and overarching theoretical framework derived from the analysis and dialogue presented in Chapter 4. This chapter will look at the nature of lived experience within the framework outlined in Chapter 5. Experiential (and practical) descriptions of the Christian life will be explored within the ontological and epistemological dynamics already expressed to prevent any false dichotomy between the concerns of theology and spirituality.

The process of Christian formation occurs in a dynamic personal relationship with the living God, involving a dialectic between divine initiation (i.e., revealed knowledge) and human response. This chapter will primarily focus on examining the nature of a response to rational-linguistic truth through use of a *worship* motif. This motif encapsulates the dynamics within the propositional framework in the previous chapter—i.e., it is characterized by both subordination and *perichoresis*.[1] True worship involves participa-

---

1. Others have also highlighted the link between worship and transformation. See Headley, *Liturgy and Spiritual Formation*; Craig-Wild, *Tools for Transformation*; Abernethy, *Worship That Changes Lives*; Bradshaw and Moger, *Worship Changes Lives*; Beale, *Biblical Theology of Idolatry*; Averbeck, "Worship and Spiritual Formation"; Smith, *Desiring the Kingdom*.

tion in the death-resurrection dialectic—in terms of self-giving/receptivity and being obedient to the will of the Father by the power of the Holy Spirit.

The next section will briefly look at the nature and means of divine knowledge within the Christian life. It will outline a holistic understanding based on a broad epistemology—while recognizing the central function of rational-linguistic communication. This will be followed by a more lengthy section exploring the holistic character of formational worship (i.e., human response to God)—with a focus on the nature of communion with God, engagement with Scripture, and ecclesiology. In the final part of the chapter, the sections on divine knowledge and human response will be brought together and explored within the context of the two "ecclesial modes" (i.e., within a gathered-scattered setting).

6.2 INTEGRAL KNOWLEDGE

6.2.1 Revelation and Transformation

This first section will outline the integral nature of divine knowledge while upholding the central function of rational-linguistic truth. The Triune God has fully disclosed himself in redemptive history. This has culminated in Christ's death, resurrection, and exaltation. Presently, the risen Christ is being revealed from heaven—expressing the fullness of God's image for the new humanity. The possibility of present formation is bound up in the church's relation to the heavenly image of Christ. Although this image will only be fully realized in the age to come, God's people are to grow in revealing what has already been inaugurated.[2] Through participating in the redemptive theo-drama, persons can increasingly come to reveal the eternal glory of the exalted Christ. By practicing Christ-orientated dispositions and virtues they put on their new creation nature rather than continuing to display an image they have constructed themselves.

Through union with Christ, the elect become grounded in the epistemological dynamics of the triune life. The self-disclosure between Father, Son, and Spirit necessitates absolute personal knowledge that is rooted in love and demonstrated in speech, presence, and act. This knowledge both determines and fulfills human experience, incorporating rational communication to the intellect, while also being a-rational in nature. While God addresses the depths of the human heart (and the whole person), rational-linguistic truth is the principal means through which this occurs.

---

2. The resurrected Christ can be understood as the distinctive ground of Christian identity and formation. See Thornhill, "Resurrection of Jesus."

6.2.2 The Means of Divine Knowledge

In the Christian life there is a need to recognize God's transcendence alongside his immanence—knowledge of him being both revealed and hidden. This correlates with the dialectic between apophatic and cataphatic categories. The term *apophatic* pertains to divine knowledge that is acquired through negation—God being known in terms of what he is not, rather than what he is. This indicates that God cannot be fully grasped or mediated through human means—it is also an appeal to knowledge through the Holy Spirit, as a result of being united to God in Christ. This is all in recognition of divine *transcendence*—in terms of God being wholly distinct, hidden, and other. In contrast, the term *cataphatic* refers to the revealed expression of divine knowledge through positive language, images, and physicality—in recognition that God can be known in some way in human terms. This is an appeal to divine *immanence*, in acknowledgment that God is present and united with his creation—with divine knowledge being mediated through physical means.

The context for a relationship with the transcendent God is physicality. It takes place within a sacramental community and (embodied) experience in daily life. All formation occurs through being-in-the-world-with-God, i.e., it involves participating in heavenly worship within the context of liturgy that is both ecclesial and cosmological. Coming to a true knowledge of the transcendent God necessitates persons engaging with that which moves them beyond self-absorption. Without divine knowledge there is no true worship and no possibility of being formed in a Christ-glorifying way. On this basis, rather than being recreated in the image of a transcendent God, persons remain (by their own determination) wholly unable to escape a self-glorifying trajectory.

6.3 FORMATIONAL WORSHIP I: ORIENTATION TOWARD GOD

6.3.1 An Integrated Response to God

This section explores the nature of a holistic response to God's self-revelation. It is only through responding that persons participate in God's transformative drama. The relation between divine initiation and human response is to reflect the dialectical relation exemplified in Christ's person. By participating in heavenly worship dynamics, God's people live within patterns characterized by both submissive obedience and dialogical perichoretic movements.

Ecclesial worship is initiated by the communication of the Scriptures—of which the gospel of Christ is the center. This remains the central catalyst by which persons grow in the knowledge of God. Although there is the initial need for rational appropriation, a "personal relationship" with God does not consist wholly of mind-to-mind communication. Indeed, rational knowledge does not only invoke a rational response, it is a prerequisite to personal knowledge of God that is participatory—while also being intellectual in character. A false dichotomy can be made between the two forms of knowing—these being unnecessarily split apart.[3] Ultimately, engaging with God at the deepest level of being (i.e., the heart) includes the rational faculties and the affections. A person's underlying need is to know God and to respond to him in faith, not simply to understand about him.

Transformational worship necessitates an integral response to God and active engagement at all levels. Although there is the need for prerequisite cerebral activity, the process of formation is to result in a response to God that incorporates the intellect, the affections, and the "practice" of knowledge within physicality. It is necessary to hold together the symbiotic union-distinction between inner and outer faculties—to integrate knowledge and praxis, and love for God/love for others. Each of these is in some form of perichoretic relation, enabling and affirming the other, while the latter element still remains subordinate to the former. For example, practice causes persons to grow in the knowledge of God while knowledge allows persons to be more effective in pursuing a virtuous life. Although reciprocity between each is needed for true formation, a proper "knowing" and "being" are required to precede "doing," while experiential knowledge is to be derived, either directly or indirectly, from the application of rational-linguistic truth in Scripture.

6.3.2 The Essence of Divine Engagement

The goal of the Christian life is to reflect the divine virtues. As persons respond to God (by engaging in the proper processes of thinking, feeling, and doing) they are able to cultivate characteristics and dispositions that match his own. To engage with God involves self-transcendent orientation (i.e., where persons are moved out of themselves) toward the eschatological heavenly image of the risen Christ. This image is not only the destiny of the

---

3. A holistic approach to epistemology is explored in Sherman, *Revitalizing Theological Epistemology*.

elect but also the means through which they are presently being formed. In repentance and faith, persons are called to turn away from themselves and live in absolute dependence on that which is outside and above them. This brings them to increasingly reflect God's glory to one another rather than glorifying themselves.[4]

Through union with Christ, the elect are called to engage in the dynamics of heavenly worship. These dynamics are characterized by subordination to God's will—following in Christ's example of obedience to the point of death. They also involve living within perichoretic expressions of giving-receiving—persons giving up their lives to Christ and receiving their true self in him.

Crucially, worship involves God's people sacrificing themselves for his glory (i.e., giving themselves to him so they may reflect his nature more). This means a continual surrender to Christ—necessitating ongoing "mortification" (i.e., putting to death the deeds of the flesh).[5] When engaging with God, self-giving includes forms of verbal self-disclosure such as confession of sin, supplication (i.e., petition and intercession), praise (or adoration), and thanksgiving. This cultivates inner dispositions of the heart and also express what is in a person's heart. Right dispositions toward God should underlie all verbal expression—so that the heart is congruent with the verbal response.

Worship also involves receiving life—by being open to more of God. This begins with moving closer to a true perception of divine revelation. The elect are to be continually attentive to God by building inner dispositions of faith and love. These may be fostered by some "contemplative" practice or non-conceptual rumination.[6] At the same time, nurturing these virtues is not dependent on such practice, for they can be cultivated through various means, chiefly in response to rational-linguistic communication.

---

4. The glory of God in the Christian life is explored in Morgan and Peterson, *Glory of God*; VanDrunen, *God's Glory Alone*.

5. The importance of mortification in the Christian life has been fully demonstrated in Owen, *Overcoming Sin*.

6. For discussion on evangelical responses to contemplation, see Schwanda, *Soul Recreation*; "Beauty of the Lord"; Strobel, "In Your Light"; Coe, "Contemplation and Contemplative Prayer"; Keller, *Prayer*.

6.4 FORMATIONAL WORSHIP II: SCRIPTURE AND PHYSICALITY

6.4.1 Introduction

While Christian formation involves participating in the triune life, it occurs in the context of human physicality. This next section will focus on the importance of responding to God through the means of Scripture and physicality—chiefly within the setting of the Christian community. It is understood that the nature of engagement with the biblical text (and the church) occurs within a framework that is characterized by subordinate-perichoretic dynamics.

Knowledge of God is reflected in Scripture, created order, and the church. Each of these has a different place within the Christian life. Divine knowledge comes primarily through the biblical text. This is the medium through which God speaks to his people as an authoritative witness. In a general sense, knowledge of God comes through created order. In a redemptive sense it is revealed through the elect (albeit imperfectly), who are called to reflect the risen Christ to the world. Unlike Scripture, the knowledge being revealed in the church is not inerrant. Given the biblical text is the objective revelation of God in history; the present rational-linguistic communication of Scripture is (either directly or indirectly) a necessary prerequisite to divine knowledge being revealed through his people. Knowledge expressed through the church comes as a result of direct or indirect subordination to *the* source of knowledge (the divinely inspired Scriptures)—so it is a secondary means.

6.4.2 Engaging with Scripture

The biblical text is to be engaged with in the context of a lived relationship with the Triune God. Scripture is given to God's people as the central means of facilitating worship—to bring persons to knowledge of God, so that they may live in obedience and be transformed.

Engagement with Scripture is to follow the same dynamics as a lived relation to the Trinity. The biblical text is to be read as worship, participating in subordinate-perichoretic dynamics. This means approaching Scripture with the disposition of humility—to be under it and conformed to it. It also involves a reading characterized by a "conversation" with the text—a giving and receiving in a perichoretic to-and-fro—so that the reader may come to embody the text. The emphasis here is on receptivity, going beyond oneself and being absorbed in the text. The continual dialogical engagement should enable self-subversion and self-transcendence. Persons are to move toward true knowledge of God, rather than being over the text—in a wholly subjective sense—and remaining unchanged.

To begin with, there is a need for the rational faculties to appropriate what God has said in Scripture. Although the biblical text communicates rational-linguistic truth (mind-to-mind), this occurs in the context of a living relationship where there is sharing of objective knowledge which is also a-rational. The possibility of persons being able to truly know and obey God is not solely dependent on their rational understanding, but on their faith and willingness to respond appropriately to divine self-revelation. Moreover, the use of Scripture must lead to a holistic knowledge of God, allowing lived experience within the triune life that is simultaneously rational and a-rational.

God is able to convey truth to the mind so that it may be understood and applied. Ultimately, a proper interpretation and application of Scripture depends on a person's relationship with God—the text being illuminated to the mind through the Holy Spirit. The possibility of formation is not wholly dependent on the intellectual skill of the interpreter. However, formation does depend on the possibility of being able to move closer to a singular interpretation—the task being faithfulness to the original intended meaning. Multiplicity is only seen in the text being applied in a variety of ways, not in a subjective interpretation that reflects the will of the individual rather than God. Any disagreement over singular meaning does not mean that there is none intended, or that the divine originator is unwilling and/or unable to communicate himself in such a clear and consistent way to be understood and applied.[7] Instead, it demonstrates how human depravity (and being given to one's own subjective inclinations) affects a person's ability to know what was originally intended. Ultimately, the reading of Scripture is not simply an isolated exercise of the individual interpreter. It is to occur in dialogue with the worshipping community—both past and present.

As well as looking for the objective meaning of the text, it is necessary to meditate on what has been heard.[8] Meditation involves engaging the heart and being absorbed into the text as an active participant. This necessitates repeated reflection and incessant attention. Rather than being a practice that is bound to a specific time and place (with the physical text) continual biblical reflection depends on memorizing the text. Rumination

---

7. A robust defense of biblical perspicuity has been outlined in Thompson, *Clear and Present Word*; "Generous Gift."

8. For a study of biblical meditation within a broader theological context, see Davis, *Meditation and Communion with God*.

on objective rational-linguistic truth in Scripture should lead to a deeper faith and affection toward God. The need is not just to understand, but to demonstrate reliance on God by placing trust in what he has said. That said, seeking the objective meaning in the text and adhering to a practice of meditation alone does not transform. The need is to apply the truth that God has spoken and to imitate Christ's obedience. It is only as a result of continual engagement with Scripture—and submission to it—that God's people can be formed in accord with his will.

6.4.3 Transformation and Physicality

Lived experience is not only grounded in relation to God, it is also fully embodied. The way in which God's people live and engage in physicality (within the church and created order) is integral to the process of Christian formation. All of creation is in one sense "sacramental." It discloses knowledge of God in some form—though not in a redemptive sense. Therefore, God's people are to appropriate the common grace present in everyday life—albeit in a different way than through the Scriptures and the church. Being absorbed in the "world" can (with discernment) be a means of enabling worship by pointing toward the transcendent God behind it.

Crucially, experiencing the divine life depends on participating in the life of the covenant community. The church is called to reveal the triune life through being grounded in the heavenly worship drama. Rather than being the means of salvation, ecclesial life is to enable persons to grow in their relationship with the Triune God and be transformed. It encourages self-transcendence so God's people can live within the redemptive drama and increasingly express it within physicality.

Ecclesial relationships are to be characterized by both subordinate and perichoretic dynamics. Firstly, through participating in the subordination demonstrated in the economic Trinity, the church is to reveal this functional characteristic, while persons maintain ontological equality. Ecclesial ministry is initiated by church leadership—who give the call to worship. This involves leading the way in sharing the Word and imaging Christ to others—revealing the knowledge of Christ through both doctrine and example. The whole church is then to respond—in both teaching and modeling to each other that which has been taught and demonstrated to them.

Secondly, ecclesial relationships are to be characterized by perichoretic dynamics. Giving and receiving occurs in the church as a result of persons participating in the life of the Trinity. Through identifying with the death and resurrection of Christ, God's people share in the trinitarian dynamics of giving-receiving—in order to corporately express perichoretic movements. In demonstrating God's love, both giver and receiver can experience change. All God's people have been given differing gifts from him for the benefit of others. Godly stewardship is demonstrated in various ways, mutually using and distributing God-given gifts. This includes speaking the truth to others and being open to God speaking truth through others. Although knowledge of God comes through both a person's example and rational-linguistic communication, both have a distinct function with the former ultimately needing to stem from the latter.

Within the Christian community there is the need for a dialectic to be held between individual and corporate dimensions. This allows a right relationship between self and other, between each person's relation to God and each other—the latter being subordinate to the former, with reciprocity between the two. Engaging in the life of the church strengthens the individual-social dialectic. It enables persons to be more distinct and more united to each other, as well as leading to greater possibility of individual obedience. However, the practice of corporate disciplines does not negate the need for personal devotions. The community is served by personal discipline and obedience. Ultimately, there is the absolute need for God's people to engage in private as well as shared practices, for both serve a different function.

6.5 FORMATIONAL WORSHIP III: ECCLESIAL MODES

6.5.1 The Gathered-Scattered Dialectic

This final section will outline how formational worship occurs within the setting of the two "ecclesial modes" (i.e., within the context of the church—both gathered and scattered. It will point toward an integral understanding that allows a central position for rational-linguistic communication. It will also speak broadly about experiential participation in the redemptive theo-drama rather than providing prescriptive means—in recognition that it is Christ who transforms persons not any specific practice or liturgy.

Along with the unfolding theo-drama in human history comes the invitation for God's people to worship and be more formed into the image of Christ. The triune life has been most fully revealed in the central "performance" of the firstborn over creation—the risen Christ. The exalted Christ has established the eternal worship drama in heaven that enfolds the communion of saints. As a result of ecclesial and cosmological liturgy, the elect come participate in this heavenly drama, engaging their senses, mind, emotions, and body.

Through being oriented toward the exalted Christ, the patterns of earthly worship are to increasingly reflect the drama of heavenly worship in sacramental form.[9] Earthly worship occurs within the two "ecclesial modes"—in a gathered or scattered context. Each of these serve a different purpose, providing different spaces for persons to be formed. Both contexts are in dynamic relation to the other based upon being subordinate to the drama of heavenly worship. There is a dialectic rather than dualistic separation between shared worship gatherings and the narrative of everyday life.

Given that the gathered setting is a corporate space to facilitate a specific "means of grace," then "scattered worship" is subordinate to "gathered worship." The central focus needs to be on the person-in-relation-to-God rather than a specific means or context. The gathered worship of the church is to be a microcosm of the Christian life, symbolizing a person's lived narrative in concentrated form. This cannot be separated from daily life. Corporate gatherings involve shared experiences (and practices) within a specific time and place. Rather than all focus being on the grace of corporate disciplines, everyday life is to be punctuated by individual disciplines such as personal Bible study and prayer. These intentional practices, whether shared or private, determine how all life is to be lived before God. Although the scattered context may be subordinate to the gathered, each is dependent on the other. There is some reciprocity because the nature of the scattered experience also informs the gathered experience, albeit in a different way.

Rather than simply being the setting for "natural" human development, the scattered context provides opportunity for Christian formation. God's people are formed through various expressions of work, play, and rest, relationships with all people, crisis and suffering, and so forth.[10] These experiences are common to all humanity. However, a life lived as worship toward God allows God's people to be formed more into the image of his Son. While formation occurs in the daily narrative, there remains value in intentional spiritual practices at a given time and place. Though everything may be involved in facilitating change, all is not sacred in the same way. Nor does it have the same function or value in the formation process.

6.5.2 The Rational-Linguistic Center

The unfolding theo-drama involves both God's initiation and human response. In his climatic redemptive performance God has revealed himself

---

9. The importance of an "otherworldly" focus for sacramentality in this present age is explored in Boersma, *Heavenly Participation*.

10. See Ford, *Shape of Living*; *Drama of Living*.

in Christ—in speech, presence, and act. In turn, God's people are called to respond (and participate) in order to express the drama of earthly worship within a ("gathered and scattered") context that is personal, ecclesial, and cosmological.

Though God may be heard through all that happens in a gathered-scattered context, the underlying catalyst is the communication of the biblical text—the center of which is the gospel of Christ. God has revealed himself through his spoken Word so that his people may know him, respond, join in the redemptive drama of heavenly worship, and grow toward revealing the knowledge of Christ to one another.

Given that hearing God's Word is imperative, there is the need for a regular reading of Scripture to punctuate daily life. Scriptural reading is also to be central in ecclesial gatherings where God's people respond to him corporately and individually. While a personal reading of the biblical text is necessary, hearing the Word in a community committed to living under the authority of Scripture aids in subverting individual subjectivity, private interpretation, and church tradition. This guards against unorthodox interpretations (that stem from the human will) being set over and against the original meaning God intended to communicate.

The elect are to listen to God speak through one another, in congruence with the scriptural witness—primarily through leadership dedicated to preaching and teaching. At the heart of corporate worship is the ministry of the Word—consisting of rational instruction and exposition. This would include a need for catechizing—systematically transmitting truth for the purpose of holistic formation. Persons also need to be open for God to speak at any time—and to glorify God in all their speech.

Although both private and shared worship include using Scripture in a variety of ways (e.g., reading, meditating, praying, or singing) these contexts assume their own distinct form and purpose. During both gathered worship and personal devotions, God's people may verbally respond to him as a means of expressing and nurturing their faith. This assumes different forms, such as confession, petition, thanksgiving, praise, lament, and so forth. Though a verbal response toward God is not limited to a specific time, certain contexts present a selected space for it to occur.

6.5.3 Integrating Presence and Act

God is being revealed in *presence* and *act* within his redemptive drama, not simply in rational-linguistic form. As the elect participate in the divine drama these elements are integrated with the pre-requisite function of rational-linguistic communication.

The presence of God has been made known in human history—being fully revealed in his Son and the revelation of the Scriptures. Through union with Christ, the elect become indwelt by the presence of the Holy Spirit—the primary agent of transformation. As persons engage with the rational-linguistic communication of the Scriptures, the Spirit can illuminate truth to the mind. God's people are called to reflect the divine presence to one another and so collectively come to express the image of the Triune God. As the glory of Christ is made known in the gathered church, they are sent out to fill the whole earth with his presence.

Persons are to encounter God's presence through liturgy within both gathered and scattered contexts. There is a dialectical relation between the sacramental expressions in both settings—ecclesial liturgy being inseparable from human personhood and cosmological liturgy. The nature and place of the worship gathering is to symbolize God's presence. The forms of physicality here can be presented to the senses for engagement—to lead persons toward the transcendent God and his redemptive drama. Redemptive dynamics can be communicated through both sign and symbol. Most notably, God's presence is known in the communion meal, which represents how all life is to be lived. It also points toward the importance of the shared meal as an everyday sacred act. Eating and drinking can involve fellowship and communal acts of "feasting" to punctuate daily life. Ultimately, the whole of creation is in one sense "sacramental," so all being-in-the-world-with-God is supposed to be "eucharistic." God's people are called to engage with him in the world, in all discernment, recognizing that the grace and nature of his presence outside the church is wholly different from the redemptive presence made known through his people.

Divine activity is also integral to the redemptive drama alongside speech and presence. God has acted within history in the giving of his Son (and the Scriptures) and continues to act within the lives of his people. He acts through his Spirit in the hearing of the biblical text, in order to shape a person's thoughts, desires, actions, and so forth. God also acts, in various ways within a "gathered and scattered" context through physicality—and most crucially—through his church.

Formation occurs as a result of the activity God's people perform in response to divine initiation.[11] The elect are to imitate what God is doing—to respond with their mind, affections, and bodies. Through the habitual practice of right affections, desires, thoughts, feelings, speech, and actions they

---

11. See Aniol, "Practice Makes Perfect"

are gradually coming to live in congruence with Christlike virtues. God's people are to give and receive sacrificial service toward each other—actions that become formational for all. This includes perceiving what God is doing in and through each other—in order to learn and respond. "Spiritual practices" may be performed at specific times—whether things persons do, or things that are done for them—which provide a special "means of grace" for formation. Also important is the performing of ritual acts, which are done to symbolize (and express) participation in the heavenly worship drama, most notably, the initiation ritual of baptism.

Gathered acts of worship and "spiritual practices" that punctuate daily life, as special "means of grace," are to set the trajectory for the activity that occurs elsewhere. In a scattered context, there is to be obedience to that which God has spoken in his written Word. At all times the elect are called to do everything out of union with Christ, to the glory of God. In carrying out specific vocations in everyday life, human beings fulfill a variety of familial and societal roles. Though the people of God participate in the same tasks and activities as non-believers, it is performing these acts as worship toward God that gives them redemptive value.

6.5.4 Transformation as Witness

The model being outlined portrays the church as the context for Christian formation—the redemptive drama being participated in by those in union with Christ. The formation that occurs in this present age is wholly bound up in a person's eschatological position in Christ. As a sign of eternal assurance, it is in continuity with the transformation that will take place in God's elect at the eschaton. In witnessing to the eschatological image of the risen Christ, the church now invite those outside into the locus of redemption.

Although there is no disconnect between the formation of the covenant community and the subsequent influence this has on wider society, it would be inaccurate to use the (redemptive) category of "Christian formation" to describe the positive development that occurs in those outside the eschatological communion of saints. There is a clear difference between the need for God's people to be formed by Christ (for the sake of the world) and the change that occurs outside the redeemed community. If the latter change were "redemptive" then it would denote a formation that is simply imposed upon all humanity, as opposed to a true and authentic (Christian) formation that stems from the response of repentance and faith. Although those outside of the covenant community may experience God's love and mercy through the church, this is not Christian transformation. What they experience instead is a redemptive witness of God's people, which is beyond the "common grace" known through other means.[12]

As God's scattered people, the church are to carry out a variety of different vocational roles in society, contributing to his temporal purposes of preserving and developing the created order for the common good. Alongside this, the distinctly ecclesial task is to worship God and be a sign of his coming kingdom, filling the earth with the knowledge of Christ—until all comes into subjection to him at the eschaton.[13] Although the witness here is to be integral (speech, presence, and act being revealed), the central need is for the rational-linguistic proclamation of the biblical gospel. Those in union with Christ are called to participate in his mediatory role—bringing others into reconciliation with God and his people. By participating in the divine "sending," the "scattered church" invite those outside into the life of the Trinity, and as a result, bring them into the community of faith—the context for Christian formation.

6.6 CONCLUSION

In this chapter, the second part of a proto-evangelical model of transformational theology has been presented. It has described how fundamental areas of the Christian life can be held together within the theoretical framework provided in Chapter 5—so outlining how a systematic propositional understanding of transformational theology relates to lived experience and practice. This removes any false dichotomy between the concerns of theology and spirituality.

This chapter has pointed toward some practical implications, without being overly prescriptive. It has demonstrated that an approach rooted in a rational-linguistic center expresses the broad diversity and common characteristics of Christian formation. Rational-linguistic communication is the means of understanding the nature of the redemptive theo-drama—and also the means of participating in it. It has a central function, with persons needing to respond to the truth of the Scriptures—in which the gospel of Christ is the center. While remaining grounded in this communication, the proposed model expresses the need for a dialectic between

---

12. A realistic proposal for Christian influence in society, with an emphasis on "faithful presence," is explored in Hunter, *To Change the World*. See also Horton, *Ordinary*.

13. See Beale, *Temple and the Church's Mission*; Beale and Kim, *God Dwells Among Us*.

integral knowledge of God and a holistic response. This is to be played out in a variety of ways within the context of the covenant community—both gathered and scattered.

Chapter 7

Conclusion

7.1 INTRODUCTION

THIS BOOK HAS SOUGHT to explore the importance of the transformation motif by developing a theological framework around it—namely, a "transformational theology." The synthesis outlined in the last two chapters has demonstrated a broad and comprehensive understanding of Christian formation and provided a framework in which to integrate its central elements.

The two-part model presents transformation as the trajectory of the Christian life. The Christian life is to be marked by change. However, there remains a dialectic (of continuity and discontinuity) between present and future transformation. Transformation can become "over-realized" (in this present age) when there is an unrealistic focus toward perfectionism or "cultural redemption." The fulfillment of God's will for his people (foreshadowed in the already-not-yet revelation of the risen and exalted Christ) only comes to fruition in the eschaton. Conversely, transformation can also be "under-realized" where there is the absence of authentic, sustainable, and significant change in God's people now. Ultimately, this latter problem stems from the depravity of the human condition, a condition characterized by the innate desire to maintain autonomy and suppress God's revealed truth.

7.2 THE NEED FOR CHRISTIAN DISTINCTIVENESS

The purpose of developing a "proto-evangelical" model of transformational theology is to move toward an understanding that is distinctly (and fully) Christian.[1] The framework outlined points toward the need to express and live out a full, integrated, and effectual vision and demonstrates how a Christian view of transformation is distinct from "natural" human development. Although common developmental concerns are not completely separate from the redemption that occurs in God's chosen people, there is confusion when a secular understanding of transformation (i.e., one that is not gospel-centered) seeps into the church in the guise of a "Christian" (or so-called evangelical) view. Rather than moving toward a distinctly Christian vision, it can lead to expressions of development that are more characteristically human-centered.

Ultimately, the Christian life has a distinct goal and means. Consequently, the framework provided has remained orientated toward an explicitly Christian approach. The distinct goal of Christian formation is seen in the eschatological vision of the exalted Christ—the archetypal image of the new humanity.[2] God's people are called to increasingly reflect the glorious image of the risen Christ throughout all creation. This stands in absolute contrast to the secular vision where the goal is "deformation"—toward a more idolatrous human-made image.

The framework has also demonstrated the distinct means through which persons become more transformed into the image of Christ. Christian formation occurs through participation in the salvific narrative—through union with Christ and God's eternal covenant community. Any development that happens apart from this is not redemptive—so it cannot be understood within the category of "Christian formation." Christ-centered change only occurs where there is a dialectic between divine initiation and the response of the worshipping community. Any form of change that does not involve this is not distinctly Christian in nature.

The two-part synthesis provides the basis on which to challenge so-called "holistic" (or "whole-life") approaches to transformation that do not maintain a clear Christian distinctive. A central focus on "broadness" and

---

1. Packer states: "In a word, evangelicalism is Bible Christianity, gospel Christianity, apostolic Christianity, mainstream Christianity. It is an understanding of the Christian revelation based upon two principles: the final authority of Holy Scripture in all matters of faith and life, and the centrality of justification by faith in the Lord Jesus Christ" (*Honouring People of God*, 330–31).

2. The distinct goal of Christian formation is related to the New Testament view of the image of God. See Blomberg, "True Righteousness and Holiness." See also Kilner, *Dignity and Destiny*, 233–273.

"inclusivity" can lead to an emphasis on using integral means for the holistic transformation of all of creation. This brings confusion between ecclesial formation (which is distinctly Christian) and other forms of (God-given) development that are common to all humanity. Though there is synergy in a holistic approach to transformation, the different areas of developmental concern can become relativized in their level of importance resulting in the loss of Christian distinctiveness.

Ultimately, the distinct goal of ecclesial mission is not human-centered development, i.e., seeking to fulfill all the needs and preferences of unregenerate humanity. Rather, the divine imperative is to redeem God's people so that they can increasingly come to express the eschatological image of the exalted Christ—filling the whole earth with his glory. Although the temporal preservation and development of created order are grounded in "common grace" (and done for the common good), this does not stem from a redemptive narrative, because it does not correlate with the new and eternal creation inaugurated through Christ.

7.3 THE IMPORTANCE OF A RATIONAL-LINGUISTIC CENTER

The means of developing a "proto-evangelical" (or "fully Christian") model of transformational theology is rational-linguistic communication. The synthesis outlined in the last two chapters has shown that this is irreplaceable. Rational-linguistic communication is the only basis from which to move toward a cohesive, integrated, broad, effectual, and distinctly Christian vision of transformational theology. It also has a central place in the formation process. Responding to the communication of the Scriptures (the center of which is the gospel of Christ) is the primary means of participating in God's transformational drama.

Undermining the central function of rational-linguistic communication only serves to remove the possibility of true worship and the imaging forth of divine glory. The rejection (or suppression) of God's spoken Word causes persons to remain grounded in subjectivism—where the authority is within rather than being outside (and above) them. This allows them to follow their own trajectory (characterized by self-glorification and idolatry) and be formed into an image congruent with their will and desires.[3] Rather than being challenged by the divine intent to direct and enable movement

---

3. The notion of self-glorification (the opposite to glorifying Christ) is explored in DeYoung, *Vainglory*.

toward Christ-exalting virtues, they find affirmation and justification of their own thoughts, beliefs, feelings, and practices.

The synthesis demonstrates that a rational-linguistic center leads toward the expression of cohesion and unity in accord with God's will. It has shown that the nature and process of Christian formation are not fragmented nor characterized by false dichotomies. As well as describing the core characteristics of a transformational theology (and expressing a cohesive outline), the synthesis remains wholly orientated around a common objective—for individuals-in-community to increasingly come to reflect Christ's image. It also demonstrates that there is commonality in how growth occurs in God's people. It is rooted in the redemptive action of God's Word and Spirit, not determined by the preferences and/or position of the individual.

The synthesis also shows that a rational-linguistic center leads toward the expression of broadness and diversity—in accord with God's will. This does not mean that a distinctly Christian view of transformation should be all-inclusive in nature—where all is being formed and all is a means of formation—without qualification. Embracing true broadness and diversity does not necessitate such "holistic universalism." Ultimately, weakening the rational-linguistic center does not lead to broadness and diversity, but to irreconcilable contradiction and conflict. While diversity is God-given, differences that stem from sinful humanity only lead toward the strengthening of individual autonomy and becoming more formed into a god (or idol) in our own image. In order to grow together toward revealing the eschatological image of the risen and exalted Christ, God's people must stay faithful to his eternal call and remain grounded in his Word.

Glossary

Affections. Inward virtues cultivated by the central disposition of faith in congruence with biblical values. The word is chiefly used in respect to the disposition of love—in terms of setting affection toward something or someone. A person's affections reveal what they desire most, and show the condition of their heart. The term is also used to refer to the actual "act" of the a-rational faculties rather than something being cultivated.

Apophatic. The dialectical opposite of cataphatic. The term pertains to knowledge of God that is obtained through negation (in terms of what he is not) rather than by positive assertions and images. It indicates that God cannot be fully known or mediated through human concepts and means, instead appealing to "direct" unmediated knowledge. It is grounded in recognition of divine transcendence, in terms of God being wholly distinct, hidden, and other. Contrast "Cataphatic."

Biblical Gospel. The *euangelion* ("good news") that is to be verbally announced by the church, so that persons may understand, believe, and come to salvation. The message to be proclaimed corresponds with the climax of the redemptive drama in history, in accord with the Scriptures: i.e., that God the Father spoke forth his Word—the Son—who lived the perfect life, died on the cross, was resurrected, and is now presently exalted—reigning as Lord and Savior.

Cataphatic. The dialectical opposite of apophatic. Refers to the revealed expression of divine knowledge through positive language, images, and physicality—in recognition that God can be known in human terms. It is most often used to refer to knowledge of God revealed through positive verbal statements, affirming from Scripture who God is. It appeals to the immanence of God, acknowledging that he is present and united with his creation—divine knowledge being mediated through human and physical means—in Scripture, church, liturgy, created order, and most centrally in Christ himself. Contrast "Apophatic"; see also "Sacramental."

Christian Formation. Refers to the distinct development that takes place in the people of God who, through union with Christ, become grounded in the redemptive work of the Triune God. God's will is for his church to be progressively conformed to the image of Christ—coming to full fruition at the eschaton. The process of formation depends on the divine agency to initiate and a cooperative human response. See also "Worship."

[Christian] Spirituality. Contemporary usage has emphasized the lived experience and practice of Christian belief, signifying how faith affects the whole of a person's life. A spiritual life is one that is being consciously lived in relation to the transcendent Triune God—so that he is glorified. One who is "spiritual" is being changed to reveal the virtues derived from faith in Christ and the work of the Holy Spirit.

Deification (Theosis). Denotes the goal of human existence to participate in the life of God and come into union with him. It literally means to become more like God or to share in the divine nature. In Eastern Orthodoxy, deification is both a transformative process that transpires through both theoria and praxis, and the goal of that process—which is to express the divine likeness. It is understood to occur through both divine activity and human effort.

Dialectic. The interaction between juxtaposed elements (or truths) that appear to contradict each other and be in conflict. The poles can be held together in paradoxical tension—affirming rather than opposing the other. This "both/and" position maintains union without confusion, providing a way of overcoming dualism and false dichotomies. See also "Unity-in-Diversity."

Evangelical[-ism]. There are two principal and contrasting means used to understand this term. A historical-sociological method would refer to a global Protestant movement that is both trans-denominational and divergent. In contrast, a biblical-theological method follows the etymology of the term *euangelion*. Here, to be evangelical is to show concern with being faithful to the "good news" of the gospel, as witnessed to in the Scriptures. Consequently, it also denotes a core commitment to the authority of the Scriptures themselves. See also "Biblical Gospel"; "Proto-Evangelical."

Grammatical-Historical. A method of biblical exegesis used to determine the author's original intended meaning, and what the original hearers would have understood. It involves a study of the grammar, syntax, and literary context of a passage—examined within its full historical context. This method presupposes the perspicuity of the Scriptures and the possibility of being able to gradually move from a subjective interpretation toward understanding the objective will of the author.

Hypostatic [Union]. A Christological designation that describes the bringing together of divinity and humanity in one individual existence, without any confusion in their substances. In Christian theology, *hypostasis* refers either to the three persons of the Trinity in one nature or to the divine and human natures of Jesus Christ as they co-exist within one person. See also "Dialectic"; "Perichoresis"; "Unity-in-Diversity."

Logoi. The plural form of the Greek word *Logos*, meaning "word" or "reason." The Logos in Christ is analogous to the *logoi* in all created things; the Logos is present in all things as uncreated *logoi*. All created things are defined, in their essence, and in their way of developing, by their own *logoi*. It denotes both the singularity and plurality of God's purpose for each thing, there being a God-given unity of meaning in the Logos, and multiplicity of meaning in the *logoi*.

Ortho-[doxy/praxy]. "Ortho-," meaning that which is "right" and "true," can be related to both beliefs (orthodoxy) and practices (orthopraxy), denoting what is to be universally normative and aspirational for the church. Through growing in the knowledge of God, persons can come to more fully express that which is right and true in a foundational sense, though this will only be wholly demonstrated at the eschaton.

Perichoresis. A term used to describe both the nature of the triune life and the hypostatic union in the incarnation. It denotes interpenetration—yet without confusion—for the purpose of upholding both union and distinction. In contemporary theology, it is most often used to describe the way the persons of the Triune God relate to each other, denoting a mutual indwelling and sharing in the lives of the other—while allowing a distinct individual identity. See also "Unity-in-Diversity."

Praxis. Refers to practice and action as a lived expression of faith, and also to outer behavior. The term is used to express the practical application of theory and active obedience, particularly in the love of neighbor.

Propositional Truth. Assertions or proposals of true rational-linguistic statements that are understood to correspond with objective universal reality or fact—and the revealed mind of God on the subject—in accord with Scripture. It is one form of *rational-linguistic* expression seen in the Scriptures, often being spoken by God himself. It is associated with indicative statements, divine promises, doctrinal affirmations, and theological systems of thought. See "Rational-Linguistic."

Proto-Evangelical. Refers to an understanding grounded in the original core message of the Christian faith—the "first gospel" that God spoke in history—which was witnessed by the early church and proclaimed as "good news," in accord with the Scriptures. Therefore, it also denotes a core commitment to the witness and authority of the Scriptures, which God has already spoken in history. Being grounded in the communication of the gospel and the Scriptures demonstrates a commitment to rational-linguistic truth. See also "Biblical Gospel"; "Rational-Linguistic."

Rational-Linguistic. A logocentric method of communication used to reveal cognitive knowledge—often propositional in nature. It is "rational" in terms of involving mind-to-mind communication that is to be understood, and "verbal"—involving the spoken word. In the Christian faith, that which is being communicated is the gospel and the fullness of biblical teaching—all in correspondence with the objective revelation of God already spoken forth in history. This performs a central mediatory function in the church—as communication to be believed and obeyed—so that persons may participate in the transformative "theo-drama."

Sacramental. Something "outward" (or material) that is endued with sacred meaning and significance beyond itself. A sacrament is often understood to be an intentional word, sign, act, symbol, or ritual conveying something hidden, mysterious, and efficacious so that divine grace may be transmitted. In a broader sense, it can refer to God being known in embodied experience in the life of the church and created order—all in some way pointing to a reality beyond the senses. See "Cataphatic."

Theandric. Literally meaning "God-human." The term is used when understanding something in relation to the union of divine and human natures in Christ or to the joint agency of divine and human.

Theo-Drama. The narrative of the eternal Triune God, revealed in speech, presence, and act—so that he may be glorified in his creation. The triune life is most fully revealed in the central "performance" of the firstborn over creation, now risen and exalted. Here, God inaugurates a new humanity and his heavenly worship drama. Through union with Christ, the church on earth is to participate in the triune life and heavenly worship of the community of saints—in order to glorify the exalted Christ. The central means of living in this formational drama is rational-linguistic communication and a subsequent response in speech, presence, and act. The drama is climaxed with the present glory of the risen Son being fully revealed in his church at the eschaton.

Theoria. From an Eastern Orthodox perspective, it has been used to refer to the highest form of contemplation, the "act" of beholding God. In a broader sense, it refers to the discursive activity of the heart toward God, involving the use of the rational and a-rational faculties for the purpose of coming to both theoretical and experiential knowledge of God.

Transformational Theology. A theological system of thought that is wholly orientated toward the distinct goal of the Christian life—namely, the transformation of the people of God into the image of Christ—to the glory of God.

Union with Christ. Refers to the believer's sharing in the life of Christ, both in his history and his eternity. Through faith, persons are identified with the death and resurrection of Christ (in history), and united with the exalted Christ (in eternity) so they may be adopted into the life of the Triune God. The nature of the relationship has implications in transforming the life of the believer that are legal, experiential, and final.

Unity-in-Diversity. The dialectic that allows for the presence of union without confusion. This paradox is central to Christian theology and praxis—first and foremost being demonstrated in the Triune God and the person of Christ. It points to the presence of both commonality and difference—allowing for broadness without a contradictory plurality. See also "Dialectic."

Virtues. Dispositions and characteristics of a person that are deemed to be morally good, right, and excellent, in accord with the person of Christ. Often described in terms of the "fruit of the Spirit" (see Gal 5:22–23)—most centrally involving love toward God and others. Rather than demonstrating moralistic self-glorification, Christian virtues are grounded in faith—in accord with the holiness of the law—to the glory of God. Virtues are demonstrated in the practice and formation of right thoughts, intentions, desires, emotions, affections, actions, and behaviors.

Worship. Worship is the proper response of God's people to his self-revelation, so that they may be formed more into the image of Christ. Most crucially, it is a response to the truth of the gospel of Christ and the Scriptures. Worship is orientated toward the Triune God, in congruence with the eschatological activity of the heavenly communion of saints. Such involves participating in the dynamics within the triune life, so that God may be glorified in his church. "Gathered worship" refers to the intentional ecclesial response that occurs in a particular time and place—allowing for specific "means of grace" to operate. "Scattered worship" refers to the broader response of God's people that occurs in daily life within societal roles.

Bibliography

Abernethy, Alexis D., ed. *Worship That Changes Lives: Multidisciplinary and Congregational Perspectives on Spiritual Transformation*. Grand Rapids, MI: Baker Academic, 2008.
Adam, Peter. *Hearing God's Words: Exploring Biblical Spirituality*. Downers Grove, IL: IVP Academic, 2004.
———. *Written for Us: Receiving God's Word in the Bible*. Nottingham, UK: IVP, 2008.
Adams, Jay E. *How to Help People Change*. Grand Rapids, MI: Zondervan, 2010.
Alexander, Donald L., ed. *Christian Spirituality: Five Views of Sanctification*. Downers Grove, IL: IVP Academic, 1988.
Allen, Michael. *Sanctification*. New Studies in Dogmatics. Grand Rapids, MI: Zondervan, 2017.
Allen, Michael, and Scott R. Swain, eds. *Christian Dogmatics: Reformed Theology for the Church Catholic*. Grand Rapids, MI: Baker Academic, 2016.
———. *Reformed Catholicity: The Promise of Retrieval for Theology and Biblical Interpretation*. Grand Rapids, MI: Baker Academic, 2015.
Allen, Pauline. "The Life and Times of Maximus the Confessor." In *The Oxford Handbook of Maximus the Confessor*, edited by Pauline Allen and Bronwen Neil, 3–18. Oxford, UK: Oxford University Press, 2015.
Anders, Max. *Brave New Discipleship: Cultivating Scripture Driven Christians in a Culture Driven World*. Nashville, TN: Thomas Nelson, 2015.
Anderson, James. *Paradox in Christian Theology: An Analysis of Its Presence, Character, and Epistemic Status*. Milton Keynes, UK: Paternoster, 2007.
Andrews, Alan, ed. *The Kingdom Life: A Practical Theology of Discipleship and Spiritual Formation*. Colorado Springs, CO: Navpress, 2010.
Aniol, Scott. "Practice Makes Perfect: Corporate Worship and the Formative of Spiritual Virtue." *Journal of Spiritual Formation & Soul Care* 10, no. 1 (2017) 93–104.
Anthony, Michael J., ed. *Perspectives on Children's Spiritual Formation*. Nashville, TN: B&H, 2006.
Armstrong, Chris. "The Rise, Frustration, and Revival of Evangelical Spiritual Ressourcement." *Journal of Spiritual Formation & Soul Care* 2, no. 1 (2009) 113–21.
Armstrong, John H., ed. *The Coming Evangelical Crisis: Current Challenges to the Authority of Scripture and the Gospel*. Chicago, IL: Moody, 1996.
Austin, Michael W. "The Doctrine of Theosis: A Transformational Union with Christ." *Journal of Spiritual Formation & Soul Care* 8, no. 2 (2015) 172–86.

Averbeck, Richard E. "Spirit, Community, and Mission: A Biblical Theology for Spiritual Formation." *Journal of Spiritual Formation & Soul Care* 1, no. 1 (2008) 27–53.

———. "Worship and Spiritual Formation." In *Foundations of Spiritual Formation: A Community Approach to Becoming Like Christ*, edited by Paul Pettit, 51–69. Grand Rapids, MI: Kregel, 2008.

Balswick, Jack O., Pamela Ebstyne King, and Kevin S. Reimer. *The Reciprocating Self: Human Development in Theological Perspective*. Downers Grove, IL: IVP Academic, 2005.

Balthasar, Hans Urs von. *Cosmic Liturgy: The Universe According to Maximus the Confessor*. 3rd ed. San Francisco, CA: Ignatius, 2003.

Barna, George. *Growing True Disciples: New Strategies for Producing Genuine Followers of Christ*. Colorado Springs, CO: Waterbrook, 2009.

Barrett, Matthew. *God's Word Alone: The Authority of Scripture*. Grand Rapids, MI: Zondervan, 2016.

Barrs, Jerram. *Delighting in the Law of the Lord: God's Alternative to Legalism and Moralism*. Wheaton, IL: Crossway, 2013.

Bass, Dorothy C., ed. *Practicing Our Faith: A Way of Life for a Searching People*. San Francisco, CA: Jossey-Bass, 1997.

Bathrellos, Demetrios. "Passions, Ascesis, and the Virtues." In *The Oxford Handbook of Maximus the Confessor*, edited by Pauline Allen and Bronwen Neil, 287–306. Oxford, UK: Oxford University Press, 2015.

Bavinck, Herman. *Reformed Dogmatics: Prolegomena*. Translated by John Vriend. Vol. 1, Grand Rapids, MI: Baker Academic, 2003.

Beale, Gregory K. *The Erosion of Inerrancy in Evangelicalism: Responding to New Challenges to Biblical Authority*. Wheaton, IL: Crossway, 2008.

———. *A New Testament Biblical Theology: The Unfolding of the Old Testament in the New*. Grand Rapids, MI: Baker Academic, 2011.

———. *The Temple and the Church's Mission: A Biblical Theology of the Dwelling Place of God*. Downers Grove, IL: IVP Academic, 2004.

———. *We Become What We Worship: A Biblical Theology of Idolatry*. Downers Grove, IL: IVP Academic, 2008.

Beale, Gregory K., and Mitchell Kim. *God Dwells Among Us: Expanding Eden to the Ends of the Earth*. Downers Grove, IL: IVP, 2014.

Beasley-Topliffe, Keith, ed. *The Upper Room Dictionary of Christian Spiritual Formation*. Nashville, TN: Upper Room, 2003.

Bebbington, David W. "About the Definition of Evangelicalism." *Evangelical Studies Bulletin* 83 (2012) 1–6.

———. *Evangelicalism in Modern Britain: A History from the 1730s to the 1980s*. London: Routledge, 1988.

Beeke, Joel R. *Developing Healthy Spiritual Growth: Knowledge, Practice, and Experience*. Darlington, UK: Evangelical Press, 2013.

———. *Piety: The Heartbeat of Reformed Theology*. Phillipsburg, NJ: P&R, 2015.

———. *What Is Evangelicalism?* Darlington, UK: Evangelical Press, 2012.

Beeke, Joel R., and Mark Jones. *A Puritan Theology: Doctrine for Life*. Grand Rapids, MI: Reformation Heritage, 2012.

Benner, David G. *Soulful Spirituality: Becoming Fully Alive and Deeply Human*. Grand Rapids, MI: Brazos, 2011.

---. *Spirituality and the Awakening Self: The Sacred Journey of Transformation*. Grand Rapids, MI: Brazos, 2012.
Benner, David G., Larry Crabb, and Gary Moon. "How We Change [Special Issue]." *Conversations: A Forum for Authentic Transformation* 8, no. 1 (2010).
Bergler, Thomas E. *From Here to Maturity: Overcoming the Juvenilization of American Christianity*. Grand Rapids, MI: Eerdmans, 2014.
Berthold, George C. "Christian Life and Praxis: The Centuries on Love." In *The Oxford Handbook of Maximus the Confessor*, edited by Pauline Allen and Bronwen Neil, 397–413. Oxford, UK: Oxford University Press, 2015.
---, ed. *Maximus Confessor: Selected Writings*. Mahwah, NJ: Paulist, 1985.
Bingaman, Brock. *All Things New: The Trinitarian Nature of the Human Calling in Maximus the Confessor and Jürgen Moltmann*. Eugene, OR: Pickwick, 2014.
Bird, Michael F. *Evangelical Theology: A Biblical and Systematic Introduction*. Grand Rapids, MI: Zondervan, 2013.
Black, Gary. *The Theology of Dallas Willard: Discovering Proto-Evangelical Faith*. Eugene, OR: Pickwick, 2013.
Bland, Dave. *Proverbs and the Formation of Character*. Eugene, OR: Cascade, 2015.
Block, Daniel I. *For the Glory of God: Recovering a Biblical Theology of Worship*. Grand Rapids, MI: Baker Academic, 2014.
Bloesch, Donald G. *The Christian Life and Salvation*. Grand Rapids, MI: Eerdmans, 1967.
---. *The Crisis of Piety: Essays toward a Theology of the Christian Life*. Colorado Springs, CO: Helmers & Howard, 1988.
---. *The Future of Evangelical Christianity: A Call for Unity Amid Diversity*. Colorado Springs, CO: Helmers & Howard, 1988.
---. *Spirituality Old and New: Recovering Authentic Spiritual Life*. Downers Grove, IL: IVP Academic, 2007.
Blomberg, Craig L. "'True Righteousness and Holiness': The Image of God in the New Testament." In *The Image of God in an Image Driven Age: Explorations in Theological Anthropology*, edited by Beth F. Jones and Jeffrey W. Barbeau, 66–87. Downers Grove, IL: IVP Academic, 2016.
Blowers, Paul M. *Maximus the Confessor: Jesus Christ and the Transfiguration of the World*. Oxford, UK: Oxford University Press, 2016.
Boa, Kenneth. *Conformed to His Image: Biblical and Practical Approaches to Spiritual Formation*. Grand Rapids, MI: Zondervan, 2001.
Boersma, Hans. *Heavenly Participation: The Weaving of a Sacramental Tapestry*. Grand Rapids, MI: Eerdmans, 2011.
Borchert, Gerald L. *Worship in the New Testament: Divine Mystery and Human Response*. St Louis, MO: Chalice, 2008.
Boulton, Matthew M. *Life in God: John Calvin, Practical Formation and the Future of Protestant Theology*. Grand Rapids, MI: Eerdmans, 2011.
Boyd, Gregory A., and Paul R. Eddy. *Across the Spectrum: Understanding Issues in Evangelical Theology*. 2nd ed. Grand Rapids, MI: Baker Academic, 2009.
Bradshaw, Paul, and Peter Moger. *Worship Changes Lives: How It Works, Why It Matters*. London: Church House, 2008.
Bridges, Jerry. *The Discipline of Grace: God's Role and Our Role in the Pursuit of Holiness*. 2nd ed. Colorado Springs, CO: Navpress, 2006.

Bibliography

———. *Growing Your Faith: How to Mature in Christ.* Colorado Springs, CO: Navpress, 2004.
———. *The Practice of Godliness.* 2nd ed. Colorado Springs, CO: Navpress, 1996.
———. *The Pursuit of Holiness.* 3rd ed. Colorado Springs, CO: Navpress, 2003.
———. *The Transforming Power of the Gospel.* Colorado Springs, CO: Navpress, 2012.
Brower, Kent. *Living as the Holy People of God: Holiness and Community in Paul.* Milton Keynes, UK: Paternoster, 2014.
Brown, Jeannine K., Carla M. Dahl, and Wyndy C. Reuschling. *Becoming Whole and Holy: An Integrative Conversation About Christian Formation.* Grand Rapids, MI: Baker Academic, 2011.
Burger, Hans. *Being in Christ: A Biblical and Systematic Investigation in a Reformed Perspective.* Eugene, OR: Wipf & Stock, 2009.
Buschart, W. David, and Kent D. Eilers. *Theology as Retrieval: Receiving the Past, Renewing the Church.* Downers Grove, IL: IVP Academic, 2015.
Calhoun, Adele A. *Spiritual Disciplines Handbook: Practices That Transform Us.* Downers Grove, IL: IVP, 2005.
Callen, Barry L. *Authentic Spirituality: Moving Beyond Mere Religion.* Grand Rapids, MI: Baker Academic, 2001.
Calver, Clive, and Robert Warner. *Together We Stand: Evangelical Convictions, Unity, and Vision.* London: Hodder & Stoughton, 1996.
Calvin, John. *The Institutes of the Christian Religion.* 2 Vols. Louisville, KY: WJK, 1960.
———. *The Christian Life.* Eugene, OR: Wipf & Stock, 1984.
Campbell, Constantine R. *Paul and Union with Christ: An Exegetical and Theological Study.* Grand Rapids, MI: Zondervan, 2012.
Caneday, A. B. "Is Theological Truth Functional or Propositional? Postconservatism's Use of Language Games and Speech-Act Theory." In *Reclaiming the Center: Confronting Evangelical Accommodation in Postmodern Times,* edited by Millard J. Erickson, Paul K. Helseth, and Justin Taylor, 137–59. Wheaton, IL: Crossway, 2004.
Carson, Donald A. "Domesticating the Gospel: A Review of Grenz's Renewing the Center." In *Reclaiming the Center: Confronting Evangelical Accommodation in Postmodern Times,* edited by Millard J. Erickson, Paul K. Helseth, and Justin Taylor, 33–55. Wheaton, IL: Crossway, 2004.
———, ed. *The Enduring Authority of the Christian Scriptures.* Grand Rapids, MI: Eerdmans, 2016.
———. *The Gagging of God: Christianity Confronts Pluralism.* Leicester, UK: Apollos, 1996.
———. "Spiritual Disciplines." *Themelios* 36, no. 3 (2011) 377–79.
———. "When Is Spirituality Spiritual? Reflections on Some Problems of Definition." *Journal of the Evangelical Theological Society* 37, no. 3 (1994) 381–94.
Carson, Donald A., and Timothy Keller, eds. *The Gospel as Center: Renewing Our Faith and Reforming Our Ministry Practices.* Wheaton, IL: Crossway, 2012.
Cattoi, Thomas. "Liturgy as Cosmic Transformation." In *The Oxford Handbook of Maximus the Confessor,* edited by Pauline Allen and Bronwen Neil, 414–35. Oxford, UK: Oxford University Press, 2015.
Chan, Simon. *Liturgical Theology: The Church as Worshipping Community.* Downers Grove, IL: IVP Academic, 2006.

———. "New Directions in Evangelical Spirituality." *Journal of Spiritual Formation & Soul Care* 2, no. 2 (2009) 219–37.
———. "Spiritual Practices." In *The Oxford Handbook of Evangelical Theology*, edited by Gerald R. McDermott, 247–61. Oxford, UK: Oxford University Press, 2010.
———. "Spiritual Theology." In *Dictionary of Christian Spirituality*, edited by Glen G. Scorgie, 52–57. Grand Rapids, MI: Zondervan, 2011.
———. *Spiritual Theology: A Systematic Study of the Christian Life*. Downers Grove, IL: IVP Academic, 1998.
Chandler, Diane J. *Christian Spiritual Formation: An Integrated Approach for Personal and Relational Wholeness*. Downers Grove, IL: IVP Academic, 2014.
———, ed. *The Holy Spirit and Christian Formation: Multidisciplinary Perspectives*. New York: Palgrave Macmillan, 2016.
Chester, Tim. *You Can Change*. Nottingham, UK: IVP, 2008.
Clark, David K. *To Know and Love God: Method for Theology*. Wheaton, IL: Crossway, 2003.
Clifford, Steve, ed. *21st Century Evangelicals: A Snapshot of the Beliefs and Habits of Evangelical Christians in the UK*. London: Evangelical Alliance, 2011.
———, ed. *Time for Discipleship?* London: Evangelical Alliance, 2014.
Cloud, Henry, and John Townsend. *How People Grow: What the Bible Reveals About Personal Growth*. Grand Rapids, MI: Zondervan, 2001.
Cockerton, John. *Essentials of Evangelical Spirituality*. Cambridge, UK: Grove, 1994.
Cocksworth, Christopher. *Holding Together: Gospel, Church, and Spirit—the Essentials of Christian Identity*. Norwich, UK: Canterbury Press, 2008.
Coe, John H. "Approaches to the Study of Christian Spirituality." In *Dictionary of Christian Spirituality*, edited by Glen G. Scorgie, 34–39. Grand Rapids, MI: Zondervan, 2011.
———. "The Call and Task of This Journal." *Journal of Spiritual Formation & Soul Care* 1, no. 1 (2008) 2–4.
———. "The Controversy over Contemplation and Contemplative Prayer: A Historical, Theological, and Biblical Resolution." *Journal of Spiritual Formation & Soul Care* 7, no. 1 (2014) 140–53.
———. "Spiritual Theology: A Theological-Experiential Methodology for Bridging the Sanctification Gap." *Journal of Spiritual Formation & Soul Care* 2, no. 1 (2009) 4–43.
Coe, John H., and Todd W. Hall. *Psychology in the Spirit: Contours of a Transformational Psychology*. Downers Grove, IL: IVP Academic, 2010.
Coffey, David. *All One in Christ Jesus: A Passionate Appeal for Evangelical Unity*. Milton Keynes, UK: Authentic Media, 2009.
Collicutt, Joanna. *The Psychology of Christian Character Formation*. London: SCM, 2015.
Collinson, Sylvia W. *Making Disciples: The Significance of Jesus' Educational Methods for Today's Church*. Carlisle, UK: Paternoster, 2007.
Confessor, Maximus the. "Ad Thalassium 61." Translated by Paul M. Blowers and Robert L. Wilken. In *On the Cosmic Mystery of Jesus Christ: Selected Writings from St Maximus the Confessor*, 131–43. Crestwood, NY: St Vladimir's Seminary Press, 2003.

———. "Ambigua to John 1–22." Translated by Nicholas Constas. In *On Difficulties in the Church Fathers: The Ambigua*, 61–451. Cambridge, MA: Harvard University Press, 2014.

———. "Ambigua to John 23–71." Translated by Nicholas Constas. In *On Difficulties in the Church Fathers: The Ambigua*, 1–373. Cambridge, MA: Harvard University Press, 2014.

———. "The Ascetic Life." Translated by Polycarp Sherwood. In *St Maximus the Confessor: The Ascetic Life, the Four Centuries on Charity*, 103–35. New York: Newman, 1955.

———. "Chapters on Knowledge." Translated by George C. Berthold. In *Maximus Confessor: Selected Writings*, 127–80. Mahwah, NJ: Paulist, 1985.

———. "The Church's Mystagogy." Translated by George C. Berthold. In *Maximus Confessor: Selected Writings*, 181–225. Mahwah, NJ: Paulist, 1985.

———. "The Four Hundred Chapters on Love." Translated by George C. Berthold. In *Maximus Confessor: Selected Writings*, 33–98. Mahwah, NJ: Paulist, 1985.

———. "Letter 2: On Love." Translated by Andrew Louth. In *Maximus the Confessor*, 84–93. London: Routledge, 1996.

———. "Questions and Doubts." Translated by Despina D. Prassas. In *St Maximus the Confessor's Questions and Doubts*, 43–157. DeKalb, IL: Northern Illinois University Press, 2010.

Conn, Joann W. *Spirituality and Personal Maturity*. Lanham, MD: University Press of America, 1996.

Constas, Nicholas, ed. *On Difficulties in the Church Fathers: The Ambigua*. 2 Vols. Cambridge, MA: Harvard University Press, 2014.

Copan, Victor. *Changing Your Mind: The Bible, the Brain, and Spiritual Growth*. Eugene, OR: Wipf & Stock, 2016.

Cosden, Darrell. *A Theology of Work: Work and the New Creation*. Eugene, OR: Wipf & Stock, 2006.

Costache, Doru. "Mapping Reality within the Experience of Holiness." In *The Oxford Handbook of Maximus the Confessor*, edited by Pauline Allen and Bronwen Neil, 378–96. Oxford, UK: Oxford University Press, 2015.

Crabb, Larry. *Inside Out*. 3rd ed. Colorado Springs, CO: Navpress, 2013.

Craig-Wild, Peter. *Tools for Transformation: Making Worship Work*. London: DLT, 2002.

Crisp, Oliver D. "Problems with Perichoresis." *Tyndale Bulletin* 56, no. 1 (2005) 119–40.

Crouch, Andy. "Reflections on Cultural Engagement." In *Loving the City: Doing Balanced, Gospel-Centered Ministry in Your City*, edited by Timothy Keller, 274–88. Grand Rapids, MI: Zondervan, 2016.

Crowe, Brandon D. *The Last Adam: A Theology of the Obedient Life of Jesus in the Gospels*. Grand Rapids, MI: Baker Academic, 2017.

Cunningham, Lawrence S., and Keith J. Egan. *Christian Spirituality: Themes from a Tradition*. Mahwah, NJ: Paulist, 1996.

Dahms, John V. "The Nature of Truth." *Journal of the Evangelical Theological Society* 28, no. 4 (1985) 455–65.

Davies, Oliver. *Theology of Transformation: Faith, Freedom, and the Christian Act*. Oxford, UK: Oxford University Press, 2013.

Davis, Andrew M. *An Infinite Journey: Growing toward Christlikeness*. Greenville, SC: Ambassador International, 2014.

Davis, John J. *Worship and the Reality of God: An Evangelical Theology of Real Presence.* Downers Grove, IL: IVP Academic, 2010.

———. *Meditation and Communion with God: Contemplating Scripture in an Age of Distraction.* Downers Grove, IL: IVP Academic, 2012.

Decker, Rodney J. "May Evangelicals Dispense with Propositional Revelation? Challenges to a Traditional Evangelical Doctrine." In *The 53rd Annual Meeting of the Evangelical Theological Society.* Colorado Springs, CO, 2001.

Demarest, Bruce. *The Cross and Salvation: The Doctrine of Salvation.* Wheaton, IL: Crossway, 1997.

———, ed. *Four Views on Christian Spirituality.* Grand Rapids, MI: Zondervan, 2012.

———. "New Dimensions in Spirituality & Christian Living." In *New Dimensions in Evangelical Thought*, edited by David S. Dockery, 374-93. Downers Grove, IL: IVP Academic, 1998.

———. "Reflections on Developmental Spirituality: Journey Paradigms and Stages." *Journal of Spiritual Formation & Soul Care* 1, no. 2 (2008) 149-67.

———. *Satisfy Your Soul: Restoring the Heart of Christian Spirituality.* Colorado Springs, CO: Navpress, 1999.

———. *Seasons of the Soul: Stages of Spiritual Development.* Downers Grove, IL: IVP, 2009.

Dennison, William D. "Dutch Neo-Calvinism and the Roots for Transformation: An Introductory Essay." *Journal of the Evangelical Theological Society* 42, no. 2 (1999) 271-91.

DeSilva, David A. *Transformation: The Heart of Paul's Gospel.* Bellingham, WA: Lexham, 2014.

DeYoung, Kevin. *The Hole in Our Holiness: Filling the Gap between Gospel Passion and the Pursuit of Godliness.* Wheaton, IL: Crossway, 2012.

———. *Taking God at His Word.* Wheaton, IL: Crossway, 2014.

DeYoung, Rebecca Konyndyk. *Glittering Vices: A New Look at the Seven Deadly Sins and Their Remedies.* Grand Rapids, MI: Brazos, 2009.

———. *Vainglory: The Forgotten Vice.* Grand Rapids, MI: Eerdmans, 2014.

Dockery, David S., ed. *The Challenge of Postmodernism: An Evangelical Engagement.* 2nd ed. Grand Rapids, MI: Baker Academic, 2001.

———. "An Outline of Paul's View of the Spiritual Life: Foundation for an Evangelical Spirituality." *Criswell Theological Review* 3, no. 2 (1989) 327-39.

Drury, Keith. *Spiritual Disciplines for Ordinary People.* Indianapolis, IN: WPH, 2004.

Dykstra, Craig. *Growing in the Life of Faith: Education and Christian Practices.* 2nd ed. Louisville, KY: WJK, 2005.

Edgar, William. *Created & Creating: A Biblical Theology of Culture.* Downers Grove, IL: IVP Academic, 2017.

Edwards, Jonathan. *The Religious Affections.* Edinburgh: Banner of Truth, 1986.

Eglinton, James. "To Transform and to Transcend: The Neo-Calvinist Relationship of Church and Cultural Transformation." In *The Kuyper Center Review: Volume 3— Calvinism and Culture*, edited by Gordon Graham, 163-84. Grand Rapids, MI: Eerdmans, 2013.

Eilers, Kent, and Kyle C. Strobel, eds. *Sanctified by Grace: A Theology of the Christian Life.* London: Bloomsbury, 2014.

Erickson, Millard J., Paul K. Helseth, and Justin Taylor, eds. *Reclaiming the Center: Confronting Evangelical Accommodation in Postmodern Times*. Wheaton, IL: Crossway, 2004.

Estep, James R., and Jonathan H. Kim, eds. *Christian Formation: Integrating Theology & Human Development*. Nashville, TN: B&H, 2010.

Fackre, Gabriel. *Ecumenical Faith in Evangelical Perspective*. Grand Rapids, MI: Eerdmans, 1993.

Fairbairn, Donald. *Life in the Trinity: An Introduction to Theology with the Help of the Church Fathers*. Downers Grove, IL: IVP Academic, 2009.

Feinberg, John S. *Light in a Dark Place: The Doctrine of Scripture*. Wheaton, IL: Crossway, 2018.

Feldmeier, Peter. *The Developing Christian: Spiritual Growth through the Life Cycle*. Mahwah, NJ: Paulist, 2007.

Ferguson, Sinclair B. *The Christian Life: A Doctrinal Introduction*. Edinburgh: Banner of Truth, 2013.

———. *Devoted to God: Blueprints for Sanctification*. Edinburgh: Banner of Truth, 2016.

———. *From the Mouth of God: Trusting, Reading and Applying the Bible*. Edinburgh: Banner of Truth, 2014.

———. *John Owen on the Christian Life*. Edinburgh: Banner of Truth, 1987.

———. *The Whole Christ: Legalism, Antinomianism, and Gospel Assurance*. Wheaton, IL: Crossway, 2016.

Finn, Nathan A., and Keith Whitfield, eds. *Spirituality for the Sent: Casting a New Vision for the Missional Church*. Downers Grove, IL: IVP Academic, 2017.

Fletcher-Louis, Crispin H. T. "God's Image, His Cosmic Temple, and the High Priest: Towards an Historical and Theological Account of the Incarnation." In *Heaven on Earth: The Temple in Biblical Theology*, edited by T. Desmond Alexander and Simon J. Gathercole, 81–99. Carlisle, UK: Paternoster, 2004.

Ford, David F. *The Drama of Living: Becoming Wise in the Spirit*. Grand Rapids, MI: Brazos, 2014.

———. *Self and Salvation: Being Transformed*. Cambridge, UK: Cambridge University Press, 1999.

———. *The Shape of Living: Spiritual Directions for Everyday Life*. Grand Rapids, MI: Baker, 1997.

Foster, Richard J. *Celebration of Discipline: The Path to Spiritual Growth*. New York: Harper Collins, 1978.

———. *Life with God: A Life Transforming Approach to Bible Reading*. New York: Harper Collins, 2007.

———. *Streams of Living Water: Essential Practices from the Six Great Traditions of Christian Faith*. New York: Harper Collins, 1998.

Fowler, James W. *Stages of Faith: The Psychology of Human Development and the Quest for Meaning*. New York: Harper Collins, 1995.

Frame, John M. *The Doctrine of God*. Phillipsburg, NJ: P&R, 2002.

———. *The Doctrine of the Knowledge of God*. Phillipsburg, NJ: P&R, 1987.

———. *The Doctrine of the Word of God*. Phillipsburg, NJ: P&R, 2010.

Gaffin, Richard B. *By Faith, Not by Sight: Paul and the Order of Salvation*. 2nd ed. Phillipsburg, NJ: P&R, 2013.

Gaffin, Richard B., and Peter A. Lillback, eds. *Thy Word Is Still Truth: Essential Writings on the Doctrine of Scripture from the Reformation to Today*. Phillipsburg, NJ: P&R, 2013.
Gangel, Kenneth O., and James C. Wilhoit, eds. *The Christian Educator's Handbook on Spiritual Formation*. Grand Rapids, MI: Baker, 1997.
Garner, David B. *Sons in the Son: The Riches and Reach of Adoption in Christ*. Phillipsburg, NJ: P&R, 2016.
Geiger, Eric, Michael Kelley, and Philip Nation. *Transformational Discipleship: How People Really Grow*. Nashville, TN: B&H, 2012.
George, Timothy, ed. *J. I. Packer and the Evangelical Future: The Impact of His Life and Thought*. Grand Rapids, MI: Baker Academic, 2009.
George, Timothy, and Alister E. McGrath, eds. *For All the Saints: Evangelical Theology and Christian Spirituality*. Louisville, KY: WJK, 2003.
Gifford, James D. *Perichoretic Salvation: The Believer's Union with Christ as a Third Type of Perichoresis*. Eugene, OR: Wipf & Stock, 2011.
Gillett, David K. *Trust and Obey: Explorations in Evangelical Spirituality*. London: DLT, 1993.
Goggin, Jamin, and Kyle C. Strobel, eds. *Reading the Christian Spiritual Classics: A Guide for Evangelicals*. Downers Grove, IL: IVP Academic, 2013.
Goldingay, John. *Evangelical Spirituality*. Cambridge, UK: Grove, 1992.
Gordon, James M. *Evangelical Spirituality: From the Wesleys to John Stott*. London: SPCK, 1991.
Gorman, Michael J. *Becoming the Gospel: Paul, Participation, and Mission*. Grand Rapids, MI: Eerdmans, 2015.
———. *Cruciformity: Paul's Narrative Spirituality of the Cross*. Grand Rapids, MI Eerdmans, 2001.
Graham, Jeannine M. "Systematic Theology and Spiritual Formation: Recovering Obscured Unities." *Journal of Spiritual Formation & Soul Care* 7, no. 2 (2014) 177–90.
Green, Bradley G. *Covenant and Commandment: Works, Obedience, and Faithfulness in the Christian Life*. Downers Grove, IL: IVP Academic, 2014.
Greenman, Jeffrey P. "Spiritual Formation in Theological Perspective: Classic Issues, Contemporary Challenges." In *Life in the Spirit: Spiritual Formation in Theological Perspective*, edited by Jeffrey P. Greenman and George Kalantzis, 23–35. Downers Grove, IL: IVP Academic, 2010.
Grenz, Stanley J. *Renewing the Center: Evangelical Theology in a Post-Theological Era*. Grand Rapids, MI: Baker Academic, 2000.
———. *Revisioning Evangelical Theology: A Fresh Agenda for the 21st Century*. Downers Grove, IL: IVP Academic, 1993.
———. *The Social God and the Relational Self: A Trinitarian Theology of the Imago Dei*. Louisville, KY: WJK, 2001.
Groothuis, Douglas. *Truth Decay: Defending Christianity against the Challenges of Postmodernism*. Downers Grove, IL: IVP, 2000.
———. "Truth Defined and Defended." In *Reclaiming the Center: Confronting Evangelical Accommodation in Postmodern Times*, edited by Millard J. Erickson, Paul K. Helseth, and Justin Taylor, 59–79. Wheaton, IL: Crossway, 2004.
Gundry, Stanley N., ed. *Five Views on Law and Gospel*. Grand Rapids, MI: Zondervan, 1996.

———, ed. *Five Views on Sanctification*. Grand Rapids, MI: Zondervan, 1987.
Hagberg, J. O., and R. A. Guelich. *The Critical Journey: Stages in the Life of Faith*. Salem, WI: Sheffield Publishing Company, 2005.
Hall, Christopher A. "Historical Theology and Spiritual Formation: A Response." *Journal of Spiritual Formation & Soul Care* 7, no. 2 (2014) 210–19.
Hardin, Leslie T. "Is a Pauline Spirituality Still Viable?" *Journal of Spiritual Formation & Soul Care* 8, no. 2 (2015) 132–46.
———. "Searching for a Transformative Hermeneutic." *Journal of Spiritual Formation & Soul Care* 5, no. 1 (2012) 144–57.
———. *The Spirituality of Paul: Partnering with the Spirit in Everyday Life*. Grand Rapids, MI: Kregel, 2016.
Harris, Brian. "Beyond Bebbington: The Quest for Evangelical Identity in a Postmodern Era." *Churchman* 122, no. 3 (2008) 201–19.
Hart, Darryl G. *Deconstructing Evangelicalism: Conservative Protestantism in the Age of Billy Graham*. Grand Rapids, MI: Baker Academic, 2004.
Hawkins, Greg L., and Cally Parkinson. *Move: What 1,000 Churches Reveal About Spiritual Growth*. Grand Rapids, MI: Zondervan, 2011.
Haykin, Michael A. G. *The God Who Draws Near: An Introduction to Biblical Spirituality*. Darlington, UK: Evangelical Press, 2007.
Haykin, Michael A. G., and Kenneth J. Stewart, eds. *The Emergence of Evangelicalism: Exploring Historical Continuities*. Nottingham, UK: Apollos, 2008.
Headley, Carolyn. *Liturgy and Spiritual Formation*. Cambridge, UK: Grove, 1997.
Hedges, Brian G. *Christ Formed in You: The Power of the Gospel for Personal Change*. Wapwallopen, PA: Shepherd Press, 2010.
Helland, Roger, and Leonard Hjalmarson. *Missional Spirituality*. Downers Grove, IL: IVP, 2011.
Helm, Paul. *The Divine Revelation: The Basic Issues*. Vancouver, BC: Regent College Publishing, 2004.
———. "The Idea of Inerrancy." In *The Enduring Authority of the Christian Scriptures*, edited by Donald A. Carson, 899–919. Grand Rapids, MI: Eerdmans, 2016.
Hermans, Chris A. M. "Spiritual Transformation: Concept and Measurement." *Journal of Empirical Theology* 26, no. 2 (2013) 165–87.
Hilborn, David, ed. *Movement for Change: Evangelical Perspectives on Social Transformation*. Milton Keynes, UK: Paternoster, 2004.
Hill, Charles E. "'The Truth above All Demonstration': Scripture in the Patristic Period to Augustine." In *The Enduring Authority of the Christian Scriptures*, edited by Donald A. Carson, 43–88. Grand Rapids, MI: Eerdmans, 2016.
Hindmarsh, D. Bruce. "Contours of Evangelical Spirituality." In *Dictionary of Christian Spirituality*, edited by Glen G. Scorgie, 146–52. Grand Rapids, MI: Zondervan, 2011.
———. "Retrieval and Renewal: A Model for Evangelical Spiritual Vitality." In *J. I. Packer and the Evangelical Future: The Impact of His Life and Thought*, edited by Timothy George, 99–114. Grand Rapids, MI: Baker Academic, 2009.
———. "Seeking True Religion: Early Evangelical Devotion and Catholic Spirituality." In *Life in the Spirit: Spiritual Formation in Theological Perspective*, edited by Jeffrey P. Greenman and George Kalantzis, 115–37. Downers Grove, IL: IVP Academic, 2010.
Hingley, Chris J. H. "Evangelicals and Spirituality." *Themelios* 15, no. 3 (1990) 86–91.

Hitchen, John M. "What It Means to Be an Evangelical Today: An Antipodean Perspective—Part One." *The Evangelical Quarterly* 76, no. 1 (2004) 47–64.

———. "What It Means to Be an Evangelical Today: An Antipodean Perspective—Part Two." *The Evangelical Quarterly* 76, no. 2 (2004) 99–115.

Hoekema, Anthony A. *Created in God's Image*. Grand Rapids, MI: Eerdmans, 1996.

———. *Saved by Grace*. Grand Rapids, MI: Eerdmans, 1996.

Holder, Arthur, ed. *The Blackwell Companion to Christian Spirituality*. Malden, MA: Blackwell, 2005.

Hollinger, Dennis. *Head, Hands & Heart: Bringing Together Christian Thought, Passion, and Action*. Downers Grove, IL: IVP, 2005.

Holmes, Stephen R. "Evangelical Theology and Identity." In *21st Century Evangelicals: Reflections on Research by the Evangelical Alliance*, edited by Greg Smith, 23–36. Watford, UK: Instant Apostle, 2015.

Hood, Jason B. *Imitating God in Christ: Recapturing a Biblical Pattern*. Downers Grove, IL: IVP Academic, 2013.

Horton, Michael S. *A Better Way: Rediscovering the Drama of God-Centered Worship*. Grand Rapids, MI: Baker, 2002.

———. *Calvin on the Christian Life: Glorifying and Enjoying God Forever*. Wheaton, IL: Crossway, 2014.

———. *The Christian Faith: A Systematic Theology for Pilgrims on the Way*. Grand Rapids, MI: Zondervan, 2011.

———. *Christless Christianity*. Grand Rapids, MI: Baker, 2008.

———. *The Gospel Commission: Recovering God's Strategy for Making Disciples*. Grand Rapids, MI: Baker, 2011.

———. *The Gospel-Driven Life: Being Good News People in a Bad News World*. Grand Rapids, MI: Baker, 2009.

———. *In the Face of God: The Dangers & Delights of Spiritual Intimacy*. Dallas, TX: Word, 1996.

———. *The Law of Perfect Freedom: Relating to God and Others through the Ten Commandments*. Chicago, IL: Moody, 1993.

———. *Ordinary: Sustainable Faith in a Radical, Restless World*. Grand Rapids, MI: Zondervan, 2014.

———. *Putting Amazing Back into Grace: Embracing the Heart of the Gospel*. Grand Rapids, MI: Baker, 1994.

Hotz, Kendra G., and Matthew T. Mathews. *Shaping the Christian Life: Worship and the Religious Affections*. Louisville, KY: WJK, 2006.

Howard, Evan B. "Advancing the Discussion: Reflections on the Study of Christian Spiritual Life." *Journal of Spiritual Formation & Soul Care* 1, no. 1 (2008) 8–26.

———. *The Brazos Introduction to Christian Spirituality*. Grand Rapids, MI: Brazos, 2008.

———. "Contributions to Evangelical Spirituality." *Journal of Spiritual Formation & Soul Care* 10, no. 2 (2017) 237–47.

———. "Evangelical Spirituality." In *Four Views on Christian Spirituality*, edited by Bruce Demarest, 159–86. Grand Rapids, MI: Zondervan, 2012.

———. *A Guide to Christian Spiritual Formation: How Scripture, Spirit, Community, and Mission Shape Our Souls*. Grand Rapids, MI: Baker Academic, 2018.

Howard, James M. *Paul, the Community, and Progressive Sanctification: An Exploration into Community-Based Transformation within Pauline Theology.* New York: Peter Lang, 2007.

Howard, Phil. "A Psychospiritual Model of Spiritual Formation: A Review of David Benner's Contribution." *Christian Education Journal* 3, no. 2 (2006) 230–39.

Hughes, Dewi A., and Jamie A. Grant, eds. *Transforming the World? The Gospel and Social Responsibility.* Leicester, UK: IVP, 2009.

Hughes, Philip E. *The True Image: The Origin and Destiny of Man in Christ.* Grand Rapids, MI: Eerdmans, 1989.

Hull, Bill. *Christlike: The Pursuit of Uncomplicated Obedience.* Colorado Springs, CO: Navpress, 2010.

———. *The Complete Book of Discipleship: On Being and Making Followers of Christ.* Colorado Springs, CO: Navpress, 2006.

———. *Conversion and Discipleship.* Grand Rapids, MI: Zondervan, 2016.

Humphrey, Edith M. "The Gifts of J. I. Packer: A Cool Head, a Warm Heart, and the Great Tradition." In *J. I. Packer and the Evangelical Future: The Impact of His Life and Thought*, edited by Timothy George, 29–41. Grand Rapids, MI: Baker Academic, 2009.

Hunter, James D. *To Change the World: The Irony, Tragedy, and Possibility of Christianity in the Late Modern World.* Oxford, UK: Oxford University Press, 2010.

Hutchinson, Mark, and John Wolffe. *A Short History of Global Evangelicalism.* Cambridge, UK: Cambridge University Press, 2012.

Issler, Klaus D. "Approaching Formative Scripture Reading with Both Head and Heart." *Journal of Spiritual Formation & Soul Care* 5, no. 1 (2012) 117–34.

———. "Inner Core Belief Formation, Spiritual Practices, and the Willing-Doing Gap." *Journal of Spiritual Formation & Soul Care* 2, no. 2 (2009) 179–98.

Jankowiak, Marek, and Phil Booth. "A New Date-List of the Works of Maximus the Confessor." In *The Oxford Handbook of Maximus the Confessor*, edited by Pauline Allen and Bronwen Neil, 19–83. Oxford, UK: Oxford University Press, 2015.

Jensen, L. Paul. *Subversive Spirituality: Transforming Mission through the Collapse of Space and Time.* Eugene, OR: Pickwick, 2009.

Jensen, Peter. *The Revelation of God.* Leicester, UK: IVP Academic, 2002.

Johnson, Andy. *Holiness and the Missio Dei.* Eugene, OR: Cascade, 2016.

Johnson, Keith L. *Theology as Discipleship.* Downers Grove, IL: IVP Academic, 2015.

Johnson, Marcus P. *One with Christ: An Evangelical Theology of Salvation.* Wheaton, IL: Crossway, 2013.

Jones, Beth F. *Practicing Christian Doctrine: An Introduction to Thinking and Living Theologically.* Grand Rapids, MI: Baker Academic, 2014.

Jones, Mark. *Antinomianism.* Phillipsburg, NJ: P&R, 2013.

Jowers, Dennis W., and H. Wayne House, eds. *The New Evangelical Subordinationism?: Perspectives on the Equality of God the Father and God the Son.* Eugene, OR: Wipf & Stock, 2012.

Kapic, Kelly M. "Evangelical Holiness: Assumptions in John Owen's Theology of Christian Spirituality." In *Life in the Spirit: Spiritual Formation in Theological Perspective*, edited by Jeffrey P. Greenman and George Kalantzis, 97–114. Downers Grove, IL: IVP Academic, 2010.

———, ed. *Sanctification: Explorations in Theology and Practice.* Downers Grove, IL: IVP Academic, 2014.

———. "Systematic Theology and Spiritual Formation: Encouraging Faithful Participation Among God's People." *Journal of Spiritual Formation & Soul Care* 7, no. 2 (2014) 191–202.

Kay, Brian K. *Trinitarian Spirituality: John Owen and the Doctrine of God in Western Devotion*. Milton Keynes, UK: Paternoster, 2008.

Keener, Craig S. *The Mind of the Spirit: Paul's Approach to Transformed Thinking*. Grand Rapids, MI: Baker Academic, 2016.

Keller, Timothy. *Prayer: Experiencing Awe and Intimacy with God*. London: Hodder & Stoughton, 2014.

Kellerman, Robert W. *Gospel-Centered Counseling: How Christ Changes Lives*. Grand Rapids, MI: Zondervan, 2014.

Kilner, John F. *Dignity and Destiny: Humanity in the Image of God*. Grand Rapids, MI: Eerdmans, 2015.

Krapohl, Robert H., and Charles H. Lippy. *The Evangelicals: A Historical, Thematic, and Biographical Guide*. Westport, CT: Greenwood Publishing Group, 1999.

Lane, Timothy S., and Paul D. Tripp. *How People Change*. Greensboro, NC: New Growth, 2008.

Langer, Rick. "Points of Unease with the Spiritual Formation Movement." *Journal of Spiritual Formation & Soul Care* 5, no. 2 (2012) 182–206.

Larchet, Jean-Claude. "The Mode of Deification." In *The Oxford Handbook of Maximus the Confessor*, edited by Pauline Allen and Bronwen Neil, 341–59. Oxford, UK: Oxford University Press, 2015.

Larsen, Timothy. "Defining and Locating Evangelicalism." In *The Cambridge Companion to Evangelical Theology*, edited by Timothy Larsen and Daniel J. Treier, 1–14. Cambridge, UK: Cambridge University Press, 2007.

Leith, John H. *John Calvin's Doctrine of the Christian Life*. Eugene, OR: Wipf & Stock, 2010.

Leithart, Peter J. *Traces of the Trinity: Signs of God in Creation and Human Experience*. Grand Rapids, MI: Brazos, 2015.

Lesniak, Valerie. "Contemporary Spirituality." In *The New SCM Dictionary of Christian Spirituality*, edited by Philip Sheldrake, 7–12. London: SCM, 2005.

Letham, Robert. *Union with Christ: In Scripture, History, and Theology*. Phillipsburg, NJ: P&R, 2011.

Lewis, Gordon R. "Is Propositional Revelation Essential to Evangelical Spiritual Formation?" *Journal of the Evangelical Theological Society* 46, no. 2 (2003) 269–98.

Lints, Richard. *The Fabric of Theology: A Prolegomenon to Evangelical Theology*. Eugene, OR: Wipf & Stock, 1993.

———. *Identity and Idolatry: The Image of God and Its Inversion*. Downers Grove, IL: IVP Academic, 2015.

Little, Christopher. "What Makes Mission Christian?" *International Journal of Frontier Missiology* 25, no. 2 (2008) 65–73.

Lloyd-Jones, David M. *What Is an Evangelical?* Edinburgh: Banner of Truth, 1992.

Lollar, Joshua. "Reception of Maximian Thought in the Modern Era." In *The Oxford Handbook of Maximus the Confessor*, edited by Pauline Allen and Bronwen Neil, 564–80. Oxford, UK: Oxford University Press, 2015.

Louth, Andrew, ed. *Maximus the Confessor*. London: Routledge, 1996.

———. "Recent Research on St Maximus the Confessor: A Survey." *St Vladimir's Theological Quarterly* 42, no. 1 (1998) 67–84.

Lovelace, Richard F. *Dynamics of Spiritual Life: An Evangelical Theology of Renewal.* Downers Grove, IL: IVP Academic, 1979.

———. "Evangelicalism: Recovering a Tradition of Spiritual Depth." *The Reformed Journal* 40 (1990) 20–25.

———. "Evangelical Spirituality: A Church Historian's Perspective." *Journal of the Evangelical Theological Society* 31, no. 1 (1988) 25–35.

———. *Renewal as a Way of Life: A Guidebook for Spiritual Growth.* Downers Grove, IL: IVP, 1985.

———. "The Sanctification Gap." *Theology Today* 29, no. 4 (1973) 363–69.

Maas, Robin, and Gabriel O'Donnell, eds. *Spiritual Traditions for the Contemporary Church.* Nashville, TN: Abingdon, 1990.

MacArthur, John, and Richard L. Mayhue. *Biblical Doctrine: A Systematic Summary of Bible Truth.* Wheaton, IL: Crossway, 2017.

Macaskill, Grant. *Union with Christ in the New Testament.* Oxford, UK: Oxford University Press, 2013.

Macchia, Stephen A. *Becoming a Healthy Disciple.* Grand Rapids, MI: Baker, 2004.

Marshall, Walter. *The Gospel Mystery of Sanctification: Growing in Holiness by Living in Union with Christ.* Eugene, OR: Wipf & Stock, 2005.

Mathis, David. *Habits of Grace: Enjoying Jesus through the Spiritual Disciplines.* Wheaton, IL: Crossway, 2016.

Mathison, Keith A. *The Shape of Sola Scriptura.* Moscow, ID: Canon Press, 2001.

Mayhue, Richard L. "Sanctification: The Biblical Basics." *The Master's Seminary Journal* 21, no. 2 (2010) 143–57.

McClendon, P. Adam. "Defining the Role of the Bible in Spirituality: 'Three Degrees of Spirituality' in American Culture." *Journal of Spiritual Formation & Soul Care* 5, no. 2 (2012) 207–25.

———. *Paul's Spirituality in Galatians: A Critique of Contemporary Christian Spiritualities.* Eugene, OR: Wipf & Stock, 2015.

McDermott, Gerald R. *Seeing God: Twelve Reliable Signs of True Spirituality.* Downers Grove, IL: IVP, 1995.

McDonald, Larry S. *The Merging of Theology and Spirituality: An Examination of the Life and Work of Alister E. McGrath.* Lanham, MD: University Press of America, 2006.

McGrath, Alister E. *Christian Spirituality: An Introduction.* Oxford, UK: Wiley-Blackwell, 1999.

———. "Engaging the Great Tradition: Evangelical Theology and the Role of Tradition." In *Evangelical Futures: A Conversation on Theological Method*, edited by John G. Stackhouse, 139–58. Leicester, UK: IVP, 2000.

———. *Evangelicalism and the Future of Christianity.* London: Hodder & Stoughton, 1994.

———. "Evangelical Theological Method: The State of the Art." In *Evangelical Futures: A Conversation on Theological Method*, edited by John G. Stackhouse, 15–37. Leicester, UK: IVP, 2000.

———. "The Great Tradition: J. I. Packer on Engaging with the Past to Enrich the Present." In *J. I. Packer and the Evangelical Future: The Impact of His Life and Thought*, edited by Timothy George, 19–27. Grand Rapids, MI: Baker Academic, 2009.

———. "The Importance of Tradition for Modern Evangelicalism." In *Doing Theology for the People of God: Studies in Honour of J. I. Packer*, edited by Alister E. McGrath and Donald Lewis, 159–73. Downers Grove, IL: Apollos, 1996.

———. "Loving God with Heart and Mind: The Theological Foundations of Spirituality." In *For All the Saints: Evangelical Theology and Christian Spirituality*, edited by Timothy George and Alister E. McGrath, 11–26. Louisville, KY: WJK, 2003.

———. *A Passion for Truth: The Intellectual Coherence of Evangelicalism*. Leicester, UK: Apollos, 1996.

———. *Roots That Refresh: A Celebration of Reformation Spirituality*. London: Hodder & Stoughton, 1991.

———. *To Know and Serve God: A Biography of James I. Packer*. London: Hodder & Stoughton, 1998.

McGrath, Alister E., and Donald Lewis, eds. *Doing Theology for the People of God: Studies in Honour of J. I. Packer*. Downers Grove, IL: Apollos, 1996.

McGuinness, Julia. *Growing Spiritually with the Myers-Briggs Model*. London: SPCK, 2009.

McIntosh, Mark A. *Mystical Theology: The Integrity of Spirituality and Theology*. Malden, MA: Blackwell, 1998.

Meadors, Edward P. *Idolatry and the Hardening of the Heart: A Study in Biblical Theology*. London: T&T Clark, 2007.

Meek, Esther L. *Loving to Know: Introducing Covenant Epistemology*. Eugene, OR: Cascade, 2011.

Merrick, James, and Stephen M. Garrett, eds. *Five Views on Biblical Inerrancy*. Grand Rapids, MI: Zondervan, 2013.

Middleton, J. Richard. *A New Heaven and a New Earth: Reclaiming Biblical Eschatology*. Grand Rapids, MI: Baker Academic, 2014.

Mohler, R. Albert. "Confessional Evangelicalism." In *Four Views on the Spectrum of Evangelicalism*, edited by Andrew D. Naselli and Colin Hansen, 68–96. Grand Rapids, MI: Zondervan, 2011.

———. "'Evangelical': What's in a Name?" In *The Coming Evangelical Crisis: Current Challenges to the Authority of Scripture and the Gospel*, edited by John H. Armstrong, 29–44. Chicago, IL: Moody, 1996.

———. "What Is Truth? Truth and Contemporary Culture." *Journal of the Evangelical Theological Society* 48, no. 1 (2005) 63–75.

Morgan, Christopher W., and Robert A. Peterson, eds. *Fallen: A Theology of Sin*. Wheaton, IL: Crossway, 2013.

———, eds. *The Glory of God*. Wheaton, IL: Crossway, 2010.

Morrow, Jonathan. "Introducing Spiritual Formation." In *Foundations of Spiritual Formation: A Community Approach to Becoming Like Christ*, edited by Paul Pettit, 31–50. Grand Rapids, MI: Kregel, 2008.

Mulholland, M. Robert. *Invitation to a Journey: A Road Map for Spiritual Formation*. Downers Grove, IL: IVP, 1993.

———. *Shaped by the Word: The Power of Scripture in Spiritual Formation*. 2nd ed. Nashville, TN: Upper Room, 2000.

———. "Spirituality and Transformation." In *Dictionary of Christian Spirituality*, edited by Glen G. Scorgie, 216–21. Grand Rapids, MI: Zondervan, 2011.

Murphy, Debra D. *Teaching That Transforms: Worship as the Heart of Christian Education*. Grand Rapids, MI: Brazos, 2004.

Murray, Iain H. *Evangelicalism Divided: A Record of Crucial Change in the Years 1950 to 2000*. Edinburgh: Banner of Truth, 2000.

Murray, John. *Redemption Accomplished and Applied*. Grand Rapids, MI: Eerdmans, 1989.

Muto, Susan. "The Unfolding Project: Science, Anthropology, and the Theology of Human and Christian Formation." *Journal of Spiritual Formation & Soul Care* 4, no. 1 (2011) 93–104.

Myers, Bryant, L. *Walking with the Poor: Principles and Practices of Transformational Development*. 2nd ed. Maryknoll, NY: Orbis, 2011.

Naselli, Andrew D., and Colin Hansen, eds. *Four Views on the Spectrum of Evangelicalism*. Grand Rapids, MI: Zondervan, 2011.

Nassif, Bradley. "An Eastern Orthodox Response to J. I. Packer." In *Reclaiming the Great Tradition: Evangelicals, Catholics & Orthodox in Dialogue*, edited by James S. Cutsinger, 176–84. Downers Grove, IL: IVP Academic, 1997.

Neff, David. "Pumping Truth: J. I. Packer's Journalism, Theology, and the Thirst for Truth." In *J. I. Packer and the Evangelical Future: The Impact of His Life and Thought*, edited by Timothy George, 43–54. Grand Rapids, MI: Baker Academic, 2009.

Nelson, Peter K. *Spiritual Formation: Ever Forming, Never Formed*. Colorado Springs, CO: Biblica, 2010.

Newton, Gary C. *Growing Towards Spiritual Maturity*. Wheaton, IL: Crossway, 2004.

———. *Heart-Deep Teaching: Engaging Students for Transformed Lives*. Nashville, TN: B&H, 2012.

Ngien, Dennis. *Gifted Response: The Triune God as the Causative Agency of Our Responsive Worship*. Milton Keynes, UK: Paternoster, 2008.

Nichols, Aiden. *Byzantine Gospel: Maximus the Confessor in Modern Scholarship*. Edinburgh: T&T Clark, 1993.

Noll, Mark A. "Defining Evangelicalism." In *Global Evangelicalism: Theology, History & Culture in Regional Perspective*, edited by Donald M. Lewis and Richard V. Pierard, 17–37. Downers Grove, IL: IVP Academic, 2014.

———. "What Is 'Evangelical'?" In *The Oxford Handbook of Evangelical Theology*, edited by Gerald R. McDermott, 19–32. Oxford, UK: Oxford University Press, 2010.

Nugent, John C. *Endangered Gospel: How Fixing the World Is Killing the Church*. Eugene, OR: Cascade, 2016.

Oden, Patrick. *The Transformative Church: New Ecclesial Models and the Theology of Jürgen Moltmann*. Minneapolis, MN: Fortress, 2015.

Olsen, Stephen E. "Evangelical Perspectives on Spirituality." *European Journal of Theology* 19, no. 1 (2010) 5–6.

Olson, Roger E. *The Mosaic of Christian Belief: Twenty Centuries of Unity & Diversity*. Downers Grove, IL: IVP Academic, 2002.

———. *Reformed and Always Reforming: The Postconservative Approach to Evangelical Theology*. Grand Rapids, MI: Baker Academic, 2007.

———. "Reforming Evangelical Theology." In *Evangelical Futures: A Conversation on Theological Method*, edited by John G. Stackhouse, 201–07. Leicester, UK: IVP, 2000.

Owen, John. *Communion with the Triune God*. Wheaton, IL: Crossway, 2007.

———. *Overcoming Sin and Temptation*. Wheaton, IL: Crossway, 2015.
Packer, James I. *18 Words: The Most Important Words You Will Ever Know*. 2nd ed. Tain, UK: Christian Focus, 2007.
———. *Celebrating the Saving Work of God. The Collected Shorter Writings of J. I. Packer*. Vol. 1, Carlisle, UK: Paternoster, 1998.
———. "Chicago Statement on Biblical Hermeneutics." In *Summit II of the International Council on Biblical Inerrancy*. Chicago, IL, 1982.
———. "The Christian and God's World." In *Transforming Our World: A Call to Action*, edited by James M. Boice, 81–97. Portland, OR: Multnomah Pub., 1988.
———. "The Comfort of Conservatism." In *Power Religion: The Selling out of the Evangelical Church*, edited by Michael S. Horton, 283–99. Chicago, IL: Moody, 1992.
———. *Concise Theology: A Guide to Historic Christian Beliefs*. 2nd ed. Nottingham, UK: IVP, 2011.
———. *Evangelism and the Sovereignty of God*. Downers Grove, IL: IVP, 2008.
———. "Faith." In *Evangelical Dictionary of Theology*, edited by Walter A. Elwell, 431–34. Grand Rapids, MI: Baker Academic, 2001.
———. *Faithfulness and Holiness: The Witness of J.C. Ryle*. Wheaton, IL: Crossway, 2011.
———. *For Man's Sake*. Exeter, UK: Paternoster, 1978.
———. *Freedom & Authority*. 2nd ed. Vancouver, BC: Regent College Publishing, 2003.
———. *Fundamentalism and the Word of God*. 2nd ed. Leicester, UK: IVP, 1996.
———. "God." In *New Dictionary of Theology*, edited by Sinclair B. Ferguson and David F. Wright, 274–77. Leicester, UK: IVP Academic, 1988.
———. *God Has Spoken*. 5th ed. London: Hodder & Stoughton, 2005.
———. "Godliness." In *New Dictionary of Christian Ethics & Pastoral Theology*, edited by David J. Atkinson and David H. Field, 410–11. Leicester, UK: IVP Academic, 1995.
———. *God's Plans for You*. Wheaton, IL: Crossway, 2001.
———. "God the Image-Maker." In *Christian Faith & Practice in the Modern World: Theology from an Evangelical Point of View*, edited by Mark A. Noll and David F. Wells, 27–50. Grand Rapids, MI: Eerdmans, 1988.
———. *Growing in Christ*. Wheaton, IL: Crossway, 1994.
———. "J. I. Packer." In *My Path of Prayer: Personal Experiences of God*, edited by David Hanes, 55–65. Worthing, UK: Walter, 1981.
———. *Keep in Step with the Spirit: Finding Fullness in Our Walk with God*. 2nd ed. Grand Rapids, MI: Baker, 2005.
———. *Knowing God*. 3rd ed. London: Hodder & Stoughton, 2004.
———. "Holy Spirit." In *New Dictionary of Christian Ethics & Pastoral Theology*, edited by David J. Atkinson and David H. Field, 445–48. Leicester, UK: IVP Academic, 1995.
———. *Honouring the People of God. The Collected Shorter Writings of J. I. Packer*. Vol. 4, Carlisle, UK: Paternoster, 1998.
———. *Honouring the Written Word of God. The Collected Shorter Writings of J. I. Packer*. Vol. 3, Carlisle, UK: Paternoster, 1998.
———. "Justification." In *Evangelical Dictionary of Theology*, edited by Walter A. Elwell, 643–47. Grand Rapids, MI: Baker Academic, 2001.

———. *Knowing Christianity*. Downers Grove, IL: IVP, 1995.

———. "Maintaining Evangelical Theology." In *Evangelical Futures: A Conversation on Theological Method*, edited by John G. Stackhouse, 181–89. Leicester, UK: IVP, 2000.

———. *Meeting God*. 2nd ed. Bletchley, UK: Scripture Union, 2006.

———. "Method, Theological." In *New Dictionary of Theology*, edited by Sinclair B. Ferguson and David F. Wright, 424–26. Leicester, UK: IVP Academic, 1988.

———. "On from Orr: Cultural Crisis, Rational Realism and Incarnational Ontology." In *Reclaiming the Great Tradition: Evangelicals, Catholics & Orthodox in Dialogue*, edited by James S. Cutsinger, 155–76. Downers Grove, IL: IVP Academic, 1997.

———. "Orthodoxy." In *Evangelical Dictionary of Theology*, edited by Walter A. Elwell, 875. Grand Rapids, MI: Baker Academic, 2001.

———. "Paradox in Theology." In *New Dictionary of Theology*, edited by Sinclair B. Ferguson and David F. Wright, 491–92. Leicester, UK: IVP Academic, 1988.

———. *A Quest for Godliness: The Puritan Vision of the Christian Life*. 2nd ed. Wheaton, IL: Crossway, 1994.

———. "Scripture." In *New Dictionary of Theology*, edited by Sinclair B. Ferguson and David F. Wright, 627–31. Leicester, UK: IVP Academic, 1988.

———. *Truth & Power: The Place of Scripture in the Christian Life*. Downers Grove, IL: IVP, 1996.

———. *Rediscovering Holiness: Know the Fullness of Life with God*. 2nd ed. Ventura, CA: Regal, 2009.

———. "Reflection and Response." In *J. I. Packer and the Evangelical Future: The Impact of His Life and Thought*, edited by Timothy George, 171–85. Grand Rapids, MI: Baker Academic, 2009.

———. "Revelation." In *New Dictionary of Christian Apologetics*, edited by W. C. Campbell-Jack and Gavin J. McGrath, 619–23. Leicester, UK: IVP Academic, 2006.

———. *Serving the People of God*. The Collected Shorter Writings of J. I. Packer. Vol. 2, Carlisle, UK: Paternoster, 1998.

———. "A Stunted Ecclesiology?" In *Ancient and Postmodern Christianity: Paleo-Orthodoxy in the 21st Century*, edited by Kenneth Tanner and Christopher A. Hall, 120–27. Downers Grove, IL: IVP Academic, 2002.

———. *Under God's Word*. London: Lakeland, 1980.

———. "The Uniqueness of Jesus Christ: Some Evangelical Reflections." *Churchman* 92, no. 2 (1978) 101–11.

Packer, James I., and Thomas Howard. *Christianity: The True Humanism*. Vancouver, BC: Regent College Publishing, 1999.

Packer, James I., and Carolyn Nystrom. *God's Will: Finding Guidance for Everyday Decisions*. Grand Rapids, MI: Baker, 2008.

———. *Praying: Finding Our Way through Duty to Delight*. Downers Grove, IL: IVP, 2006.

Packer, James I., and Thomas C. Oden. *One Faith: The Evangelical Consensus*. Downers Grove, IL: IVP, 2004.

Packer, James I., and Gary A. Parrett. *Grounded in the Gospel: Building Believers the Old-Fashioned Way*. Grand Rapids, MI: Baker, 2010.

Palmer, G. E. H., Philip Sherrard, and Kallistos Ware, eds. *The Philokalia: The Complete Text* Vol. 2. London: Faber and Faber, 1990.

Parker, David. "Evangelical Spirituality Reviewed." *The Evangelical Quarterly* 63, no. 2 (1991) 123–48.

———. "Review of Evangelical Experiences: A Study in the Spirituality of English Evangelicalism 1918–1939." *Evangelical Review of Theology* 28, no. 4 (2004) 375–76.

Payne, Don J. "J. I. Packer's Theological Method." In *J. I. Packer and the Evangelical Future: The Impact of His Life and Thought*, edited by Timothy George, 55–68. Grand Rapids, MI: Baker Academic, 2009.

———. "Theological Anthropology and the Formation of Piety: A Study in James I. Packer." Ph.D. diss., University of Manchester, 2003.

———. *The Theology of the Christian Life in J. I. Packer's Thought: Theological Anthropology, Theological Method, and the Doctrine of Sanctification.* Milton Keynes, UK: Paternoster, 2006.

Peppiatt, Lucy. *The Disciple: On Becoming Truly Human.* Eugene, OR: Cascade, 2012.

Perrin, David B. *Studying Christian Spirituality.* New York: Routledge, 2007.

Peters, Greg. "Historical Theology and Spiritual Formation: A Call." *Journal of Spiritual Formation & Soul Care* 7, no. 2 (2014) 203–09.

———. "On Spiritual Theology: A Primer." *Journal of Spiritual Formation & Soul Care* 4, no. 1 (2011) 5–26.

Peterson, David G. *Encountering God Together: Biblical Patterns for Ministry and Worship.* Nottingham, UK: IVP, 2013.

———. *Engaging with God: A Biblical Theology of Worship.* Downers Grove, IL: IVP Academic, 1992.

———. *Possessed by God: A New Testament Theology of Sanctification and Holiness.* Downers Grove, IL: IVP Academic, 1995.

Peterson, Eugene H. *A Long Obedience in the Same Direction: Discipleship in an Instant Society.* 2nd ed. Downers Grove, IL: IVP, 2000.

Peterson, Robert A. *Salvation Accomplished by the Son: The Work of Christ.* Wheaton, IL: Crossway, 2012.

———. *Salvation Applied by the Spirit: Union with Christ.* Wheaton, IL: Crossway, 2014.

Piper, John. *Desiring God: Meditations of a Christian Hedonist.* Colorado Springs, CO: Multnomah, 2011.

———. *Future Grace: The Purifying Power of the Promises of God.* Colorado Springs, CO: Multnomah, 2012.

———. *A Peculiar Glory: How the Christian Scriptures Reveal Their Complete Truthfulness.* Wheaton, IL: Crossway, 2016.

———. *Reading the Bible Supernaturally: Seeing and Savoring the Glory of God in Scripture.* Wheaton, IL: Crossway, 2017.

Piper, John, and David Mathis, eds. *Acting the Miracle: God's Work and Ours in the Mystery of Sanctification.* Wheaton, IL: Crossway, 2013.

Plantinga, Cornelius. *Engaging God's World: A Christian Vision of Faith, Learning, and Living.* Grand Rapids, MI: Eerdmans, 2002.

———. *Not the Way It's Supposed to Be: A Breviary of Sin.* Grand Rapids, MI: Eerdmans, 1996.

Plummer, Robert L. "Are the Spiritual Disciplines of Silence and Solitude Really Biblical?" *Southern Baptist Journal of Theology* 10, no. 4 (2006) 4–12.

Porter, Steve L. "The Gradual Nature of Sanctification: Σάρξ as Habituated, Relational Resistance to the Spirit." *Themelios* 39, no. 3 (2014) 470–83.
———. "Is the Spiritual Formation Movement Dead?" *Journal of Spiritual Formation & Soul Care* 8, no. 1 (2015) 2–7.
———. "On the Renewal of Interest in the Doctrine of Sanctification: A Methodological Reminder." *Journal of the Evangelical Theological Society* 45, no. 3 (2002) 415–26.
———. "Philosophy and Spiritual Formation: A Call to Philosophy and Spiritual Formation." *Journal of Spiritual Formation & Soul Care* 7, no. 2 (2014) 248–57.
———. "Sanctification in a New Key: Relieving Evangelical Anxieties over Spiritual Formation." *Journal of Spiritual Formation & Soul Care* 1, no. 2 (2008) 129–48.
———. "Spiritual Formation in the Academy and the Church: A State of the Union." *Journal of Spiritual Formation & Soul Care* 7, no. 2 (2014) 175–76.
———. "The Willardian Corpus." *Journal of Spiritual Formation & Soul Care* 3, no. 2 (2010) 239–66.
Porter, Steve L., Gary Moon, and J. P. Moreland, eds. *Until Christ Is Formed in You: Dallas Willard and Spiritual Formation*. Abilene, TX: ACU, 2018.
Powlison, David. *How Does Sanctification Work?* Wheaton, IL: Crossway, 2017.
Poythress, Vern. *In the Beginning Was the Word: Language—a God-Centered Approach*. Wheaton, IL: Crossway, 2009.
Prassas, Despina D., ed. *St Maximus the Confessor's Questions and Doubts*. DeKalb, IL: Northern Illinois University Press, 2010.
Prior, Kenneth. *The Way of Holiness: A Study in Christian Growth*. 3rd ed. Tain, UK: Christian Focus, 1994.
Quicke, Michael J. *Preaching as Worship: An Integrative Approach to Formation in Your Church*. Grand Rapids, MI: Baker, 2011.
Ramey Jr, Robert H., and Ben Campbell Johnson. *Living the Christian Life: A Guide to Reformed Spirituality*. Louisville, KY: WJK, 1992.
Randall, Ian M. *Evangelical Experiences: A Study in the Spirituality of English Evangelicalism 1918–1939*. Milton Keynes, UK: Paternoster, 1999.
———. "Evangelical Spirituality." In *The New SCM Dictionary of Christian Spirituality*, edited by Philip Sheldrake, 289–91. London: SCM, 2005.
———. "Recovering Evangelical Spirituality." *European Journal of Theology* 19, no. 1 (2010) 33–44.
———. "'Take My Life': Evangelical Spirituality and Evangelical Identity." In *British Evangelical Identities Past and Present: Volume 1*, edited by Mark Smith, 215–37. Eugene, OR: Wipf & Stock, 2008.
———. *What a Friend We Have in Jesus: The Evangelical Tradition*. London: DLT, 2005.
Rankin, Stephen W. *Aiming at Maturity: The Goal of the Christian Life*. Eugene, OR: Cascade, 2011.
Reeves, Rodney. *Spirituality According to Paul: Imitating the Apostle of Christ*. Downers Grove, IL: IVP Academic, 2011.
Rice, Howard L. *Reformed Spirituality: An Introduction for Believers*. Louisville, KY: WJK, 1991.
Rickabaugh, Brandon L. "Eternal Life as Knowledge of God: An Epistemology of Knowledge by Acquaintance and Spiritual Formation." *Journal of Spiritual Formation & Soul Care* 6, no. 2 (2013) 204–28.
Ridgely, Susan B. "Connected Christians: New Practices in Evangelical Spirituality." *Spiritus: A Journal of Christian Spirituality* 14, no. 1 (2014) 84–93.

Rognlien, Bob. *Experiential Worship: Encountering God with Heart, Soul, Mind, and Strength.* Colorado Springs, CO: Navpress, 2005.

Roxburgh, Kenneth B. E. "Spirituality for the Twenty-First Century." *Scottish Bulletin of Evangelical Theology* 17, no. 2 (1999) 129–44.

Rybarczyk, Edmund J. *Beyond Salvation: Eastern Orthodoxy and Classical Pentecostalism on Becoming Like Christ.* Carlisle, UK: Paternoster, 2004.

Ryken, Leland. *J. I. Packer: An Evangelical Life.* Wheaton, IL: Crossway, 2015.

Sager, Allan H. *Gospel-Centered Spirituality.* Minneapolis, MN: Augsburg Fortress, 1990.

Samra, James G. *Being Conformed to Christ in Community: A Study of Maturity, Maturation, and the Local Church in the Undisputed Pauline Epistles.* London: T&T Clark, 2006.

Samuel, Vinay, and Chris Sugden, eds. *The Church in Response to Human Need.* Eugene, OR: Wipf & Stock, 2003.

———, eds. *Mission as Transformation: A Theology of the Whole Gospel.* Eugene, OR: Wipf & Stock, 2009.

Saucy, Robert. *Minding the Heart: The Way of Spiritual Transformation.* Grand Rapids, MI: Kregel, 2013.

Schmemann, Alexander. *For the Life of the World: Sacraments and Orthodoxy.* 2nd ed. Crestwood, NY: St Vladimir's Seminary Press, 2000.

Schneiders, Sandra M. "Christian Spirituality: Definition, Methods, and Types." In *The New SCM Dictionary of Christian Spirituality,* edited by Philip Sheldrake, 1–6. London: SCM, 2005.

Schreiner, Thomas R. *Faith Alone: The Doctrine of Justification.* Grand Rapids, MI: Zondervan, 2015.

———. *The King in His Beauty: A Biblical Theology of the Old and New Testaments.* Grand Rapids, MI: Baker Academic, 2013.

———. *New Testament Theology: Magnifying God in Christ.* Nottingham, UK: Apollos, 2008.

Schwanda, Tom., ed. *The Emergence of Evangelical Spirituality: The Age of Edwards, Newton, and Whitefield.* Mahwah, NJ: Paulist, 2016.

———. "Evangelical Spiritual Disciplines: Practices for Knowing God." *Journal of Spiritual Formation & Soul Care* 10, no. 2 (2017) 220–36.

———. *Soul Recreation: The Contemplative-Mystical Piety of Puritanism.* Eugene, OR: Pickwick, 2012.

———. "'To Gaze on the Beauty of the Lord': The Evangelical Resistance and Retrieval of Contemplation." *Journal of Spiritual Formation & Soul Care* 7, no. 1 (2014) 62–84.

Scorgie, Glen G., ed. *Dictionary of Christian Spirituality.* Grand Rapids, MI: Zondervan, 2011.

———. "Overview of Christian Spirituality." In *Dictionary of Christian Spirituality,* edited by Glen G. Scorgie, 27–33. Grand Rapids, MI: Zondervan, 2011.

———. "True Spirituality: The on-Going Evangelical Quest." In *The 56th Annual Meeting of the Evangelical Theological Society.* San Antonio, TX, 2004.

Seamands, Stephen. *Ministry in the Image of God: The Trinitarian Shape of Christian Service.* Downers Grove, IL: IVP, 2005.

Seddon, Philip. *Gospel and Sacrament: Reclaiming a Holistic Evangelical Spirituality.* Cambridge, UK: Grove, 2004.

Senn, Frank C., ed. *Protestant Spiritual Traditions*. Eugene, OR: Wipf & Stock, 2000.
Sheldrake, Philip. "Christian Spirituality as a Way of Living Publicly: A Dialectic of the Mystical and Prophetic." *Spiritus: A Journal of Christian Spirituality* 3, no. 1 (2003) 19–37.
———, ed. *The New SCM Dictionary of Christian Spirituality*. London: SCM, 2005.
———. *Spirituality: A Brief History*. 2nd ed. Chichester, UK: Wiley-Blackwell, 2013.
———. *Spirituality and Theology: Christian Living and the Doctrine of God*. London: DLT, 1998.
———. *Spirituality: A Very Short Introduction*. Oxford, UK: Oxford University Press, 2012.
———. *Spirituality: A Guide for the Perplexed*. London: Continuum 2014.
Sherman, Steven B. *Revitalizing Theological Epistemology: Holistic Evangelical Approaches to the Knowledge of God*. Eugene, OR: Pickwick, 2008.
Sherwood, Polycarp, ed. *St Maximus the Confessor: The Ascetic Life, the Four Centuries on Charity*. New York: Newman, 1955.
Smith, Christian. *The Bible Made Impossible: Why Biblicism Is Not a Truly Evangelical Reading of Scripture*. Grand Rapids, MI: Brazos, 2011.
Smith, David W. *Transforming the World? The Social Impact of British Evangelicalism*. Carlisle, UK: Paternoster, 1998.
Smith, Gordon T. *Called to Be Saints: An Invitation to Christian Maturity*. Downers Grove, IL: IVP Academic, 2014.
———. *Evangelical, Sacramental & Pentecostal: Why the Church Should Be All Three*. Downers Grove, IL: IVP, 2016.
Smith, James K. A. *Desiring the Kingdom: Worship, Worldview, and Cultural Formation*. Grand Rapids, MI: Baker Academic, 2009.
———. *Imagining the Kingdom: How Worship Works*. Grand Rapids, MI: Baker Academic, 2013.
———. *You Are What You Love: The Spiritual Power of Habit*. Grand Rapids, MI: Brazos, 2016.
Smith, Timothy. "The Evangelical Kaleidoscope and the Call to Christian Unity." *Christian Scholars Review* 15 (1986) 125–40.
Sproul, Robert C. *Getting the Gospel Right: The Tie That Binds Evangelicals Together*. Grand Rapids, MI: Baker, 2003.
———. *Pleasing God: Discovering the Meaning and Importance of Sanctification*. Colorado Springs, CO: David C. Cook, 2012.
Stackhouse, John G. "Evangelical Theology Should Be Evangelical." In *Evangelical Futures: A Conversation on Theological Method*, edited by John G. Stackhouse, 39–58. Leicester, UK: IVP, 2000.
Stamoolis, James, ed. *Three Views on Eastern Orthodoxy and Evangelicalism*. Grand Rapids, MI: Zondervan, 2004.
Stanley, Brian. *The Global Diffusion of Evangelicalism: The Age of Billy Graham and John Stott*. Downers Grove, IL: IVP Academic, 2013.
Stellman, Jason. *Dual Citizens: Worship and Life between the Already and the Not Yet*. Sanford, FL: Reformation Trust, 2009.
Stetzer, Ed, and Eric Geiger. *Transformational Groups: Creating a New Scorecard for Groups*. Nashville, TN: B&H, 2014.
Stetzer, Ed, and Thom S. Rainer. *Transformational Church: Creating a New Scorecard for Congregations*. Nashville, TN: B&H, 2010.

Stewart, Kenneth J. "Did Evangelicalism Predate the Eighteenth Century?: An Examination of David Bebbington's Thesis." *The Evangelical Quarterly* 77, no. 2 (2005) 135–53.

———. *In Search of Ancient Roots: The Christian Past and the Evangelical Identity Crisis.* Downers Grove, IL: IVP Academic, 2017.

Stiller, Brian C., Todd M. Johnson, Karen Stiller, and Mark Hutchinson, eds. *Evangelicals around the World: A Global Handbook for the 21st Century.* Nashville, TN: Thomas Nelson, 2015.

Storms, Sam. *Packer on the Christian Life: Knowing God in Christ, Walking by the Spirit.* Wheaton, IL: Crossway, 2015.

Stott, John. *Christ the Controversialist.* Leicester, UK: IVP, 1970.

———. *Evangelical Truth: A Personal Plea for Unity, Integrity, and Faithfulness.* Nottingham, UK: IVP Academic, 2005.

Strobel, Kyle C. *Formed for the Glory of God: Learning from the Spiritual Practices of Jonathan Edwards.* Downers Grove, IL: IVP, 2013.

———. "In Your Light They Shall See Light: A Theological Prolegomena for Contemplation." *Journal of Spiritual Formation & Soul Care* 7, no. 1 (2014) 85–106.

Sugden, Chris. "Transformational Development: Current State of Understanding and Practice." *Transformation* 20, no. 2 (2003) 71–77.

Sunquist, Scott W. *Understanding Christian Mission: Participation in Suffering and Glory.* Grand Rapids, MI: Baker Academic, 2013.

Tan, Siang-Yang, and Douglas H. Gregg. *Disciplines of the Holy Spirit: How to Connect to the Spirit's Power and Presence.* Grand Rapids, MI: Zondervan, 1997.

Tang, Alex. *Till We Are Fully Formed: Christian Spiritual Formation Paradigms in the English-Speaking Presbyterian Churches in Malaysia.* Singapore: Armour, 2014.

Taylor, Iain, ed. *Not Evangelical Enough: The Gospel at the Centre.* Milton Keynes, UK: Paternoster, 2003.

Thiselton, Anthony C. *Systematic Theology.* Grand Rapids, MI: Eerdmans, 2015.

Thomas, Gary L. *The Glorious Pursuit: Embracing the Virtues of Christ.* Colorado Springs, CO: Navpress, 1998.

———. *Sacred Pathways: Discover Your Soul's Path to God.* Grand Rapids, MI: Zondervan, 2010.

Thompson, James W. *The Church According to Paul: Rediscovering the Community Conformed to Christ.* Grand Rapids, MI: Baker Academic, 2014.

———. *Moral Formation According to Paul: The Context and Coherence of Pauline Ethics.* Grand Rapids, MI: Baker Academic, 2011.

Thompson, Mark D. *A Clear and Present Word: The Clarity of Scripture.* Downers Grove, IL: IVP Academic, 2006.

———. "The Generous Gift of a Gracious Father: Toward a Theological Account of the Clarity of Scripture." In *The Enduring Authority of the Christian Scriptures*, edited by Donald A. Carson, 615–43. Grand Rapids, MI: Eerdmans, 2016.

———. *Saving the Heart: What Is an Evangelical?* London: St Matthias, 1995.

Thompson, Marjorie J. *Soul Feast: An Invitation to the Christian Spiritual Life.* 2nd ed. Louisville, KY: WJK, 2005.

Thornhill, Anthony C. "The Resurrection of Jesus and Spiritual (Trans)Formation." *Journal of Spiritual Formation & Soul Care* 5, no. 2 (2012) 243–56.

Thunberg, Lars. *Man and the Cosmos: The Vision of St Maximus the Confessor.* Crestwood, NY: St Vladimir's Seminary Press, 1985.

———. *Microcosm and Mediator: The Theological Anthropology of Maximus the Confessor*. Chicago, IL: Open Court, 1995.

Tidball, Derek J. "The Bible in Evangelical Spirituality." In *The Bible in Pastoral Practice: Readings in the Place and Function of Scripture in the Church*, edited by Paul Ballard and Stephen R. Holmes, 258–74. Grand Rapids, MI: Eerdmans, 2005.

———. *Who Are the Evangelicals?: Tracing the Roots of Today's Movements*. London: Marshall Pickering, 1994.

Tiller, John. *Puritan, Pietist, and Pentecostalist: Three Types of Evangelical Spirituality*. Cambridge, UK: Grove, 1982.

Tisdale, Theresa C. "Psychology and Spiritual Formation: The State of the Union." *Journal of Spiritual Formation & Soul Care* 7, no. 2 (2014) 220–28.

Tizon, Al. *Transformation after Lausanne: Radical Evangelical Mission in Global-Local Perspective*. Eugene, OR: Wipf & Stock, 2008.

Tollefsen, Torstein T. "Christocentric Cosmology." In *The Oxford Handbook of Maximus the Confessor*, edited by Pauline Allen and Bronwen Neil, 307–21. Oxford, UK: Oxford University Press, 2015.

———. *The Christocentric Cosmology of St Maximus the Confessor*. Oxford, UK: Oxford University Press, 2008.

Tomlinson, Dave. *The Post-Evangelical*. Grand Rapids, MI: Zondervan, 2003.

Törönen, Melchisedec. *Union and Distinction in the Thought of St Maximus the Confessor*. Oxford, UK: Oxford University Press, 2007.

Torrance, Andrew B. *The Freedom to Become a Christian: A Kierkegaardian Account of Human Transformation in Relationship with God*. London: T&T Clark, 2016.

Tripp, Paul D. *Instruments in the Redeemer's Hands: People in Need of Change Helping People in Need of Change*. Phillipsburg, NJ: P&R, 2002.

Turnball, Richard. *A Passionate Faith: What Makes an Evangelical?* Oxford, UK: Monarch, 2012.

Twombly, Charles C. *Perichoresis and Personhood: God, Christ, and Salvation in John of Damascus*. Eugene, OR: Pickwick, 2015.

Van De Walle, Bernie A. *Rethinking Holiness: A Theological Introduction*. Grand Rapids, MI: Baker Academic, 2017.

Vander Lugt, Wesley. *Living Theodrama: Reimagining Theological Ethics*. Farnham, UK: Ashgate, 2014.

Vander Lugt, Wesley, and Trevor A. Hart, eds. *Theatrical Theology: Explorations in Performing the Faith*. Eugene, OR: Wipf & Stock, 2014.

VanDrunen, David. *God's Glory Alone: The Majestic Heart of Christian Faith and Life*. Grand Rapids, MI: Zondervan, 2016.

———. *Living in God's Two Kingdoms: A Biblical Vision for Christianity and Culture*. Wheaton, IL: Crossway, 2010.

Vanhoozer, Kevin J. "Augustinian Inerrancy: Literary Meaning, Literal Truth, and Literate Interpretation in the Economy of Biblical Discourse." In *Five Views on Biblical Inerrancy*, edited by James Merrick and Stephen M. Garrett, 199–235. Grand Rapids, MI: Zondervan, 2013.

———. "The Drama of Discipleship: A Vocation of Spiritual Formation." In *Pictures at a Biblical Exhibition: Theological Scenes of the Church's Worship, Witness, and Wisdom*, 180–99. Downers Grove, IL: IVP Academic, 2016.

———. *The Drama of Doctrine: A Canonical-Linguistic Approach to Christian Theology*. Louisville, KY: WJK, 2005.

———. "A Drama-of-Redemption Model." In *Four Views on Moving Beyond the Bible to Theology*, edited by Stanley N. Gundry and Edward P. Meadors, 151–99. Grand Rapids, MI: Zondervan, 2009.

———. *Faith Speaking Understanding: Performing the Drama of Doctrine*. Louisville, KY: WJK, 2014.

———. "Lost in Interpretation? Truth, Scripture and Hermeneutics." *Journal of the Evangelical Theological Society* 48, no. 1 (2005) 89–114.

———. "May We Go Beyond What Is Written after All? The Pattern of Theological Authority and the Problem of Doctrinal Development." In *The Enduring Authority of the Christian Scriptures*, edited by Donald A. Carson, 747–92. Grand Rapids, MI: Eerdmans, 2016.

———. "Putting on Christ: Spiritual Formation and the Drama of Discipleship." *Journal of Spiritual Formation & Soul Care* 8, no. 2 (2015) 147–71.

———. "Response to R. Albert Mohler Jr." In *Five Views on Biblical Inerrancy*, edited by James Merrick and Stephen M. Garrett, 71–76. Grand Rapids, MI: Zondervan, 2009.

———. "The Voice and the Actor: A Dramatic Proposal About the Ministry and Minstrelsy of Theology." In *Evangelical Futures: A Conversation on Theological Method*, edited by John G. Stackhouse, 61–106. Leicester, UK: IVP, 2000.

Vanhoozer, Kevin J., and Daniel J. Treier. *Theology and the Mirror of Scripture: A Mere Evangelical Account*. Downers Grove, IL: IVP Academic, 2015.

Vishnevskaya, Elena. "Divinization and Spiritual Progress in Maximus the Confessor." In *Theosis: Deification in Christian Theology*, edited by Stephen Finlan and Vladimir Kharlamov, 134–45. Eugene, OR: Pickwick, 2006.

———. "Divinization as Perichoretic Embrace in Maximus Confessor." In *Partakers of the Divine Nature: The History and Development of Deification in the Christian Tradition*, edited by Michael J. Christensen and Jeffery A. Wittung, 132–45. Grand Rapids, MI: Baker Academic, 2007.

Volf, Miroslav, and Dorothy C. Bass, eds. *Practicing Theology: Beliefs and Practices in Christian Life*. Grand Rapids, MI: Eerdmans 2001.

Vorster, Nico. *Created in the Image of God: Understanding God's Relationship with Humanity*. Eugene, OR: Pickwick, 2011.

Waaijman, Kees. "Conformity in Christ." *Acta Theologica Supplementum* 8 (2006) 41–53.

———. *Spirituality: Forms, Foundations, Methods*. Translated by John Vriend. Leuven, Belgium: Peeters, 2003.

———. "Transformation: A Key Word in Spirituality." *Studies in Spirituality* 8 (1998) 5–37.

Waggoner, Brad J. *The Shape of Faith to Come: Spiritual Formation and the Future of Discipleship*. Nashville, TN: B&H, 2008.

Walker, Andrew G., and Robin A. Parry. *Deep Church Rising: Recovering the Roots of Christian Orthodoxy*. London: SPCK, 2014.

Waltke, Bruce. "Evangelical Spirituality: A Biblical Scholar's Perspective." *Journal of the Evangelical Theological Society* 31, no. 1 (1988) 9–24.

Ward, Timothy. *Words of Life: Scripture as the Living and Active Word of God*. Nottingham, UK: IVP Academic, 2009.

Ware, Corinne. *Discover Your Spiritual Type: A Guide to Individual and Congregational Growth*. Herndon, VA: The Alban Institute, 1995.

Warner, Robert. *Reinventing English Evangelicalism, 1966–2001: A Theological and Sociological Study*. Eugene, OR: Wipf & Stock, 2007.

Watson, David. *Discipleship*. London: Hodder & Stoughton, 2014.

Wax, Trevin. *Eschatological Discipleship: Leading Christians to Understand Their Historical and Cultural Context*. Nashville, TN: B&H, 2018.

Webb-Mitchell, Brett P. *Christly Gestures: Learning to Be Members of the Body of Christ*. Grand Rapids, MI: Eerdmans, 2004.

Webber, Robert E. *Ancient-Future Faith: Rethinking Evangelicalism for a Postmodern World*. Grand Rapids, MI: Baker, 1999.

———. *Common Roots: The Original Call to an Ancient-Future Faith*. Grand Rapids, MI: Zondervan, 2009.

———. *The Divine Embrace: Recovering the Passionate Spiritual Life*. Grand Rapids, MI: Baker, 2006.

———. *Evangelicals on the Canterbury Trail: Why Evangelicals Are Attracted to the Liturgical Church*. New York: Morehouse, 2013.

———. *Worship Old and New*. 2nd ed. Grand Rapids, MI: Zondervan, 1994.

Webber, Robert E., and Donald G. Bloesch, eds. *The Orthodox Evangelicals*. Nashville, TN: Thomas Nelson, 1978.

Webster, John. *Holiness*. London: SCM, 2002.

Wellum, Stephen J. "Postconservatism, Biblical Authority, and Recent Proposals for Re-Doing Evangelical Theology: A Critical Analysis." In *Reclaiming the Center: Confronting Evangelical Accommodation in Postmodern Times*, edited by Millard J. Erickson, Paul K. Helseth, and Justin Taylor, 161–97. Wheaton, IL: Crossway, 2004.

Westberg, Daniel. *Renewing Moral Theology: Christian Ethics as Action, Character, and Grace*. Downers Grove, IL: IVP Academic, 2015.

Whitlock, Luder G. *The Spiritual Quest: Pursuing Christian Maturity*. Grand Rapids, MI: Baker, 2000.

Whitney, Donald S. "Defining the Boundaries of Evangelical Spirituality." In *The 53rd Annual Meeting of the Evangelical Theological Society*. Colorado Springs, CO, 2001.

———. *Spiritual Disciplines for the Christian Life*. 2nd ed. Colorado Springs, CO: Navpress, 2014.

———. *Spiritual Disciplines within the Church: Participating Fully in the Body of Christ*. Chicago, IL: Moody, 1996.

Wilbourne, Rankin. *Union with Christ: The Way to Know and Enjoy God*. Colorado Springs, CO: David C. Cook 2016.

Wilder, Terry L., ed. *Perspectives on Our Struggle with Sin: Three Views of Romans 7*. Nashville, TN: B&H, 2011.

Wilhoit, James C. "Only God's Love Counts: Van Kaam's Formation Theology." *Journal of Spiritual Formation & Soul Care* 1, no. 2 (2008) 168–81.

———. *Spiritual Formation as If the Church Mattered: Growing in Christ through Community*. Grand Rapids, MI: Baker Academic, 2008.

Wilkins, Michael J. *In His Image: Reflecting Christ in Everyday Life*. Colorado Springs, CO: Navpress, 1997.

Willard, Dallas. "Discipleship." In *The Oxford Handbook of Evangelical Theology*, edited by Gerald R. McDermott, 236–46. Oxford, UK: Oxford University Press, 2010.

———. *The Divine Conspiracy: Rediscovering Our Hidden Life in God*. New York: Harper Collins, 1998.

———. *The Great Omission: Reclaiming Jesus' Essential Teaching on Discipleship.* New York: Harper Collins, 2006.

———. *Hearing God: Developing a Conversational Relationship with God.* 2nd ed. Downers Grove, IL: IVP, 2012.

———. *Knowing Christ Today: Why We Can Trust Spiritual Knowledge.* New York: Harper Collins, 2014.

———. *Renewing the Christian Mind: Essays, Interviews, and Talks.* New York: Harper Collins, 2016.

———. *Renovation of the Heart: Putting on the Character of Christ.* Colorado Springs, CO: Navpress, 2002.

———. *The Spirit of the Disciplines: Understanding How God Changes Lives.* New York: Harper Collins, 1991.

———. "Spiritual Formation as a Natural Part of Salvation." In *Life in the Spirit: Spiritual Formation in Theological Perspective*, edited by Jeffrey P. Greenman and George Kalantzis, 45–60. Downers Grove, IL: IVP Academic, 2010.

———. "Spiritual Formation in Christ Is for the Whole Life and the Whole Person." In *For All the Saints: Evangelical Theology and Christian Spirituality*, edited by Timothy George and Alister McGrath, E., 39–53. Louisville, KY: WJK, 2003.

Willard, Dallas, and Gary Black. *The Divine Conspiracy Continued: Fulfilling God's Kingdom on Earth.* London: Harper Collins, 2014.

Williams, Janet P. "Pseudo-Dionysius and Maximus the Confessor." In *The First Christian Theologians: An Introduction to Theology in the Early Church*, edited by G. R. Evans, 186–200. Malden, MA: Blackwell, 2004.

Wolters, Albert M. *Creation Regained: Biblical Basics for a Reformational Worldview.* Grand Rapids, MI: Eerdmans, 2005.

Wooldridge, Darryl. *Relationship Is the Transformative Space: Living in the Not Yet.* Eugene, OR: Wipf & Stock, 2016.

Worthen, Jeremy. *Responding to God's Call: Christian Formation Today.* Norwich, UK: Canterbury Press, 2012.

Wright, Christopher J. H., ed. *The Cape Town Commitment: A Confession of Faith and a Call to Action.* Peabody, MA: Hendrickson, 2011.

———. *The Mission of God's People: A Biblical Theology of the Church's Mission.* Grand Rapids, MI: Zondervan, 2010.

———. *The Mission of God: Unlocking the Bible's Grand Narrative.* Leicester, UK: IVP Academic, 2006.

Wright, N. T. *After You Believe: Why Christian Character Matters.* New York: Harper Collins, 2010.

www.ingramcontent.com/pod-product-compliance
Lightning Source LLC
Chambersburg PA
CBHW051739230426
43670CB00012B/2088